To Yolanda —
You do great work! Thanks
so much !

P THE ower
OF Service

KEEPING CUSTOMERS FOR LIFE

Petra Marquart

Ponderosa Press
Hackensack, Minnesota

Third printing, 2001.

Ponderosa Press, P.O. Box 55, Hackensack, Minnesota 56452

Cover multi-media collage by Thomas M. Cassidy.
Collage photo by Dominick Fucci.
Book design by Dorie McClelland.
Printed in the United States of America.

Publisher's Cataloging-in-Publication
(Provided by Quality Books, Inc.)

Marquart, Petra A.
    The power of service: keeping customers for life / Petra A. Marquart. — 1st ed.
    p. cm.
    Includes bibliographical references and index.
    ISBN 0-9662716-0-2

    I. Customer services.   I. Title.

HF5415.5.M37   658.8'12
                            QBI98-103

This book is dedicated to the true spirit of service
and to those caring souls and simple systems
that bring service to life.

Acknowledgements

Thanking everyone who contributed to or influenced the writing of this book is a daunting task. At the top of the list are all of the wonderful service providers with whom I have had the pleasure of doing business. They have assured me that wonderful service is not only possible, but that it is also alive and well. I also offer a big thanks to Peg Beauchaine, Eileen Grumley, Judy Clark, my aunt Junnis, my cousin Joyce and all my other wonderful friends and family members who so often asked, "How's the book coming? How are you?" and, on occasion, "Why are you doing this?" A special thank you to Pam Cain, M.D. for her medical terminology research and for being the standard bearer for extraordinary service in medicine. In addition, I offer my sincere thanks to Sue Morem, Bev Johnson, and Jane Bunting for their editorial feedback and suggestions; to Vina, my sister and guiding light, for her hard work and dedication in helping me write this book; and to my life-long friend and soul mate, M (Mary Quain), who edited my original manuscript. Finally, I thank Lonna Mosow for inspiring me to reach for great things.

Contents

The Power of Service

By serving others, not ourselves, we derive lasting satisfaction. And by leaving something of lasting value, we cheat death out of its sting.

Charles E. Watson and Pamela Johnson

At its purest level, service is a relationship between the customer and the organization. It's as simple as that. But the quality of that relationship and the foundation on which it is built depend on a multitude of variables, many of which will be covered in this material.

From my work with numerous organizations, both large and small, I have come to the conclusion that real customer satisfaction comes from two basic relationship questions:

Did I get my needs met?

How did I get my needs met?

Although there are two other critical components of the service relationship, price and time, they play a distant second to meeting the customers' needs and treating them well in the process.

A number of organizations hire consultants to come up with programs filled with bells and whistles that guarantee customer satisfaction. And the fancier the bells and whistles, the more excited everyone becomes. Throw in a few matrixes that measure feedback, and computer programs that track customer data, and you'll find people in near ecstasy. But many of these shiny bells and whistles are only that, bells and whistles. Nothing gets better. Nothing changes. And customers are anything but satisfied. What makes this even worse is that all of this costs a ton of money.

You might ask, why do basically bright people with good intentions spend so much money on things that don't work? The answer is simple—real service is just too basic. It is so basic that everyone misses the point: Good service comes from the hearts of the people providing the service and from the values underlying the systems that support the service process. Good service comes from the people, the politics, the procedures, and the policies of an organization. For service to be real, everyone and everything involved in the customer's experience must be driven by an overwhelming desire to serve.

1

Why Service?

There's a great deal of talk about service today, but what's really being accomplished? According to TARP (Technical Assistance Research Programs) of Arlington, Virginia, not much. They reported that in 1996, out of all of the organizations investing in service and quality training, about 75 percent were failing to bring service and quality to life. Why? Because front-line workers aren't buying in. The people closest to the customers are not emotionally, psychologically, or spiritually on board the service/quality bandwagon. And without those front-line employees on board, service and quality are nothing more than banners on the wall.

There are a number of reasons why this is so, but recurring themes are (1) downsizing, right-sizing, and re-engineering have taken their toll, (2) leaders and managers don't model the new service values, and (3) fewer resources (budget, people, time), more work, and incredible demands have damaged people's spirits beyond their ability to perform. Yet, this is the exact time in history when service is most important to the success of any organization. The American marketplace is finally getting the picture that service is absolutely foundational for a business, industry, or organization to even compete.

As incredible as it might seem, not all industries believe this is true. Some manufacturing companies and their employees insist that they aren't close enough to the customer to worry about service. We hear, "We never have any interaction with the customer," or "I'm just a shipping clerk. Service doesn't really matter to me." But in today's world, that thinking is naive and down-right dangerous. Everyone has customers. And the treatment of each person along the service chain affects the next person, and then the next, and on it goes until it eventually ends up in the face of the external customer.

It is often within the organization, from co-worker to co-worker, that the downward spiral of bad service begins. People who believe that they don't have any customers often act like they don't have any customers, and that behavior can be devastating. Instead, people need to adopt the philosophy of author and service guru Karl Albrecht: "If you're not serving the customer, serve someone who is." In other words: If you're not serving the customer, you are probably supporting and serving someone who is. Either way, you are part of the service process. All for one and one for all.

History of success is no guarantee

In addition to front-line workers who aren't on board the service express, another sure killer of a successful service reputation is, "We've been around for such a long time that our durability will sustain us; we're not really too concerned about service." But being around for a long time doesn't insure being around in the future. A number of once-successful organizations have slowly died on the vine simply because they were hanging their future on their past. In fact, during the 1980s, 230 companies (46 percent) quietly disappeared from the Fortune 500 list.

Obviously, neither size or reputation guarantee continued success. Even if companies haul out new products, run expensive ads, and spend thousands of dollars on marketing programs, they will fail if they don't earn and sustain a good reputation. And how is reputation in the marketplace achieved and sustained? By the way companies do business and how they treat their customers. Many of those companies lost from the Fortune 500 list may have done nothing wrong other than losing sight of what mattered most—the customers.

Service: a formidable economic presence

Service represents an enormous part of the U.S. economy. According to TARP, 79 percent of Americans work in the service industry, while

19 percent work in manufacturing. And of those 19 percent in manufacturing, 90 percent do service work such as designing, engineering, finance, marketing, distribution and so on. Service represents about 91 percent of all jobs in this country. According to *Time* magazine, it accounts for 70 percent of the entire U.S. economy. In other words, it's huge. And indicators suggest that the service industry is continuing to grow. The Department of Labor reported that, in a single month, 153,000 new service jobs were created. During that same period, 40,000 new manufacturing jobs were created. There is little question that the service industry will continue to play an enormous part in our future economic reality.

With that in mind, wouldn't you think that the largest segment of the U.S. economy would be the best in the world, or at least a global contender? If the largest contributor to the U.S. economy was chewing gum, wouldn't we be moved to produce the finest chewing gum in the world? But, does the United States have the finest service in the world? Not according to most people. When asked how they perceive the quality of service in America, people often respond, "It's fair to poor," "Hot and cold," or "Rotten."

Customers say over and over that they can visit a store one day and be treated well, come back the next day and be treated like a virus. They don't trust service to be consistent. So, instead of venturing out to do business with the confidence that they will be satisfied, they have adopted a wait-and-see attitude, which is not only discouraging but stressful. People like to know what to expect, not only of the products and services they purchase, but in the way they are going to be treated along the way. Unpleasant surprises are unwelcome and will send customers out the door in droves and into the well-stocked aisles of any other company carrying those same products or services.

The "cancer" of indifference

Just how bad has service become in the United States? A study conducted by TARP discovered that service in the United States needed to improve by whopping 300 percent to be considered okay. Three hundred percent! That seems almost impossible. It's partly because we don't know what customers consider bad service. For instance, when people are asked what they consider unacceptable, most respond: rudeness, employees not knowing the answer to a question, being ignored, no one available to help, being given incorrect information, waiting in line, employees standing around gabbing, feeling like an interruption, being put on hold (telephone), being given the run-around, being lied to, and being talked down to.

Indeed, these are all elements of poor service, but they aren't what make the need for improvement as high as three hundred percent. What made customer dissatisfaction soar to these heights is a disease spreading through many organizations aptly referred to as the *cancer of indifference*. People can either quit and leave or quit and stay. When they quit and stay, there is always indifference. Has your organization been afflicted yet? You will know it has when you see employees robotically going through the motions of service when it's obvious that they could not care less. They say all of the right things: "May I help you?" or "I'll see if we can order another one." And even though customers may eventually get the items they're looking for, these employees make it perfectly clear that they don't care.

The cancer of indifference is a giant, cosmic nothingness that is spread throughout an organization by the walking dead—those who have emotionally quit their jobs but keep showing up for work. You may have seen them in the office hallway or talked to them over the phone. You'll recognize them by their "Pardon me, but you have me confused with someone who cares" attitude. You can't miss it. It's written all over their faces and wrapped in the tone of every word they speak. Customers who experience indifference from someone within an organization walk out the door or hang up the phone feeling empty, frustrated, and discounted. But the purveyor of indifference, the employee, is often oblivious to her or his own indifference. Somewhat like a hit-and-run driver, they don't know the damage they've caused, yet there is incredible damage just the same.

The scariest thing about the walking dead is that they seldom act out or do anything that would qualify them for dismissal. They show up for work everyday, usually on time, and go through all the proper motions. They never hit anyone or use foul language. The problem is that at no level do they care about what they do or for whom they do it. They don't care about their customers, their jobs, their co-workers, and, in many instances, themselves.

Disgruntled employees are terrorists. They are out to sabotage the customer's experience by their alienation, anger, and resentment.
Paul Goodstadt

One of the tragedies of the cancer of indifference is that, unlike physical cancer, it is contagious. An employee suffering from it, and I do mean suffering, often infect other employees. In the break room or by the copier, the walking dead spew their disdain for the organization and all for which it stands. All of the horrible tales from the past are retold until people's spirits are broken; the cancer's ugly seeds are planted in a fresh soul. In meetings, the walking dead always focus on the negative, and any new idea is a bad idea. They carry around the organization's trash and dirty laundry like a purple heart. There is no reward for this destructive behavior that kills the very root of service—the spirit of the people.

Indifference is so damaging because of the critical role service plays in an organization's success. Manufacturing gurus Dr. W. Edwards Deming, the godfather of the quality movement, and Joseph Juran, another highly esteemed quality expert, both believe that customers are more important than the production process itself. Organizations where the importance of customers is understood also understand the correlating importance of service. And if that correlation isn't clear in your organization, consider this: The Strategic Planning Institute states that organizations with high service priorities realize a 12 percent return on sales (most good companies realize 4 to 6 percent) and gain 6 percent of new market share each year at higher prices (most good companies gain 1 to 2 percent). Awareness of this bottom-line impact can give your organization the impetus to put service at the top of its efforts in the future.

The impact of service

When customers have experienced poor service (anything from rudeness to indifference), we know that only about 4 percent of those unhappy customers will tell us. But, we also know that they tell others. In fact, according to Richard Whitely, author of *The Customer-Driven Company*, dissatisfied customers tell, on average, 14 to 20 other people about their dissatisfaction with a product or service. This doesn't mean that a person receives poor service, runs home, dials up a friend, bad-mouths the organization, and says, "I've gotta go. I've got twelve other people to call." The message is often spread instead through grunts and shrugs. "Where did you buy that shirt?" "Oh, this thing. I got it at Bob's Shirt Shop." By the tone of voice and body language, you know this person is not happy about the shirt, Bob's shop, or both. Without a lot of words, it's pretty clear that Bob's isn't a cool place to buy shirts.

In contrast to telling 14 to 20 other people about bad service, customers tell only three others when they have received dazzling service. But those three people are powerfully important to the future of the organization. Not only are happy customers more loyal, they stay loyal longer. This gives us some breathing space to make better decisions and expand products and services in a more controlled manner.

What motivates customers to tell three other people about the service they have received? The experience must be *dazzling*. Good simply motivates customers to silence.

This happened to me when I saw the Broadway stage play *Joseph and His Technicolor Dream Coat*. A friend had asked me months prior if I wanted to see the play. I didn't know much about it at the time, but it sounded like fun, so I said sure, sign me up. Months passed, and then one evening I received a phone call from my friend informing me that I owed her $75.00. For what? Had she bought me snow tires or something? Seventy-five dollars? Then she reminded me of my commitment to attend the play with her. Me and my big mouth! It was the middle of the week, the middle of a Minnesota winter, and the highlight of the show was going to be Donny Osmond in a loin cloth. How could I get out of this? But being a woman of my word, I martyred myself and went. And guess what: I was blown away! I grinned from ear to ear and absolutely loved every minute of it—especially Donny Osmond in a loin cloth. The next morning when I arrived at work, I couldn't wait to tell everyone to go see Joseph and his robe.

About two months after that, I had the chance to see *Phantom of the Opera* (another seventy-five bucks). Unfortunately, I wasn't blown away. And the next day, when I went to work, I didn't mention the play to anyone. This wasn't some deliberate sabotage like, "Oh, I didn't like *Phantom* that much. I've got to remember not to talk about it." It just didn't come to my mind. If someone asked, "Have you seen *Phantom of the Opera?*" I responded "Yes, it was good."

Here's the lesson: If you ignore, anger or upset customers, in any way, they will tell 14 to 20 other people about you. If you, as author Kristen Anderson says, "knock their socks off with dazzling service," they will tell three others. If you are simply good, they will tell no one. Good is what is expected. It will not get you where you want to go.

The service edge in small business

The bigger we grow, the smaller we've got to think.

Sam Walton

Although some small business owners claim that they can't compete with large businesses, one area where small businesses can significantly outshine their larger counterparts is service. Small business comprises an extraordinarily large portion of our business community. Eighty percent of our jobs come from companies with 100 or fewer employees. If small businesses are to compete with larger ones, they must fuel those elements that allow them to compete. And of all the things small businesses can do better than larger companies, the most critical is to provide good service.

In small business, every level and every layer of the organization has the opportunity to interface with the customer either by phone or in person. Customers are looking for intimacy and personal attention in their business interactions, and there is no large business that can compete with the opportunities small businesses have to provide both.

Why customers seek our products and services

There's a difference between selling and helping people to buy.
People love to buy, but hate to "be sold." About 75 percent of
all buying decisions are based on unconscious needs or wants
such as prestige, habit, or perceived value.

Michael LeBeouff

There are two basic reasons why a person ventures out to do business with an organization. One is to **solve a problem,** and the other is to **feel good.**

In most instances, people contact their dentist, accountant, mechanic, or plumber to solve a problem. A tooth hurts, taxes need to be paid, or the car needs new brakes. We want the problem solved so we can continue on without inconvenience or pain. It isn't often that someone visits her accountant for a few laughs or his dentist for some relaxation and fun. We go to these places primarily because we need to solve a problem.

On the other hand, we see a movie, go to the theater, have dinner at a fine restaurant, or travel to a vacation resort to have a good time. The pure pleasure of the experience is our goal.

Successful organizations of the future will provide both a solution to a problem and a pleasurable experience. Does this mean that we will go to the dentist to have a good time? Probably not. But we will be aware that the treatment by the dentist and the dental staff is contributing either to a positive or negative experience.

I experienced this recently when I visited my dentist, Dr. Dodds. I had been bothered with a painful tooth and finally decided that avoiding it wasn't working; so I made an appointment. When I arrived at the clinic, pale and full of fear, the staff welcomed me, made me feel safe, and assured me that everything would be fine.

Unfortunately, everything wasn't fine. The tooth that had been causing the pain was cracked and had to be extracted (translation: yanked out). I panicked as the dentist advised me of my options. I could (a) seek another opinion, (b) avoid it all together, take medication, and live with the pain, or (c) just do it. Since living in pain or staying drugged for the rest of my life didn't seem attractive, I agreed to let him just do it.

I'll admit I was sweating profusely during the procedure, but what really surprised me was that this wasn't one of the worst experiences of my life. What made it bearable was how I was treated by the dentist and his staff. They comforted me, assured me, laughed with me (or at me, I'm not entirely sure) and, when it was over, praised me for my bravery. Would I want to go through it again? No way. But if I have to, I know I will be treated with respect and cared for in the process.

In organizations where the primary product is entertainment, such as movie theaters or fine restaurants, a greater market share will be gained if, somewhere in providing pleasure, there is an additional service that could be perceived as a solution to a problem. For instance, in addition to having dinner at a fine restaurant, perhaps the parking valet would take your car to a partnering service station for an oil change and car wash. All of this could be added to the dinner bill so that, when you are finished dining, you would be on your way in a clean, freshly-oiled car.

The customer relationship evolves

Today's customers have evolved to be more than simply passive participants of the business interaction. In the beginning of the customer relations evolutionary process, the organization is simply the vendor and the customer the receiver. This interaction is no more than a transaction, "I've got it, you want it, and I'll sell it to you."

The second stage in the evolution of the customer relationship is that of supplier and client, "I still have something you want and I will give it to you, but I also am going to be available to assist you if you need my help."

And the ultimate stage of the customer relationship is one of partnership, "I know who you are, I know what you need, I see where you're going, and I will help you in any way I can." This stage hinges on trust and open communication. The customer must be confident that she can trust you with confidential information, and you will keep her apprised of new opportunities or issues that may affect her organization's success.

Each of these evolutionary stages depends to varying degrees on service at different levels. Without service, there will be no relationship on which to build a partnership or, as in the first step of the process, for a customer to return again. We must conclude that service at all three stages is foundational.

Why service is such a "hot" topic today

Thus far we have discussed some of the reasons why service needs to be fundamental to any organization's vision. But why are organizations rallying around the call to service in such droves? There are four key elements that seem to be driving this movement: competition, expectations, technology and, industry changes.

Competition

Competition drives organizations to set higher standards. Unfortunately, many organizations fail to compete simply because their standards are based on the premise that they're no worse than anyone else. It's easy to conclude that, for those companies, the biggest threat to success lies within. Most organizations today know their main competitors. In some instances, they are obvious; in others, they've been ferreted out and dissected by a research firm. Regardless how they are identified, the competitors your organization faces today are pretty clear.

What isn't as clear is the competition your organization will face tomorrow, or in five or ten years. No one knows who that will be. (If they did, it would be a little spooky.) In all probability, there is a talented, smart someone, somewhere on earth, thinking about a new way to deliver your product or service to the world. The frightening fact is that when that new competitor hits town, your customers are going to take a long, hard look. No matter how long they've been doing business with you, they're going to look. They always do, it's human nature. And when your customers' heads are turned, you will be completely dependent on the quality of the relationship they have with you today.

If their view of the relationship is bad, they're gone. If it's so-so, maybe they'll stay, maybe they won't. But if their relationship with you is basically wonderful, they're going to look, but they will not leave. Will some? Of course. But you will improve your odds considerably by creating wonderful relationships with your customers today.

From satisfaction to indebtedness

To insure the customer's commitment to you in the future, your level of customer service and satisfaction can't simply be okay. Your customers must have a sense of indebtedness associated with their relationship with you. They must believe that if they do business with anyone else, they will be cheating on you. And the only thing that assures that kind of indebtedness is the degree to which you have satisfied them in the past. If their degree of satisfaction has been only marginal, there will no sense of debt. If you have consistently gone the extra mile and shown a deep loyalty and commitment to them, you can count on their loyalty to you.

The kind of behaviors that create customer loyalty and indebtedness are those which elicit a spontaneous "Wow" when people hear about them. For instance, consider the story about a gentleman looking for a special gift for the holidays at Nordstrom. He approached a sales clerk at the perfume counter and asked for a specific kind of perfume. The clerk responded with genuine disappointment that they didn't carry that particular brand. But she asked if he was going to be in the store for a while. He responded that he was; she asked that he not leave until they connected again.

With that, the customer left for another department. The clerk put on her coat, took some money out of the till, went out the door, down the street to a competitor, bought the perfume, returned, gift-wrapped it, tracked down the gentleman, apologized for taking such a long time, and discounted it 30 percent. Wow! Do you think that guy can shop any place other than Nordstrom and not feel guilty? He became indebted through a heroic act which in all likelihood will reward Nordstrom with his continued loyalty. Not all organizations can go that far to please a customer, but what all organizations must ask is: How far can we go to satisfy our customers beyond their wildest expectations?

Raising customer expectations out of the competitors' reach

Value added must be a surprise. It can't be expected.

Bill Murray

Michael Treacy and Fred Wiersema wrote in an article for the *Harvard Business Review*, titled "Customer Intimacy and Other Value Disciplines," how Dell Computer, Home Depot, and Nike overshadowed their formidable competitors by raising their customers' expectations beyond their competitors' reach. They did this by changing what customers valued and how it was delivered, then boosted the level of value that customers expected.

Customers used to define value as quality and price. Today that's expanded. In addition to quality and price, value is also defined by convenience of purchase, after-sale service, dependability, and so on. Successful companies have narrowed their focus on delivering superior customer service to one of three value disciplines: operational excellence, customer intimacy, or product leadership. They have become champions in one of these and met industry standards in the other two.

Operational excellence means that the organization will provide customers with reliable products or services at competitive prices with hassle-free delivery. Customer intimacy targets specific markets and then tailors offerings to exactly match the demands of those niches. Product leadership offers leading-edge products and services that consistently enhance the customer's use or application of the products, thereby making rival goods obsolete. For instance, Nike excels in product leadership in the athletic shoe industry. They consistently push the envelope in the development of their product line. But they also maintain, at industry standards, customer intimacy and operational excellence. Competitors have a hard time keeping up with a company that focuses on one of these value disciplines, maintains high standards in the other two, and uses service as the thread interwoven through all three.

Expectations

People buy expectations, not things.

Ron Zemke and Chip Bell

Organizations need to know what the customer values most in doing business with them, and then must manage every aspect of those expectations. Anyone who has been in a primary, significant relationship knows that poorly managed expectations can cause conflict. In fact, at the center of most conflict is some kind of misguided expectation:

"I expected you home at 6:00."

"You did? I thought you wanted me home at 7:00."

"You know we always eat at 6:00. I expected you'd call."

And on it goes. Most conflict doesn't occur because people are bad. It occurs, instead, because one person expects one thing and the other person expects something else. When that happens, there's instant conflict. Now, if people get into "expectation" trouble with someone they've known for five, ten, fifteen, or twenty years, how many times a day do you think a customer comes in contact with your organization expecting something and is let down? It happens all the time. And what's really frightening is that often the person letting the customer down doesn't realize anything happened.

I experienced this first hand while doing training at a local hospital. During a brief break, I went to the gift shop to buy some chewing gum. As I entered the gift shop, I noticed that the two clerks behind the counter were chatting with another shopper. If I remember correctly, they were discussing the flowers in Pella, Iowa. As I entered, both clerks looked up at me but said nothing. Instead, they continued with their conversation. I went to the candy counter, picked up the gum, and returned to the check-out counter to pay. As I approached, I said hello. The two clerks said nothing as I put the gum on the counter. One of the clerks took it, rang it up on the cash register, and said, "That'll be a dollar nine." I dug in my purse, handed her the dollar nine, picked up the gum, and said thank you. Neither of the two clerks said anything to me.

How did I feel? Invisible. The really frightening part of this encounter is that, had their supervisor asked if they had offended or provided poor service to anyone that day, they both would have sincerely answered no. Yet I couldn't have been more offended.

What is your product?

Expectations are as deep as beliefs because what you absolutely expect to happen, happens. What delights customers today is then expected tomorrow, creating the need for continuous improvement and growth. So what do customers expect when they do business with you today?

Before an organization can discuss its customers' expectations, it must answer the question what is our product? It sounds like an easy question, but for many organizations the answer is not that clear. If an organization manufactures a specific product or product line, the question is relatively easy to answer, "We manufacture blue sticks." And if your answer is blue sticks, or some other tangible item, it's fairly easy to measure the quality of the product. Anything that can be carried, touched, driven, held, tasted, or worn is relatively easy to measure in product quality. It lives up to the customers' expectations, has the features that they will use, and comes with zero defects.

Simply put, when your product is a thing, you can measure the quality of that thing by how it works in relationship to how it is supposed to work. If it doesn't work, it will be viewed as an inferior or poor-quality product.

And what's the big deal about poor quality in products? According to Jeremy Main in *Quality Wars*, poor quality costs 20 to 30 percent of total sales. It's a terrible loss for the company and, with today's acute awareness of the need for good quality, inexcusable.

If the product works about the same as it is expected to work, the customer will probably be satisfied. If it works much better than the customer expects, that customer often becomes an advocate of the product and an unsolicited member of your marketing force.

When your product is service

Service is the only product that you can never recall.

Anonymous

If there are no tangible products being manufactured, chances are your product is service. If you get up in the morning, go to work, and stand at a work bench, conveyor belt, or machine, most likely you are in the manufacturing business. But if you get up, go to work, and sell your time, knowledge, or talent, you are in the service industry and your product is service.

We can clearly understand the importance of quality in manufacturing, but what does quality mean to service? We know that the quality aspect of service isn't easy to measure. W. Edwards Deming, Joseph Juran, and Philip Crosby are all modern-day gurus of quality who have outlined points dealing with the organization's need for quality in process and procedure. Deming created 14 points, Juran 10, and Crosby 14. Incredibly, not one of these gurus mentions the word customer in any of their points. But if all of these gurus' points are to make a difference in the end, quality must be delivered as the customer defines it.

How do the quality aspects of service and products compare? Or do they compare? According to Performance Research Associates, Minneapolis, the quality of products compared to the quality of service isn't identical but is closely related. Look at their findings on quality products versus quality service on page 18.

Even in manufacturing, customer value equals the ratio of financial sacrifice (cost) to the perceived benefit. Because this is hard for the customer to really determine (cost vs. benefit), it is his expectations of these factors that are most important. And his expectations are shaped by his perceptions. Customers use more than twenty attributes by which they judge products. Over one-third of those elements are service attributes. Why is this relevant? The cost of poor service quality and loss due to poor service rivals the cost of poor quality in products. It has been reported that nearly 25 to 30 percent of gross sales are lost due to poor service quality. And, according to

Quality Products and Service

QUALITY PRODUCTS
   Zero defects
   Technical quality
   Precise standards and performance
   Treating errors as mortal sin
   Creating standards and protocols for every aspect of transactions
   Mechanizing the human element
   No surprises, standard operating procedures, rote and drill
   Production quality
   Developing satisfactory and mutually beneficial relationships
   Customer satisfaction
   Reworking every policy and procedure to perfection, and
      creating an absolutely seamless performance

QUALITY SERVICE
   Zero defections
   Customer quality
   Transactions that delight customers
   Treating errors as opportunities
   Standards for technical quality, empowerment and solutions
   Capitalizing on the human element
   Speed and flexibility in responding to unique demands
   Performance quality
   Building lasting, creative customer partnerships
   Customer retention
   Experimenting, leapfrogging the competition, taking mea-
      sured risks then learning from them

Earl Naumann, Professor of Marketing at the College of Business at Boise State University, service expectations are constantly evolving, making it increasingly difficult to achieve service success.

When service is the product, a new question needs to be asked: What is the difference between service and quality? Karl Albrecht says that "service is work done by a person for the benefit of another, and that quality is a measure of the extent to which a thing or experience meets a need, solves a problem, or adds value for someone."

Although I agree with Albrecht's definition, I would like to expand it.

The value of the service product is based on four judgments:

Service
> How did you treat me? (interpersonal)

Quality
> What was the process I had to go through to receive your service? What was the outcome? (systemic/performance)

Price
> What was the cost compared to the perceived value?

Time
> Did you do what you said you would do within the time frame you said you would do it?

Or in other words, your service is being judged by (1) the interpersonal aspect, caring, (2) the process and outcomes, (3) the perceived value, and (4) being true to your word. In a nutshell, brilliant service is delivered with care and competence within sensible, customer-driven systems.

Quality service includes both processes and outcomes

> *The reason to be concerned with quality is that*
> *the customer is concerned about quality.*
>
> Joseph Juran

While the majority of this book focuses on the interpersonal aspect of service, I don't want to diminish the importance of the quality in service. Quality in service includes both *processes* and *outcomes*. The first aspect of service quality is process. Ron Zemke and Chip Bell have said that the product *is* what the product *does*. It is the total package. The same is true when your product is a service. How many times have you visited a shop or business and wondered if the organization is deliberately trying to make it hard for you to do business there? You find their process so cumbersome or complicated that you think it would be easier to forget about doing business with them all together. It's too much work.

These hassles show up as inconvenient parking, limited business hours, incompetent employees ("I don't know." "That's not my department." "You'll have to call back."), not enough check-out lines, strict return policies, busy telephone lines, and never being able to speak to anyone in charge, to name a few. If a customer experiences any of these situations when dealing with an organization, the quality of that organization's service is in jeopardy.

The second aspect of quality is outcomes. Your customers will ask themselves, "Was the problem resolved? Was the part fixed? Am I better? Did I get what I needed?" If the answer to any of these questions is no, chances are customers will conclude that they have received poor-quality service. If you hear customers saying, "I'm still sick," or "It doesn't work right," or "I didn't get the right information," or "You said you'd call me back," you probably have a customer questioning the quality of your service.

When it comes to quality in the marketplace, the only thing that really matters is the customer's experience. No matter how wonderful you believe your product or service to be, it means nothing unless the customer feels the same way. As unbelievable as it sounds, there are organizations that not only ignore customers' expectations, but seem to actually disdain them. "If they want that, they'll have to go elsewhere." "They can't have it by then. They'll just have to wait or go someplace else." "We can't do that," or "They can't have that," are the battle cries of organizations bound for failure. Reasonable customers, which means most (90 to 95 percent), understand that they can't always get what they want, when they want it. What frustrates most customers is not being able to receive those things that are reasonable to expect. "But you are in the tire business, how can you consistently be out of the most common tire size?" "You told me my VCR would be ready on Tuesday, and now on Thursday you tell me it's still not ready. Why didn't you call me so I didn't drive all the way down here?" These things are pretty reasonable to expect.

There are even some organizations, or representatives of organizations, who seem to have an adversarial attitude regarding their customers. What makes that truly unfortunate is that the customers probably sense their lack of interest in the relationship. No matter how quick the service or effective the process, that lack of interest will diminish the quality of the organization's service in the customers' eyes.

Process vs. outcomes in manufacturing

The distinction between manufacturing and service is now arbitrary and obsolete. In the modern sense, all work is service work. Both manufacturing and service meet needs, solve problems, and add value for people.

Karl Albrecht

In the manufacturing business, quality and service play as important a role as when service is your product, but they are judged on a different basis. In manufacturing, service is still based on how the customer is treated, but the process aspect is judged at the service level. In other words, when customers order a product from a manufacturing company, they will ask, "How did the people treat me, and what process did I to go through to get this product?" The outcome in manufacturing generally lies in the quality of the product itself.

The life of an organization depends on quality and service

Doing business with any organization, whether it provides products or services, needs to be pleasant, quick, and easy. And its products or services must meet its customers' needs. To make this possible, the organization must be grounded in both service (treatment) and quality (process and outcomes).

An organization is much like a living, breathing, growing organism. In this organism, quality is the nervous system, or brain, and service is the heart. Both must be healthy in order for the organism to be strong and resilient. You may know someone who suffers with heart disease. Although their brain is strong and healthy, their life is diminished because their heart is not well. Organizations with high-tech systems that are snappy and efficient, but whose customers are treated poorly, will find their image, and ultimately their life, diminished.

You may also know someone suffering from Alzheimer's or dementia. Even though their brain is diseased, their strong heart beats on. But their life is diminished. The service image is also diminished in organizations where everyone is really nice but nothing gets done right and tasks are not effectively completed. Customers say, "Yes, these people are really nice to work with, but I won't go back because they never do anything right."

In order for an organization to thrive today, its service reputation (how they treat people), and its quality image (the process and outcomes) must be world-class. If either of these is diminished in the eyes of the customer, the reputation of the entire organization is also diminished and the customer's loyalty is at risk.

Price and value

Why would I buy from your organization instead of one of your competitors? In order for me or anyone else to choose your organization over another, is if we see the difference between you and your competitors. If we don't, the only way you can compete is through price.

Ron Zemke

According to a survey by The Conference Board, customers were asked which was more important: Having all of your needs met or price? Sixty-five percent responded having all their needs met, and 35 percent answered price. Price is always a factor in deciding whether to purchase a product or service, but it is seldom the only factor.

Imagine for a minute going out to dinner with your significant other and spending a hundred dollars. I don't know what part of the world you're from, but I do know that in my world spending a hundred dollars for dinner would seem quite extravagant. Still, if the food was wonderful, the service impeccable, and the ambiance delightful, we might think back on that experience as very special.

But, if we spent a hundred dollars for dinner where the food was poor, service was poor, and nothing was done right, we would probably spend the next few days trying to decide whose dumb idea it was to eat there.

In reality, it is often not what we pay for something, but what we perceive that we get in exchange. We must perceive an even exchange. We need to believe that we got a hundred dollars worth of something at the restaurant or we will not be happy about the experience. Consequently, when customers complain about your prices, on some level they don't believe there was a fair exchange between the product or service and what they paid.

According to a story that appeared in *The Wall Street Journal*, for a number of years Mobil Oil had been losing ground in the competitive gasoline business. Mobil decided not to lower prices again, but rather to raise the standards by which they served their customers and thus increase the perceived value. They found that only 20 percent of gasoline purchases are based on price. The other 80 percent comes from a fluid mix of standards by which value will be perceived.

The new strategy that Mobil decided to implement, called "Friendly Service," has increased sales by about 25 percent at stations where it is being tested. Just making the facility cleaner and safer by additional lighting sparked gains in sales of 2 to 5 percent. Adding helpful attendants pushed sales up another 15 to 20 percent. At some sites, concierge attendants can be seen dashing into the station's store to buy coffee or soft drinks for people who can't or prefer not to leave their car. Eighty-five percent of the 8,000 Mobil independent owners have said they will be on board the Friendly Service bandwagon as soon as training is available.

Dick Schaaf, who with Ron Zemke wrote *The Service Edge*, was featured in a Dick Youngblood column in the business section of the *Minneapolis Star Tribune*. He cautioned service providers that dazzling service is not the only aspect that is being measured when customers decide with whom they want to do business. "A twist in customer expectations is that, along with exceeding their service expectations, they also want to get the biggest bang for their buck."

They want to be treated well, get their money's worth, and find real value in their trading. The people who say, "Yes, I still shop at this hardware store even though the people are rude or indifferent, simply because of the price," will almost always leave if they have a chance to go where they can get both good value and be treated well.

Price is important in part because we are a bargain-hunting people. Maybe it's a hangover from our primitive ancestors, but we love to go on the hunt to see if we can get something really great for a low price. But beware. We are also a people who expect to be treated with a certain respect. Organizations that over estimate the importance of price will be in for a rude awakening the day a new competitor, featuring the same products at about the same price and committed to treating people like royalty, opens its doors.

Timeliness

> *Perception is reality.*
> Tom Peters

Customers have many expectations regarding time, and most of them are based on the organization's promises. "Your order will be in tomorrow." "We'll call you on Tuesday." "It will be ready by noon." "Someone will be right with you." "I'll be right back."

What on earth is meant by "I'll call you right back," or "I'll be right with you," or "I'll be right back?" What is the exact length of time of "right back?" There is no good answer to that question other than to say that right back is always shorter to the customer than it is to the service provider. If you call back in ten minutes, the customer was expecting five. If you called in the afternoon, they were expecting the morning. And on it goes. A key element in dazzling customers with your service is to respond to them in less time than expected, even if you don't have the answer or information in question. The important element in timeliness is to continue to communicate as often and as promptly as possible until the problem is resolved or the question has been answered.

Which expectation is most critical?

The loss of the focus that the customer is a human being is probably the single most important fact about the state of service and service management in the western world today.

Karl Albrecht

All four expectations—service (caring, or how was I treated?), quality (systems or process; and competence or outcomes), price (even exchange and equal value), and time (time frame)— are crucial to the success of an organization. However, of the four, the customer will judge you most critically by service—how they are treated. Why? Of these four essential criteria, service is the only one that the customer will take personally. Because it is harder to detach from the interpersonal, the performance of people will effect the customer more than the performance of the product.

Many companies are espousing the goal to become world-class. The opportunity to make that happen will be won or lost with every interaction its customers have with the organization. Customers compare the service they receive to the service they expect, and they take it personally. When expectations aren't met, the relationship with the organization will suffer.

Building customer relationships

If customers put the need to be treated well first and foremost, organizations must be clear as to what behaviors customers value in their interactions. Wanting to treat people well and actually doing it are two separate things. The following were posted on a company's bulletin board as to what their customers expect:

To be recognized (regard);
To be treated with courtesy (respect);
To be served but not pressured;
To receive our undivided attention;
To be given practical information;
To have their problem solved;
To be treated with honesty and openness;
To be treated like individuals;

To have easy and open channels of communication;

To have your loyalty;

To see your sincere appreciation for their continued loyalty.

All of these behaviors affect customers on a personal level. When most of us believe we've been given special treatment, by anyone, we believe that treatment has to do with us, "It's because I am special that I am treated this way. You went out of your way to help me because I am special. You took the time to call me and tell me my car wasn't ready. You took the time to call because I'm special. It's all about me." And I, in return, will think those people who recognize and value me are equally special in return.

Treating people well is not some policy gimmick. It's letting customers know that someone wants to help them and, at some level, cares about them. People feel better about themselves when others treat them well. We need not be dependent on others treating us well to feel good about ourselves, but the cumulative effect of positive interactions with people reaffirms that we're basically okay.

Being talked down to, or treated like a nuisance or an interruption, hits us right in the gut. We feel discounted and, in some instances, bad about ourselves. Most of us don't need to go out and pay good money for someone to help us feel bad about ourselves.

If the process is cumbersome, the outcome ineffective, or the product substandard (all quality issues), it is about the organization. If the price is too high for what the customer perceives they get in return (price), that is about the organization. The same is true for time. If the service provider calls back late or doesn't live up to his or her word, that is about the organization. But when service providers talk to customers with an edge to their voice, rudely, or in any way that feels negative, the customer takes that poor treatment personally. Treating the customer poorly is, without question, the most devastating aspect of any organization's service reputation and the hardest one to overcome.

From lip service to real service

Don't misunderstand this point. An organization cannot rate zeros on a ten-point scale in quality, time, and price, treat the customer nicely, and expect nice behavior to overcome poor performance in those other areas. Instead, your service will be viewed as only lip service. Eventually the recipient comes to the conclusion that it just isn't real, much like faith without works or love without affection.

If the level of quality is rated seven on a zero to ten scale, price at eight, time at seven, and service at ten, the inefficiencies of quality, price, and time will probably be forgiven. In other words, customers will forgive some reduction in quality, price, and time if you treat them like royalty in the process. However, no matter how excellent your quality, fair your price, or responsive your timeliness, your customers will not forgive you if you treat them poorly. They will take it personally. Customers who are treated poorly may stay and do business with you for a while, but will leave as soon as there is a reasonable alternative.

Judging the organization from the inside out

Service, quality, price, and time are also four criteria by which employees judge the organizations for which they work. Employees ask about service, "How does this organization serve me? Am I treated fairly? Is my contribution valued? Am I treated with respect, regard, honor?" There are people all over the world who would give their right arm for an employer who treats them like a valued asset instead of something that needs to be managed, controlled, or dealt with.

In addition to service, employees within an organization ask the quality questions, "What is the process I have to follow to accomplish my work? How easy is it for me to do my job?" Systems that encumber job tasks instead of enhancing them will be viewed as poor quality and obstacles to quality work performance. Employees also question the competency, or quality, of their leaders and co-workers. Are they continuing to learn and grow from those around them? Are there sound decisions and clear directions?

Employees judge the organization by compensation (price). Everyone wants to earn as much money as possible in exchange for the work they do. Although some employees may have exaggerated expectations concerning salary and other benefits, most people simply expect their remuneration to be fair. Just as customers expect a fair exchange for the money they spend, employees expect a fair exchange for their time, knowledge, and talent. Leaders and managers who think they pull a fast one by getting people to work for less than what is fair don't understand the depth of the effect of this mistreatment. These leaders and managers are looking for short-term, quick gains. They don't care at whose expense those gains are made or about the long-term ramifications of their actions.

Finally, employees judge the organizations they work for by time: Does my manager get back to me in a timely manner when I have a question? Was my review done in the time frame promised? Do I get information regarding decisions that affect me in a timely manner?

Once again, out of these four criteria, service, quality, price, and time, the employee will judge the organization most critically by service: Yes, I want to work with processes that make sense, I want to be paid well, and I expect answers in a timely manner, but most of all, I want you to treat me with respect, regard, honor, and decency.

This was shown beautifully in the movie, *Mr. Saturday Night.* In the movie, Billy Crystal plays an aging comedian much like the late George Burns or Georgie Jessel, always on the come-back trail, always another gig. Throughout his entire career, his brother has been his agent, manager, gofer, whatever. If it needed doing, he was there.

One day his brother came to him and said what many managers in many organizations hear. "I'm going to quit. I just want to go sit on the beaches of Florida and be old." The response was also typical of many managers. "How dare you leave me? I've given you all kinds of opportunities, paid you well, taught you everything you know." With a sad look on his face, his brother looked at him and said, "Yes, that's all true. But you could have been nicer to me."

At the end of his career, the brother's spirit had been broken. Broken not by the way he had been paid or by the skills he had acquired, but by the way he had been treated. In the end, all that mattered was personal. It was about how he had been treated as a person, a human being. And that's why service, how employees are treated, is so important. Poor treatment breaks spirits, and broken spirits lose the will to serve.

Service Is an Inside-Outside Job!

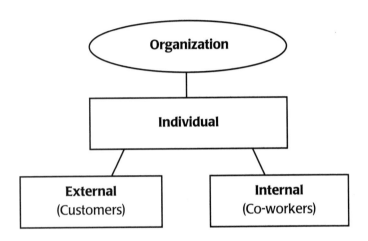

Technology

> *The factory of the future will have only two employees: a human and a dog. The human will be there to feed the dog. The dog will be there to keep the human from touching the equipment.*
>
> Warren Bennis

Most, if not all, businesses and industries depend on technology to an extensive degree and technology has changed the way we do business. For instance, twenty-five years ago there were fewer than 50,000 computers. Now there are 50,000 computers sold every day. More than anytime in history, we can compete, though only for short spans of time, solely because we have the technological, competitive edge. But there is a frightening reality about technology—the speed at which it changes. According to *Nation's Business*, two million workers a year lose their jobs because of shifts in technology.

To understand the ramifications of technological change, consider this: There has been more technological change in the past 50 years than in all of history. Then consider how quickly and profoundly these technological advancements have affected our daily lives. In 1980, there were no ATMs (automatic teller machines), no laser printers, no cellular phones, few, if any, remotes for TVs, no compact disks, few VCRs, no video rental stores, only restaurants had microwave ovens, fax machines cost several thousand dollars and took about five minutes to transmit, no personal computers, and no World Wide Web.

The impact of technological changes is made clear in this scenario detailed in Peter Large's book, *The Micro Revolution Revisited*: "You are in Paris, and you decide to use your American Express card. Getting credit approved involves a 46,000 mile journey over phones and computers. The job can be completed in five seconds." And whether you're ready for it or not, over the next five years, fax machines will be in fifty percent of American homes. (They are in thirty percent of Japanese homes today.)

Even more staggering is the fact that there will be twice again as much change in technology over the next twenty-five years as there has been in all previous history. This begs the question: Who in the world can keep up with this incredible speed of change? A recent newspaper cartoon showed a woman buying a computer. She asked the computer salesman, "Will this computer be obsolete next week?" The salesman laughed and said, "Are you kidding, it's obsolete right now."

The computer is extending the reach of the human brain the way machines extended the reach of the human muscle.

Based on a quote by Malcolm S. Forbes, Jr.

Just as the industrial revolution brought new jobs into the workplace, so the technological revolution is taking them away. With virtual factories and sales outlet centers, the need for people in labor positions is decreasing. A steel company that once employed 120,000 people now employs 20,000 people—who produce more steel thanks to technology and automation.

How will people in the future compete for the few jobs that will be available? One vital factor will be the person's ability to get along with others and their willingness to serve at all levels both internally and externally. In fact, many organizations are taking the position that technical skills can be trained. They are hiring people who are nice and who get along well with others. If you are in one of those companies that is tired of putting up with the bad apples and chronic complainers, try a different approach to your interviewing process. Along with focusing the interview on questions about skills, experience, and adaptability to change, ask: Do you work with any charities? What kind of community activities are you involved with? In other words, what kind of person are you? What is your commitment to service of others? Who are you at your very core? Most tasks can be taught or trained, but the willingness to care and put other's needs first can not.

The impact of service on technology

What does the speed of changing technology have to do with service? The answer is simple. If an organization is hanging its reputation on its *stuff*, it will almost always be behind the curve. As soon as a bank invests millions of dollars in a machine that takes deposits over the phone, its competitor will purchase the latest, greatest version of that machine. Tragically, the minute that new machine goes into action, the first bank's machine is out of date. The same is true in medicine. One clinic will spend millions of dollars advertising the ease of use and advantages of a new diagnostic instrument that assesses the health of a patient by her simply walking through it. But sure as shootin', the next week that clinic's major competitor will purchase an instrument that diagnoses in some other magical way. No one will be able to keep up with the speed of technological changes in the future.

An organization cannot depend on keeping ahead of its competitors with technology. What it can depend on, even during the most aggressive technological competition, is its service. If your service is impeccable, no matter what new, fancy gizmo your competitor uses to lure your customers away, customers will say, "Thanks, but no thanks. I'm satisfied with how they take care of me right here." Does that mean that you can stagnate in your technological advancements? Not at all. But it does mean that you don't have to panic every time your competitors get something new. You can rest assured that your customers value your service and how you treat them more than they value your stuff.

Industry changes

Price Pritchett writes in his book, *New Work Habits for a Radically Changing World*, that in 1950, 73 percent of U.S. employees worked in manufacturing or production, but now less than 8 percent of us make our living in these areas. Today 91 percent of U.S. employees work in the service sector. Quickly, knowledge is becoming our most important product. Established companies are down-sizing, others are starting smaller and staying that way. The 500 largest U.S. companies have not created one net new job since 1974.

Things change. Times change. And industries change—which leads to another reason for the current rush to service. Almost every consumer experience, from buying a car, to taking out a bank loan, to seeing a doctor, has changed over the years almost beyond what we could have imagined. But as industries change, we find that customers are not always pleased with those changes.

Take the experience of visiting a doctor. It wasn't that many years ago that doctors would come to the house to care for their patients. If someone had told people that the day would come when the doctor would no longer make house calls, no one would have believed it. But the day obviously has come. Not only does the doctor no longer come to the house, but there are times when people don't see the same doctor on subsequent visits to the same clinic. Do dramatic advances in medicine mean everyone is happy with today's healthcare? Not at all.

The same is true with the experience of getting a bank loan. Many people remember when a loan was made with only the security of a hand shake. Can you imagine that today? Today if you want to get a loan from a bank, you had better bring along your first-born. Some banks are becoming so automated that they prefer you don't even come into the bank to make transactions. This is unfortunate for those banking customers who can't rest without seeing the face of the person taking their deposit. But those customers had better get used to it. Once change occurs, things seldom return to the old way.

The telecommunications industry is on the leading edge of change. And yet, here's a common example of what it all boils down to for customers. A friend of mine discovered during the process of relocating her business that the telephone company no longer provides phones. Because of this, she spent days running around trying to find appropriate business telephones. All of this in the name of progress? Customers ask: Progress for whom?

I even remember the days when people called one another with the help of the telephone operator. You'd pick up the phone and hear an operator say, "Number, please?" Once you'd given her the number, she (it was almost always a woman in those days) would magically connect you with your desired party. But as the telephone industry progressed, the operator became a thing of the past and the dial was introduced. This was not a good thing for my grandmother. Until this new-fangled dial arrived, she had been able to call her brother, Nils, in Norway with only the aid of the operator. But when progress was made and automation took over, she could not adapt to the change. So, for the rest of her life, someone in her family would have go to her home to dial Norway for her.

Changes in industries are not always welcomed by the customer. But as the world moves forward and things do change, organizations can soften the blow and ease the confusion by continuing to treat the customer with dignity and genuine concern. They can concentrate first and foremost on their service. Doctors no longer come to our homes, but they can remember the need for personal commitment to their patients. Banks can't give away the store with only a handshake, but they can remember that there is potential for a lifelong relationship. And communications companies will continue to lead the world in technology, but they can remember that their customers need help when technology moves faster than customers' ability to understand.

Good service just makes good sense

*It's a new ball game for America's business. The plays
are changing and customers are calling the shots.*

Barbara Trimarco Gulbranson

In addition to the fact that customers expect service, competition is coming out of the woodwork, technology is changing at lightening speed, and changes don't always please customers, there is another reason to provide good service—it makes good business sense.

John Tschohl, author of *Achieving Excellence Through Customer Service*, talks about the benefits to an organization for providing dazzling service. They include:
- Increased market share;
- Increased sales and profit;
- Repeat business, larger sales, order upgrades;
- More new customers;
- Increased yield from advertising budgets;
- Fewer complaints; more complaints favorably resolved;
- Enhanced reputation;
- Competitive edge;
- Lower turnover;
- Improved employee morale; happy customers = happy employees = happy customers.

And if these aren't enough reasons to inspire royal treatment for customers, then consider the powerful effect of customer retention and loyalty.

Retention

More than serving the customer's needs, we service the customer's loyalty.

Darby Checketts

According to the American Management Association, 65 percent of a company's business volume comes from customers who return again and again because of their sense of satisfaction. Frederich F. Reichheld, author of *The Loyalty Effect*, and director of Bain & Co., a

Boston-based strategy consulting firm, adds further that "sales equal opportunity, and retention equals profits." No matter how many new customers you acquire, you have no net gain if there's a revolving door with as many going out as coming in. The mentality we are moving into today is that of cradle to grave. We want customers for life—not just a one-time transaction. And yet, in spite of the clear benefits of long-term, happy customers, most businesses over spend in customer acquisition and under spend in customer retention.

Retention depends on knowing your customer

No statistics, marketing, or financial statements or strategies will ever take the place of devoted customers—those who simply would not buy elsewhere.

Michael LeBeouff

Many companies don't acknowledge their customers and employees as people. They are statistics, or assets, or expenses, or potential. They are seldom human beings with thoughts, feelings, needs, wants, and values. The old way of doing business was to think of something that someone might want, create it, and then try to convince the public that they want it. Today's thinking is not about mass production but is about meeting the customer's needs, one customer at a time.

Organizations spend millions of dollars each year on advertising and marketing. Yet, without customer retention, marketing dollars are as good as thrown down the drain. Most organizations lose up to 25 percent of their customers each year. If that is cut by as little as 5 percent, the bottom line will increase by 100 percent. No matter how you slice it, it's more economical to keep your current customers than to go out and find new ones.

This is true even if you sweeten the pot occasionally by throwing in a perk or two. An auto repair shop decided that it needed to reward its long-term customers for doing business with them. They decided to throw in something extra that the customer might appreciate on occasion. This wasn't a program where everyone got a free air-freshener on their third visit; it was more personal than that. If the mechanic noticed that the windshield washers were bad, he would put on a new pair free. Or if the washer fluid was low, it would be filled and the remaining amount given to the car owner at no charge. And on occasion, if the repair person could sense that a customer was getting impatient because of the lengthy repair process, the customer would be asked if anything could be done to help them out.

The owner of this station had learned, first-hand, the value of a devoted customer. His customers have every reason to trust that the mechanics will fairly repair anything that may need to be repaired. And to insure this interdependent relationship, the station owner understands that spending a few dollars on windshield wipers or window washer fluid is really a very small investment.

Research has shown one of the reasons why those small investments are so important. It costs one-fifth as much to keep a current customer as it does to find a new one. Organizations get 85 to 95 percent of their current business from satisfied customers coming back, buying more, and telling others. Served well, customers will generate more money each and every year they remain. And as purchases rise, operating costs decline. Reichheld says, "The only way to get rich is to earn a loyal customer base. To give customers outstanding value, you really need loyal employees who are going to stay with you and learn how to serve them."

Reichheld further contends that U.S. corporations lose half of their customers in five years, half of their employees in four years, and half of their investors in less than a year. He suggests that this disloyalty stunts corporate performance by 25 to 50 percent. Long-term customers are willing to pay more over time as long as they perceive that there is equal value in the exchange. Long-term customers who are satisfied will not only purchase on a continuing basis, but will buy more frequently and purchase higher-end products. The willingness of customers to increase the frequency of purchase and to order higher-priced products is directly related to their degree of satisfaction with previous buying experiences. Not only do current, satisfied customers create a more valuable financial base, the customers they refer will purchase more products and be more loyal than customers attracted through advertising and marketing.

There are probably additional reasons why more and more organizations are putting service at the top of their list. But these basics—competition, expectations, technology, industry changes, good sense, and retention— comprise a compelling case for focusing on service as a foundational value. The importance of these issues and their impact on service will be reiterated throughout this material and, most likely, through your increasing encounters with the global-market community.

Conclusion

Why service? Because of competition. Because customers expect it. Because technology changes too quickly to hang your reputation on your past. Because industry changes don't always delight customers. And, finally because service guarantees loyalty and customer retention. Service is, if not the only, then one of the most critical, components of success, no matter how large or small the organization.

Critical Service Influences

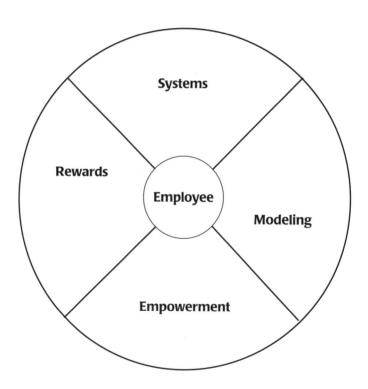

2

What Is Service?

Definition of customer

Before we can discuss the meaning of genuine service, we need to agree on what is a customer and who are our customers. The word customer has been defined in a number of ways by a number of people. Some define customer as a consumer who wants your products or services, or someone willing to trade one thing of value for another. Others have defined customer as anyone who receives the benefit of what you do, or anyone who expects something from you. All of these definitions seem to work. In spite of that, many industries choose not to define the receivers of their services as customers. In fact, some choose to avoid using the word altogether. For instance, in the health industry, we are patients. In education, we are students. To the airlines, we are passengers. In the automobile industry, we're buyers. Has the word customer become so misaligned that we need to use other words to describe the relationship between service providers and receivers?

To further assess this, let's use the definition of customer as *anyone who receives the benefit of what you do.* With this definition, can't we easily call patients, students, car buyers, and passengers customers? Could it be that the words that often seem to cause problems are those used in place of customer, such as student, patient, car buyer, and passenger? Why? Because of what the word customer implies compared to what the other words imply. For example, the word customer implies choice. As a customer, I can choose from all of the options available to me. It also implies expectations. As a customer, I expect certain things from you. As a customer, I have rights that you cannot violate. Any violation of those rights will terminate the relationship and I will seek your products or services elsewhere.

For many of us, the term patient has a special and important meaning. It implies a degree of intimacy. But it also implies submission. Patients don't believe that they have the same power in the clinic as they have as customers elsewhere. They generally don't shop around or demand better service or argue with a decision. Patients are often intimidated by the authority of the care provider, and this is due, in part, to the term patient itself.

The same is true for the word student. Can a student demand a specific outcome from the educational service provider or school? For instance, should a student be able to demand to know how to read or write the same way a customer can demand satisfaction with a product or service? Not today. Students are often asked to stand in long lines, eat marginal food, and put up with all kinds of inconveniences that we would never impose on a real customer. Students are expected to demand very little. They're only students! Imagine the paradigm shift that would be needed to think of a five-year-old kindergarten student as a customer. But that is exactly what she or he is.

We all know that car buyers mean more to the automobile industry than just the purchasers of cars. Car buyers are customers who, if treated right, could be embarking on a life-long relationship with the dealer. Corporate consultant Tom Peters says that 25 percent of car buyers return to the same place over and over to purchase their cars. If a dealer plays his or her cards right, this relationship could mean hundreds of thousands of dollars in income from both service and sales.

Sewell Cadillac in Texas is committed, first and foremost, to treating car buyers as customers. Because of its lifetime commitment to customers, it has also enjoyed 97 percent customer satisfaction. In today's critical society that is extraordinary. To insure that customers are treated like the most important part of the business, Sewell has a well-paid work force that consistently delivers good work performance. To make doing business with them easy, they give out free loaner cars and are open at times convenient for the customer. In addition, cars go back to the same mechanic each time they are brought in so a personal relationship is established. Mechanics are paid by the job; if it's not done right the first time, they do it over at no cost.

A passenger, as the word implies, is not just sitting idly by on the plane. Instead a passenger is involved in a journey that is often dependent on the service received from baggage handlers at one end to claims attendants at the other. The word passenger implies a passive observer; customer, on the other hand, demands attention and requires that all airline employees do whatever it takes to bring this traveler back.

In the end, every industry, profession, and business must realize that the people who receive their services are customers—no matter what else they may be called. The term need not be augmented or diminished. *Customers are, and always will be, people who have choices, expectations, and rights.*

Customers come in different packages

Although all customers are people, all customers are not alike. Our customers may have similar needs and expectations but they are significantly different from one another. They don't exist in the aggregate nor do they have the same needs and expectations. As a marketer, you need to be cognizant of that and approach each customer from that premise.

For example, coming from the same demographic group doesn't mean that customers are the same. Although around the same age, from the same generation, and in the same business, can we say that Madonna and Amy Grant are the same? Demographically, yes. But are they the same person? Do they want the same things? Maybe some things. But you really need to know about each of them as an individual to satisfy their needs.

Co-workers are customers

If a customer is someone we interact with for business purposes, we need to include our co-workers as our customers. This makes sense since customer service always occurs from the inside out. An organization's service attitudes and behaviors effect everyone who comes in contact with the organization.

The concept of internal customer (co-worker) isn't easily accepted. People intellectually may *get it* but they may not *buy it*. Probably a more favorable definition of co-worker would be partner in service or co-server. But, no matter what they are called, employees must be treated well and must treat each other well. If people within the organization are treated with less dignity or respect than external customers, the organization will crumble from the inside out. Just as abusive homes often produce people who abuse, organizations that treat their workers poorly produce a work force that treats people poorly as well. And this is only one side-effect of the poor treatment of employees. Other residual effects include low morale, low productivity, high turnover, high absenteeism, and a lot of dispirited human beings.

Service defined

We have defined the word customer; now we need to define the word service. While writing a service program for a major retailer, one company executive asked that the program clearly dictate to *their people* (the front-line workers) the behaviors of *what to say* and *how to act* in any given situation. He also insisted that everyone should know that if they did not consistently exhibit these behaviors, they would be fired. These requests were clearly at odds with what I believe to be the core meaning of service.

Service at its very best is invisible. It is so integrated into the behavior of the service providers that the recipient doesn't even see it coming. All they know is that it feels good and that the experience is pleasurable. If the customer is pressed to define what makes it pleasurable, they can probably do so. But a truly good service interaction is so much a part of the process that it doesn't stand out as a separate effort. At its most elementary level, service is anything that delights the customer, eases the process, or inspires the customer to return to do business again. The key word here is anything. *Good service is created on the spot by well-trained, empowered employees in response to anything the customer needs at that exact moment.*

Some organizations believe that they will deliver good service simply by emphasizing a behavior, such as using a customer's name.

Using a customer's name is often a good thing. But it means nothing if the customer needs or expects something from you and you fail to deliver. Good service providers are highly empowered employees. The entire organization lives by the rule: whatever it takes. To make this happen, training needs to include good service philosophies and ideals, but few how-to directives. One can't be trained on what to say or how to act in every given situation. Service is simply created in the moment and on the spot.

Service as a marketing strategy

The best kept secret in the global economy today is that if your service is awesome you get so stinking rich you have to keep buying new bags to take all of the money home.

Tom Peters

While customer service is people and systems, it also can be viewed as a brilliant marketing strategy. Not a scheme, but a strategy.

John Tschohl says that service works as a multiplier or booster to advertising. If the consumer's mindset about an organization is positive before the advertising is observed, the message is accepted at a deeper level. We have all experienced something or someone whose reputation has preceded them. When Nordstrom opened at the Mall of America in Bloomington, Minnesota, its reputation had already created an excitement for shoppers. Long heralded as one of the leaders in satisfying customers, the well-known retailer was flooded with people anticipating that long-sought-after "primo" service experience. People expect the sales associates at Nordstrom to be service-driven. And most of the time they are. A casual smile or nod of the head at Nordstrom reinforces their image.

The opposite can be true as well. Some government agencies have suffered from poor service reputations. Unfortunately, that reputation precedes the customer's experience and almost anything, from a somber look to a slight glance, can be taken as bad government behavior. At Nordstrom, that look might not have even been noticed.

Taking this a step further, however, when an employee at Nordstrom really blows it and gives bad service, it stands out like a sore thumb. And when a government employee bends over backwards to provide extraordinary service, people seem surprised. The benefit of service as an enhancer is dependent on the degree of good or bad service given. If an organization has a good service reputation going into the experience, a marginal experience will be overlooked. If an organization has a bad service reputation going into the experience, any error will be magnified.

Good service means being "present"

One of the keys to good service is being present. Although this is hard to define, most people understand its meaning. It means paying full attention to someone and having the willingness to understand their needs. Stephen Covey, author of *First Things First*, addresses it this way: "When you acknowledge the presence of others and adapt your presentation in an effort to reach them, in effect you say to them, 'You matter. You're a person of worth. You have intrinsic merit, and I'm not comparing you with anyone else. You are precious.'" He concludes, "As a customer, I can usually tell if front-line service providers are totally present during the few seconds we interact as they take my order or deal with my request. If they are totally present, I sense that they really care."

Willingness to understand and letting people know they really care are two of the reasons Saturn is rated number three in customer satisfaction for car manufacturers, only behind Lexus and Infinity. Long ago, Saturn made the commitment that service would be more important than the quality of the car itself. The quality of the car would be excellent, but the commitment to service excellence would be the number one goal. How? Through willingness to understand and listen to what truly matters to their customers.

Ken Blanchard, author of *The One Minute Manager*, tells this story about a man who wanted to buy a Saturn for his wife. He had just found out that she had beaten cancer following a five-year remission. On the fifth anniversary of that terrifying diagnosis, he wanted to surprise her with the white Saturn she had been admiring for a long time. He called the local Saturn dealer to ask whether they had any white Saturns in stock. They had only one. He assured the dealer that he would take the car, and guaranteed that he would be in the next day to close the deal. That day, he told his wife that he wanted her to go with him for a quick ride. As they walked into the Saturn showroom, he saw that the dealership had moved the white car to the center of the room. His wife moved toward it like a magnet. Then, with a yell and some tears, she read aloud the sign sitting on the front of the car, "Congratulations, Jane, Five Years Cancer-Free—Here's to Life!" What they didn't notice at first was that the Saturn people had moved all of the other customers and sales people outside so Jane could enjoy the moment with some privacy. However, when the people outside saw Jane and her husband hug, everyone started to applaud. Saturn's incredible reputation is made just like this—its people knowing what matters most to the customer—one customer at a time.

Relationships

*The spirit of service comes from very basic personal
feelings about self, work, and other people.*

Karl Albrecht

Jill Janov writes in her book, *The Inventive Organization*, "Our ability to achieve our highest potential at work rests on the relationships we create. If we can reframe our relationships, we can revitalize ourselves and reinvent our organizations." This reinvention is dependent on the person-to-person interface organizations have with customers, either on the phone or in person. Everything else in the organization supports that event.

As stated earlier, customer service is, ultimately, a relationship between the organization and a person seeking a product or service. In order for service to be extraordinary, companies need to achieve deep, rather than broad and shallow, relationships with their customers.

Relationships are about people

When people say that they had a certain kind of experience with an organization, what do they really mean? An organization is not the entity that deals with the customer. It is the people within the organization. Granted, these relationships are often dependent on the rules, policies, culture, and procedures of the organization. But, in reality, the customer relationship is about the interaction between one human being and another.

Most of the time, the customer relationship begins at the time of inquiry. One could even argue that the relationship begins at the time the customer becomes aware of your organization. Right from the beginning, the relationship establishes itself to be either positive or negative. One of the reasons for potential difficulty is the difference in perception between the seller and buyer. For the seller, the point of sale is usually considered the end of the process. But for the buyer, it's just the beginning. The seller must understand that the sale is the beginning of a long-term relationship. In the words of Ron Zemke and Chip Bell, the "art of the deal" must "balance with the long-term relationship."

The definition of relationship

The definition of relationship for our purposes is to "interact with meaning." Simply passing a stranger in the hallway and smiling or nodding does not constitute a relationship. But once we have spent time with someone, helped them identify needs or solve a problem, we have indeed interacted with meaning and have created the foundation of a relationship. With this definition of relationship, to interact with meaning, it is quite clear that we have a relationship with every person with whom we meaningfully interact throughout our business day. No matter how small the sale or infrequent the visit, you and the customers you serve are bound by a relationship based on their needs and expectations and your willingness to live up to their expectations and resolve their needs.

The elements of relationship

Everyone is trying to accomplish something big,
not realizing that life is made up of little things.

Frank A. Clark

Relationships of all kinds must include certain elements to thrive as well as survive. Football coach Lou Holtz teaches us to ask three things about the people with whom we have relationships:

46

- Can I trust you?
- Are you committed to doing your best?
- Do you care about me and my well-being?

These questions aren't answered by words, but by deeds or actions. The same is true with our customer relationships. In order for them to thrive, we must exhibit trustworthiness, show our commitment to always performing at our best, and let the customer know we care about them and their well-being. How would your customers answer these three questions about you and your organization?

When people are asked about their personal, significant relationships, we discover that the quality of those relationships often depends on the presence of certain elements including trust, commitment, honesty, respect, communication, some sense of comfort with the individual, a desire to understand the other's point of view, and sharing common interests. In addition, most people desire some sense of intimacy within their personal relationships. Intimacy, as we will use it here, refers to disclosure. I share certain things about myself with you and you share certain things about yourself with me. The closer we are to people, the more we choose to share emotionally, physically, and spiritually.

If we analyze our relationships with people with whom we interact for business purposes, we will likely discover that they, too, value the above elements. These elements are not at the intensity of our personal relationships, but they are a valuable part of professional relationships where a degree of intimacy or disclosure is appropriate.

For example, shortly after the death of her husband, an elderly woman came into her doctor's office for an appointment. While taking her blood pressure, the nurse casually asked the woman how she was doing. The woman quietly responded that she had not been herself since her husband's death. The nurse sensed that this had not been an easy thing to admit for this private woman. Instead of simply patting her on the arm and telling her that time will heal all things, the nurse disclosed the pain she had felt when her father died. At that moment, two people disclosed information about themselves that opened the door to intimacy and common understanding. The nurse did not take over and dominate the conversation concerning her own pain, but she did disclose that she understood the power of grief and why the patient had not been herself.

You will notice in this example, that the nurse did not say, "I know how you feel." No one knows how another person feels about anything. It is insulting and presumptuous to assume that we do. The preferred response is, "I remember how I felt when my father died. This must be very painful for you."

Maintaining good relationships

The natural tendency of relationships, whether in marriage or business, is toward erosion of sensitivity and attentiveness.

Theodore Levitt

Like other assets, relationships can appreciate or depreciate. For instance, when companies try to boost short-term sales by over selling and over promising, they set themselves up for relationship failure. As soon as they can't keep their overblown promises, they retreat from their responsibilities, and act dishonestly to cover up their failures; the relationship begins to depreciate.

On the other hand, good relationships are well-managed. This takes many forms. For instance, some relationships can be better served by simply spending time rather than doing something. In the relationship between service provider and customer sometimes all that is needed is simple acknowledgment that says: I see you.

Remember the story about the hospital gift shop clerks who ignored me when I went to buy gum? Their primary failure was in not acknowledging me. They were completely void of "I see you," and because of that, I felt invisible. Had either of them simply nodded at me or looked up and smiled when I entered the shop, it would have been an entirely different experience.

Communication is at the core of relationship

Although all of the previous elements of a good relationship are vital, one is the centerpiece. That is communication. Communication is simply an exchange of meaning that leads to mutual understanding.

We will discuss communication in detail in a later chapter, but because communication plays such an important part in providing dazzling service, it will be introduced here.

Service providers communicate all kinds of messages to customers when using phrases such as "How are you," "It's good to see you today," "Next," or "I'd be glad to help you down here." Each one of these statements has a different result. If you are going to sustain a wonderful service reputation, you must find gracious ways to phrase your everyday statements. "I'd be glad to help you down here," is far better than, "Next." And, "It was my pleasure to help you," leaves a more powerful impression than, "Oh, it was nothing." Each of these responses creates an impression on the customer that impacts your service reputation. Ask yourself what customers consistently hear when they come in contact with your organization. If it is your goal to have good relationships with your customers, you must communicate to them that they are important and that they are the only reason you opened the doors or answered the phones that day.

Managing relationships

In addition to good communication, good relationships need to be effectively managed. There are four primary components to successfully managing relationships. They are awareness, assessment, accountability, and action.

Awareness asks the question: Does the relationship exist and who is involved? Assessment asks: How is the relationship doing? Are there problems? Is it working? Accountability asks: What is my role in the relationship? What have I contributed? How has that contribution effected the relationship? Action asks: What can I do to improve the relationship or situation? Who needs to do what?

Managing relationships creates a culture of goodwill in which the tasks that need to be accomplished are done. In organizations where relationships are well managed, the tangible results are improved. In places where people value their relationships and feel like they are a part of a group, more work gets done and gets done better.

Relationship accountability on the front line

We must remember that customer service is about relationships. There is a relationship between the organization and the customer and between the customer and the product or service. At the center of these relationships are the organization's front-line employees. In fact, the primary relationship in customer service is usually the relationship between the customer and the organization's front-line employees. Unfortunately, these are often the lowest paid and least empowered people on the payroll. Why is that a problem? Because employees who feel devalued by the organization tend to pass that message on to the customer. That message is so powerful that we could conclude that service is dependent on how valuable the employee perceives she/he is to the organization. Employees who feel highly valued have reinforced self-esteem. Those who are rewarded and celebrated share their enthusiasm every day by delivering impeccable service. They are inspired by great leadership and reflect the mirrored image of the impeccable service their manager has bestowed on them.

Conclusion

We know that customers come in all shapes and sizes. Some come from across the street, some from across town, some from across the globe, and others from across the office. No matter who your customers are or where they come from, each one has a relationship with you and your organization. The extent to which they value that relationship is equal to their commitment to continue doing business with you over time.

3

Cornerstones of Service

There are four basic, critical cornerstones to insure that service will be an integral part of an organization's philosophy:

> Genuineness
> Attitude
> Congruence
> Paradigm

GENUINENESS

> *Genuine: Sincerely and honestly felt or experienced and free from hypocrisy or pretense.*
>
> Webster's Dictionary

At the heart of providing genuine service, we must care about our work and the people we serve. Dale Carnegie said it best: "People don't care how much you know until they know how much you care." As I've worked with a number of organizations, front-line workers have said to me: "You've got to be kidding. I don't even like a lot of our customers; now you're telling me that I have to care about them." I'm afraid so. But the care I'm talking about here is not a feeling, it is a *behavior*. It doesn't really matter what is felt for the customer because service caring is not about feelings. It is about our day-to-day actions and willingness to perform.

When a number of top executives were asked who they admired most, three names stood out: Lee Iacocca, Albert Einstein, and

Mother Theresa. The first two were obvious, but Mother Theresa? When asked why they chose Mother Theresa, the executives explained, "Because of her ability to care for people in spite of who they are." Her act of love was always the same. Leaders of organizations know that this needs to be true within their organizations as well. Sustained success will only come when all employees genuinely serve all customers, internally and externally, in spite of who they are or how they deserve to be treated. (There is a line that customers can't cross in their treatment of workers. If they do, it is an exception to this. Inappropriate customer behavior will be discussed in chapter 19 about complaints.)

Standards of genuine service

Most people don't like hypocrisy or pretense. They can almost sense it when they walk into a room. People want the real thing, the genuine article, the real McCoy. But no matter where you go today, you can find a number of imitations of the real thing. Watches that look like a Rolex. Cars that resemble Mercedes Benz. Jewelry that looks like Cartier. But nothing replaces the real thing. People get passion in their lives from things that have genuine meaning or are perceived to be real or valuable.

The same is true with service. Customers can tell from the moment they walk in the door whether or not an organization's service is genuine or not. Below are four standards that establish whether service will be perceived as genuine or viewed simply as a cheap imitation of the real thing.

First, the genuineness of service is judged *by the way it works*. Just as you might suspect that the watch you bought from the beach-side shop in Mexico is not a real Rolex by the way it works, you will also conclude whether service is real or not by the way it works. People experience genuine service from you according to:
- how far out of your way you go to help them;
- how hard you work to solve their problem;
- how much time you spend with them;
- how you remedy breakdowns.

All of these processes are essential for us to believe that service is genuine. Service breakdowns, just as product breakdowns, must be remedied efficiently and effectively. For example, if a real Rolex breaks, chances are that the people who repair the watch are attentive and responsive. However, just try to get that imitation Rolex repaired back at the beachside shop in Mexico. The people providing the real product are dependent on it working and working well. They realize that their reputation depends not only on this but also on the customer's willingness to return and purchase products in the future. The same is true with genuine service. The customer will judge service, in part, by the ease and commitment with which the providers fix problems when they do occur. (We will explore how to do this later.)

Secondly, we get an impression of service *by the way things look*. A cluttered, messy work station may make us think twice about leaving an expensive watch to be repaired. Or a dirty waiting area may make us question the decision to have a haircut at that salon. Looks can be deceiving, but sometimes they are all we have to go on, and we draw a number of conclusions from what we see. How does genuine service look?

- **Clean,** organized and open for business.
- **Alert** and ready to move into action. People just hanging around never give the impression that they want to help. In fact, we often feel like we are imposing when we approach them to do business.
- **Groomed** and appropriately dressed. Sue Morem, a Minneapolis based expert on professionalism and author of *How to Gain the Professional Edge,* has dedicated her career to helping people appear appropriate for their line of work. In her research, she has confirmed the importance of looking the part and presenting oneself in the best possible light. Can you imagine your heart transplant surgeon chewing on gum or having dirty fingernails or dressing in bib overalls? Something tells me you'd ask for a second opinion. The same is true about everyone in every professional role. They are judged, fairly or not, by the way they look.
- **Confident.** We judge the genuineness of service by the confidence exuded by the service provider. If we walk into a shop and ask

a question about a product or service, and the person we ask seems uncertain or uninformed, we will not trust the answer or be able to rely on the response. Customers do business with organizations where employees are trained well and empowered to help. The customer does not believe that service is genuine if the person providing the service is not confident about what they do or what they know.

Thirdly, genuine service *has a special sound to it.* People who genuinely want to serve share that desire in their tone of voice and in the words they use. A tone of voice that indicates a genuine willingness to serve is friendly, warm, and sincere. We read a great deal into the service provider's tone of voice. One tone saying, "May I help you?" may sound genuine and sincere while another tone, using the same words, may say, "Must you be here now? Can't you see I'm busy?" We will talk in greater detail about the importance of tone in the discussion concerning congruency.

The words that communicate service in a genuine manner are known as customer-friendly language. These include:

• Using the **customer's name.** Few things are more appealing to a person than the sound of his/her own name. Refer to the person by their formal name unless they ask you to do otherwise, e.g.: "Ms. Jones, Mr. Smith, Dr. Anderson." Don't overdo this. A lot of sales people evidently took a class in which they were told to use the customer's name. Many now do so to such an extent that it becomes more irritating than not using their name at all. Use the customer's name a couple of times and only when it is most appropriate. This might be in greeting the customer or when the customer is departing. This is especially important in organizations where a customer does repeat business and their name is often in front of the service provider either on a check, service order, or chart. This is true in doctors' offices, dental clinics, banks, car repair shops, and attorneys' offices. There is rarely any excuse not to use the customer's name in these settings. Organizations where this is not consistently done are neglecting a simple, inexpensive, and effective customer-friendly tool.

• Using **pedestal phrases** such as, "That sounds like a good idea" or, "You know what? I think you're right" or "I really appreciate your input."

• Using **please and thank you.** As kids, most of us were taught to use these words and they are as valuable today as they were then.

Finally, customers will know service is genuine *by the way it feels.* When customers are asked, "Why didn't you go back to that place to do business," a lot of times they will answer, "It just didn't feel friendly" or "I always felt like an intruder" or "They always seemed too busy to help me." Much of what we do in life is predicated on how we feel. We trust our gut and depend on those feelings to help us make decisions. The same is true with service. People seek services and products from doctors, clothiers, mechanics, plumbers, dentists, clinics, and restaurants, because they liked someone or felt confident about the quality of their work or service. Here are the subconscious feeling questions people ask about the organizations with which they do business:

Do I feel welcome in your presence?

Do I feel safe? Do you have my best interests in mind?

Do I feel comfortable or are you busy putting on airs and trying to impress me?

Do I feel important to you or am I just another interruption to your busy day?

Do I feel calm or is doing business with you hectic and stressful?

ATTITUDE

> *Service as gift-giving is a selfless act, not a tactical decision.*
>
> Chip R. Bell

If there were a single most important element of service, it would be attitude. Attitude is like a filter that hangs over our eyes through which we view our lives. If our attitude is bad, everything looks bad. If it is good, things look good. In addition to being a screen through which our reality is filtered, attitude also creates our emotional climate, positions our mind for the direction it will take, and is a choice.

Attitude creates our emotional climate

Most people dislike being in the presence of a person with a bad attitude. My least favorite bad attitude is *martyr.* I don't enjoy being with

The longer I live, the more I realize the impact of attitude on life. Attitude, to me, is more important than facts. It is more important than the past, than education, than money, than circumstances, than failures, than success, than what other people think or say or do. It is more important than appearance, giftedness, or skill. It will make or break a company, a church, a home. The remarkable thing is we have a choice everyday regarding the attitude we will embrace for that day. We cannot change our past...we cannot change the fact that people will act in a certain way. We cannot change the inevitable. The only thing we can do is play on the one string we have, and that is our attitude...I am convinced that life is 10 percent what happens to me and 90 percent how I react to it. And so it is with you...

Charles Swindoll

people who believe that life has been especially difficult for them and that the rest of us have gotten off with nary a worry. (Yes, life has been harder for some people than others and I sympathize with them. There are some horror stories in life and they break my heart.) But I'm talking about the woe-is-me and ain't-it-awful people, who spend precious time basking in their own misfortune. What's really at the center of their trouble is their attitude. In fact, it doesn't really matter what happens to a person in life; what really matters is how they react to what has happened. What matters is attitude.

If attitude creates our emotional climate, then we really are each other's weather and daily environment. Do you feel depressed at the end of the day? Maybe it's because everyday you work across from drizzle. Or maybe you sit in meetings with fog, rain, dark skies, or thunder. All of these climates affect you just as powerfully as meteorological climates. If you go home every night feeling down, there's a good chance that someone has been raining on your parade.

More important than the weather others bring to your world is the weather you bring to others. Are you thunder, rain, drizzle, dark clouds, or fog; or are you a ray of sunshine, a breath of fresh air, and blue skies? The weather you bring affects someone else's ability to serve.

Attitude positions our mind

> *Attitudes are more important than facts.*
> Karl Menninger

It's amazing how easy it is to do the things in life that we have a good attitude about. We get up on a Saturday morning and we can (a) clean the garage, (b) have brunch with friends, or (c) play golf. In which descending order do you think these will be done? The answer: The one you have the best attitude about will get done first. The same is true with service. If you have a positive attitude about service, look forward to helping people, and realize your paycheck ultimately depends on the quality of your service, you will put service at the center of your professional world and build everything else around it. And if you don't care about people or your job, service will be the last thing on your mind.

Attitude is a choice

Of all of the concepts regarding attitude, this is the hardest one for many people to accept. They contend, "I am what I am." This is me. What you see is what you get. Don't ask me to be all sugar and spice to my customers, it's not my style. But in truth, we are not etched in granite. We are fluid and, although it can be challenging to change, we are capable of changing. According to Deepak Chopra, what we really are is the "sum total of all of our choices." Choose one thing and we're this. Choose another and we're that. Not that change is easy; it's not. Personal change is always a challenge, whether it's smoking cessation, starting to exercise, or changing our attitude. But what we ultimately do about these things is always our choice.

The biggest obstacles to change are our habits and comfort zone. We never like being too far from either. Imagine your conscious mind as a guard standing at the door of a library which is your sub-conscious mind. Taking it a step further, let's say you work for a com-pany where everyone knows you are not the friendly type. In fact, you're down right crabby. Whenever you meet a co-worker in the hallway, you put your head down, grunt, and pass on by. Nobody pays much attention to this because that's just you and no one expects anything different. Right? What's really happening is that your conscious mind (the guard) sees a co-worker coming down the hall, reaches back into your subconscious mind (the library), grabs the tape closest to the door (your habits and comfort zone), plugs the tape into your behavior, and you, as always, put down your head, grunt, and pass on by. Why? Because that's you? No. Because that behavior has become your habit, and from your habit you have cre-ated your comfort zone.

Let's say you decide that being an unfriendly, grunting co-worker is not how you want to spend the rest of your professional life. You realize that you are lonely and empty and have few friends. You decide you want to change. (Always step number one.) You have a lot of tapes in your head. You even have one about being nice to people. You know how people act when they are friendly and how good rela-tionships work. You may even have read something on interpersonal relationships or have seen someone interact well with people. With this new understanding, the next time you're walking down the hall and a co-worker approaches, you choose to reach into the back of the library for the tape on how to be nice to people and plug it in. This time you stop, smile, and say, "Hello, Mary, how have you been? I haven't seen you in a while." And your life is never the same.

One of the best examples of this comes from the late Viktor Frankl, the author of *Man's Search for Meaning*. During World War II, Frankl, a psychiatrist from Vienna, was sent to Auschwitz. He had seen all that he loved destroyed in front of his eyes. People he knew and loved had been brutally taken from him. Devastation of this magnitude can barely be imagined. Unbelievably, at the end of the war, Victor Frankl walked out of the concentration camp whole. "How did you do this?" he was asked. His answer, "I chose." The next time you're having a bad day, or don't like your job, or the boss, or the customer, remember that you will always choose how you act, what you say, and how you are. You will choose to serve or not to serve. It is always up to you.

The attitude of service is in the heart

The attitude of service is based on a definition shared with me by friend and author Lawrence Harmon. It is this:

> *Customer, tell me what it is you need, how you need it, and when you need it, and I will do everything in my power to give it to you just that way. You see, I'm here to serve you. That is the purpose of my work.*

If we serve for a living, if service is our product, we are servants. Period. At the core of service, at its very root, is the servant's heart. And the depth and quality of our relationship with our customers, especially a servant relationship, is equal to the degree to which we are willing to sacrifice for them.

Sacrifice is part of any relationship built on depth and commitment. Relationships with customers are no different. If there is little or no sacrifice, the quality of the relationship will suffer. In the midst of sacrifice is commitment to the job, the customer, and ourselves. In the end, even career success comes from the committed—those who work from the heart.

A lot of us don't like the word servant. Our Japanese counterparts don't seem to have the same aversion to the concept of servanthood. In fact, the word for customer in Japanese translates literally to "honored guest." I'm not on the bandwagon that everything regarding Japanese business is good and everything regarding American business bad. I know that isn't true. But, in this instance, American workers could learn something about the art of service from their Japanese neighbors.

Part of the reason that the concept of servant is so hard to internalize is that so many American workers already feel like second-class citizens within their organizations. But servanthood is not about second-class citizenship. In true servanthood, no one is made to feel less than another, humiliated, abused, used, ignored, belittled, taken advantage of, or treated poorly in any way. These cruel behaviors are not about servanthood but slavery. Slavery is not a choice; it is imposed and always wrong. Servanthood, instead, is a chosen position one has in relationship to another.

Humbleness: the missing link in service

When humans created the mirror, they began to lose their soul.
They became more interested in image than character or substance.

Stephen Covey

True servanthood is about a change of heart: the servant's heart. It is about being humble—an attitude which long ago succumbed to greed, power, and success. But as Sam Walton said, "The bigger you get, the smaller you've got to think." Humbleness is about thinking small. About one person, one customer, at a time.

Sajeela Moskowitz Ramsey, author and consultant, writes in *Executive Excellence*, "If we are obsessed with success, control, answers, ascendance, prestige, materialism, winning, and going for it all, we cannot serve. To serve well, we must focus on the opposite. To be humble, imaginative, patient, and to go for the best solution." This is about devoting our whole being toward a higher purpose in our work.

To achieve the humbleness needed to drive the servant's heart, you must commit to three steps. The first step in creating the servant's heart is to *leave your needs at home* or in the car when you come to work each day. The needs of others must be in front of you all day long instead of your own problems and concerns.

The second step in creating the servant's heart is to *leave your ego at the door.* Bring your self-esteem, that is your healthy partner in life. But leave that puffed up part of you that wants others to know how much you know, what you think, and what you have done. Get the spotlight off yourself and onto the needs of others. To paraphrase a saying by Dale Carnegie: You can gain more commitment and dedication from others in two hours of being interested in them than you can in two months of trying to get them interested in you.

Finally, you must *leave your need to be right at the door,* in the car, or at home when you come to work each day. You know people who will fight tooth and nail to prove they're right. And what do they gain? TV talk show host, Oprah Winfrey, said that she had given up participating in arguments in which she was trying to prove she was right. She realized that they wasted valuable time and lost people's goodwill. It was simply no longer worth the fight. She realized that she gained nothing in the end.

The same is true with customers. Is the customer always right? No! An emphatic no. No matter what you have read or been taught in customer service classes, the customer is not always right. Not only are they often wrong, but they are sometimes mean-spirited, underhanded, crabby, or bullheaded. But they are always the customer and you will always choose how you are going to treat them.

Climbing the servant's ladder to success

We make a living by what we get. We make a life by what we give.
Winston Churchill

The dichotomy concerning servanthood is that the higher up in the organization you climb, the greater your servanthood grows. In fact, leaders are super servants who are in place to serve those who serve the external customer. Super servants have enormous responsibility and are profoundly important to the life of the organization. They create avenues and remove barriers to serving the customer. But if they become barriers themselves instead, they are no longer functioning as leaders and cease to be valuable.

Dan Hanson, author of *A Place to Shine: Bringing Special Gifts to Light*, believes that to be an effective leader, you must bring your heart to the workplace. He also teaches that the work place should be a caring community of workers engaged in a shared purpose for the common good. But he laments that that caring community and common good seem to go out the window when the health of the organization is challenged. When deficits begin to rear their ugly head or resource materials dramatically change cost projections, organizations go back to hiding behind the invisible shield of imperialism. Servant leaders, on the other hand, rise above the fray and maintain their sense of service even during the most difficult and challenging times.

The system is also a servant

In addition to the front-line worker and the leader, the system, that black hole that seems to create frustration for employees and customers alike, is there for one reason and one reason only—the system is in place to serve. If the system impedes or encumbers service, it must be taken apart and reassembled with one goal in mind: It must serve the customer or someone who is serving the customer.

In the end, if the only thing someone has available is an attitude driven by the need to delight and serve the customer, this is all that is needed. If nothing else in this book makes sense, just look in the mirror and ask: Who am I deep in my heart and what am I willing to do for others? An honest answer will set the course for the rest of your life.

CONGRUENCE

Nothing has any meaning in life except the meaning we give it.
Anthony Robbins

The definition of communication, as we will define it throughout this material, is an *exchange of meaning*. If service is going to be communicated—and it must be communicated— it needs to be communicated with congruence. This means to communicate an effective message, words, tone, and body language all need to say the same thing.

The problem with incongruence is that the meaning of the communication is not clear and consequently it cannot be trusted. When people are communicating with us, all of our senses are involved. And contrary to common sense, the greatest sensory tool in communication is not hearing but sight. If you see it, you can believe it. Often, what you see is telling you the opposite of what you hear. When this happens, the incongruence renders the words virtually powerless.

Mehrabian's theory

Dr. Albert Mehrabian, author of *Silent Messages*, developed a theory that is still perceived as valid by many communication specialists. His theory suggests that

> 7 percent of our meaning is communicated through words,
>
> 38 percent through tone of voice, and
>
> 55 percent through body language or physiology.

If Mehrabian is right, and most suspect that he is, we could conclude that it makes little difference what we say since the real meaning comes from how (tone) it is said and in what manner (body language) it is presented.

One of the most familiar examples of this theory can be witnessed in the expression, "I'm sorry." The conversation goes something like this, "I said I was sorry." "No, you didn't." "Yes, I did. Didn't you hear me?" "I know you said you were sorry, but I know you're not sorry." And on it goes. This kind of conversation makes people feel crazy. The real problem with this apology is incongruence. The minimally powerful words (7 percent) are saying I'm sorry, but the tone and body language are saying get off my back and leave me alone. Unfortunately, those big messengers—tone, and body language—are all that the receiver is hearing.

Incongruence and service

How does incongruence affect service? It is probably at the core of more bad service and customer dissatisfaction than any other issue. It is what causes a service provider to slowly shuffle toward a customer and, in a completely disinterested tone, ask, "Can I help you?" Or if the customer has had a problem, the service provider says in a couldn't-care-less voice, "We're really sorry." But everyone knows the truth. The truth could be heard through body language and tone of voice, and it's perfectly clear that this service provider was anything but sorry.

I experienced incongruence first hand when Lonna Mosow, Susan Vass, Sue Morem, and I were making plans to present our seminar *The Power Behind the Promise*. We had previously presented it at the Sheraton Airport Hotel in Bloomington, Minnesota, where the staff had done a wonderful job serving us and helping make the event a success. But due to greater than anticipated attendance, we needed to move our next presentation to a larger hotel. We selected a reputable hotel in another Minneapolis suburb where we were given a verbal commitment on our room. The confirmation papers were to follow. We cleared our calendars, began working on the promotional materials, and announced the seminar's date and place during many of our personal appearances. As the date for registration approached, I received a phone call from the hotel's events department informing me that they could not honor their commitment to us and that we should not be upset because their commitment to us was "only verbal." The reason for bumping us was that a larger group wanted our room plus fifty sleeping rooms; this was a deal the hotel "couldn't pass up."

We were extremely disappointed. But what made this such an irritating experience was not the fact that we were "bumped." We all know that at times organizations have to make business decisions where someone is going to be at the short end of the stick. What upset us was the way it was handled. The woman from the events' department called and said in her sweetest little, I-could-not-care-less voice how sorry she was that this had happened. But in reality, there was not one morsel of sorry in her voice. Had she genuinely said how hard the decision was to make, how deeply they regretted having to make it, and, maybe, had they given us a little "spiff" (e.g., upgrade the sound system at no charge) to encourage us to pick another date, we might have chosen a new date, booked the hotel, and walked away happy customers. But that's not how it was handled.

This hotel lost the goodwill of four potential customers (who all speak for a living, by the way) not so much because of their decision, but because of the way the message was delivered. At the very core of the message, we needed to believe that there was some honest remorse. But her tone of voice made it clear that there was none. The entire conversation had been steeped in incongruence.

An important lesson to be learned from this is that anytime you are dealing with people over the telephone, you have lost fifty-five percent of your communication power. What this means is that communication over the phone must be exaggerated. In person, someone can get by with a sad look, slumped shoulder, and a meager "I'm sorry." But over the telephone, that sad look and slumped shoulder are missing. This means that you need to verbally express a more emphatic, "I'm sorry." The speaker must project the image of the sad look and slumped shoulder into the mind of the receiver. This image is created and projected by words and tone. Expressions that would be considered over done and far too dramatic in person are needed to create the picture for the cerebral eye of the telephone recipient.

Finally, the least powerful of the communicators, words, need to be expressed clearly and chosen deliberately, especially when communicating in writing. In today's business culture, where communications transpire over fax machines, e-mail, and computers, writing is quickly becoming a rediscovered art. But the written word can be mired in ambiguity. People aren't always clear as to what was meant by what was written. Because of this, when people say they are reading between the lines, they are actually looking for meaning in the missing tone and body language. How did she look and what was her tone when she wrote, "Dear John?" When people are able to be concise and express themselves clearly in writing, the reader can relax and grasp the true meaning of the message. If not, the reader spends a great deal of time and energy trying to decipher the truth.

Being congruent with the customer

In addition to being congruent with oneself—making certain that your words, body language, and tone all say the same thing—you must be congruent with the customer. A practice that supports this is

Neuro Linguistic Programming (NLP). Although NLP is much more sophisticated than I have the time or ability to explain here, its basic premise is that the skill of influencing comes, in part, from mirroring the style of the person you want to influence. Based on the theory that likes attract, it concludes that we will do more business with people like us than people who are considerably different from us. This, in essence, is about congruence.

A delightful example of a service encounter gone bad due to incongruence is a scene in the movie *Trains, Planes and Automobiles*. In the story, John Candy and Steve Martin are trying to get home for the Thanksgiving holiday. A winter storm grounds their plane, their bus runs out of route, and their train breaks down several miles away from the nearest road. Steve Martin, whose character is just a teensy bit up-tight, can tolerate the nightmare no longer.

Needing to separate himself from the just-a-little-too-friendly Candy, he decides to rent a car. He's taken by bus to the car rental lot which is, of course, at the farthest part of the airport. There, he gets off of the bus and walks to the space where his rental car should be parked. But the only thing in this parking spot is skid marks. He can't believe it. He throws his briefcase to the ground and flails his arms in the air in a fit of anger.

Once calmed down, he begins his three-mile walk back to the terminal. During his trek, he falls down an embankment, watches as his hat gets run over by a speeding truck, and ends up walking into the airport terminal wearing his necktie as a scarf. Now a customer wearing a necktie as a scarf should be an indication that there is a problem. But the rental agent didn't notice this since she was on the telephone with a personal call. She finally ended her telephone conversation with, "Gobble, gobble," and turned to look at Steve Martin, who looked like he'd been shot out of a cannon into a wall. She remembered her customer service training, smiled, and said in a sweet-as-sugar voice, "How may I help you?" I will not repeat his response, but it involved the maniacal repetition of a very bad word. I believe, had he been able, he would have reached across that counter and scratched that smile right off her face.

I submit that had the rental agent hung up the phone, looked at him, and said in a caring and concerned voice, "Oh, my word. What happened? What can I do to help you?" He would have been angry that the car wasn't there, but he would not have gone ballistic. What made him crazy was her smile and her complete oblivion to his situation. She pretended she didn't see anything wrong and chose, instead, to ignore all of his obvious signs. This is an example of being incongruent with the customer's mood or frame of mind. Providing dazzling customer service is (1) recognizing the customer's frame of mind, and then (2) responding in an appropriate manner. If the customer is angry, you are concerned. If the customer is upset, you are calm and caring. And if the customer is happy, you mirror that joy. You become a key part of their experience.

PARADIGM

The significant problems we face cannot be solved at the same level of thinking we were at when we created them.

Albert Einstein

Because it is not a perfect world, the only true and lasting service comes from the paradigm or foundation on which it was built. According to Thomas Kuhn in *The Structure of Scientific Revolutions*, a paradigm is "a model or a way of viewing things." Or more simply put, according to Karl Albrecht, a paradigm is "a mental frame of reference that dominates the way people think and act." Our paradigms become our filter of reality. They are important because they govern the way we view the world and the way we make decisions regarding that world.

Organizations committed to service can adopt one of these three things, **thinking, behavior,** or **paradigm,** to change their service reputation. Each is a valid change agent, but the depth and transcending quality of the change depend upon which you choose.

Change thinking

Thinking is linear and typically one-directional. For instance, an organization can adopt a service policy about waiting in line. This service thinking is about one thing, waiting in line, and has little effect on any of the other activities within the organization. Many times thinking is reinforced with slogans and signs such as, "You will never have to wait in line." Thinking is limited to one process at a time and is managed by everyone's collective understanding of the process.

In order to change an entire organization's thinking, each issue the organization faces needs to be discussed, a decision must be made, and everyone needs to buy into that decision. In order to have any effect on the overall image of the organization, each worker needs to be aware of, and committed to, each appropriate decision for every customer transaction. In organizations committed to changing thinking, you probably hear employees frequently ask, "What did they decide our policy was concerning this?" Every situation would have a policy or concluded thought, and everyone would need to know each of those policies and thoughts. Needless to say, this would be a daunting task.

Change behavior

The second method for bringing an entire organization "on board the service bandwagon" is for all workers to adopt certain customer service behaviors. When behaviors drive an organization's performance, workers are programmed to behave in a certain way based on a specific stimulus. For instance, an organization could mandate that all employees say, "Hi, my name is [Petra], and I would be more than happy to show you around" every time a customer walked in. Even though this sounds nice at first, it loses much of its appeal as customers hear this exact statement repeated 25 times by 25 different people. Pre-scripted statements also lose their charm for customers making four or five trips and always hearing the same thing. Even mild-mannered Minnesotans have even been known to snap, "Enough already with the happy talk. Can't you think of something else to say?"

If you remember when I was asked to write a service program for a major retail center, they asked me to design a script that would tell *their people* how to act and what to say in any given situation. What they really wanted me to do was program their employees' behaviors. But workers at retail centers face so many diverse situations that it would be impossible to be scripted for every situation. As an example, one of the retail workers told about a customer who approached the guest services desk carrying a brown paper bag. The customer asked the guest services worker, "Would you mind watching this bag for me? My snake eggs are in here and they're about to hatch." Something tells me we would not have included how to handle snake-egg requests in our script, and that guest services worker would have been incapable of handling the situation effectively.

Service thinking and service behavior create shallow and empty experiences for customers. In addition, they are not reliable. They often depend on the moods of employees and the situations they face. When the stars are all properly aligned and the moon is full, in other words when everything is perfect, workers can think about each service concept and act out the behaviors mandated by the organization. The unfortunate reality is that this is not a perfect world, the moon isn't always full, and clouds often cover the stars.

Change paradigms

Paradigms are constantly in flux. They are dynamic and changing. As soon as an old paradigm loses the power of its explanation, a new paradigm is in the making. Joel Barker, author and futurist, teaches that there are a number of ramifications as new paradigms begin to infiltrate the changing body. There is turbulence, disagreement, dissension, and, finally, gradual acceptance. And as soon as this new paradigm loses it usefulness, another new paradigm will begin.

Our paradigms are essentially what we believe to be true. Each paradigm is made up of entire thinking patterns, not simply one linear thought. Joel Barker has done considerable work on the concept of paradigms. His powerful example of Swiss watchmakers illustrates the considerable magnitude paradigms have on decisions as well as decision makers. In his film, *Discovering the Future: The Business of Paradigms*, Barker tells how 60 percent of the Swiss work force made its living making watches. In fact, Switzerland was known universally as the country where watches were made. But, as Barker points out, the Swiss were stuck in their paradigm on what made watches work. Because of that, they lost out on an opportunity that changed the watch-making industry.

Several Swiss workers had approached their managers with a new, revolutionary idea on how to make a watch run. But the managers had been in the watch-making business for a long time and knew how to make a watch. To make a watch run, there had to be gears and those gears needed to be wound up. These workers were talking about something that didn't have any gears and never needed to be wound up. They were talking about quartz. Unfortunately, the Swiss managers couldn't see the potential of quartz because their watch-making paradigm was in the way. So the Swiss workers took their idea to a New York trade show where it was adopted by competitors who revolutionized the watch-making industry.

Just as the Swiss watchmakers' ability to accept change was clouded by their paradigm, numerous other leaders' and great thinkers' abilities to accept changing concepts or see possibilities was clouded by paradigm. Consider these:

> *Radio has no future.*
>
> Lord Kelvin, President, Royal Society

> *Everything that can be invented has been invented.*
>
> Charles H. Duell, Director U.S. Patent Office, 1899

> *Sensible and reasonable women do not want to vote.*
>
> Grover Cleveland, 1905

> *There is no likelihood that man can ever tap the power of the atom.*
>
> Robert Milikan, Physics Nobel Laureate 1923

> *Who wants to hear actors talk?*
>
> Harry Warner

> *I think there's a world market for about five computers.*
>
> T.J. Watson, Chairman, IBM

> *There is no reason for any individual to have a computer in their home.*
>
> Ken Olsen, President, DEC

As astounding as these statements now seem, they were made by bright people with great talent. Is it any wonder that change is so difficult for so many of us?

Stephen Covey tells a story in his book, *The Seven Habits of Highly Effective People*, which further helps bring the concept of paradigm to light. It takes place on a bright Sunday morning in New York. On this quiet, sunny morning, he was enjoying the ride across town on a city bus. Basking in the solitude and quiet, he noticed a man with three children get on board. The children immediately began running around the bus, yelling and carrying on. Covey, who had up until then been enjoying the trip, could feel himself becoming more and more agitated. What could he do to cope with this interruption? Well, he reasoned, he could change his thinking. After all they were only kids. He could get over it by using the power of positive thinking his friend, Norman Vincent Peale, had taught. He also knew he could change his behavior. He could move to a different part of the bus to distance himself from the disturbance. But what happened in real life changed his paradigm. He approached the father, "You know your kids are really misbehaving. Do you think you could do something to keep them under control?" "I'm really sorry," responded the father, "we're on our way home from the hospital. Their mother died last night." With that news, Covey didn't have to change his thinking or his behavior. His paradigm had changed. The children looked different, the father looked different. The day looked different. Everything had changed. He was transformed.

In order for organizations to serve at the level that matters, service must come from the organizational and personal paradigm of service. Without this, service will be hollow and fixed and will not withstand the day-to-day pressures that organizations face.

Paradigms are spiritual

Jack Hawley, in his book, *Reawakening The Spirit in Work: The Power of Dharmic Management*, writes that transformation or paradigm change usually occurs at a spiritual level. It is at the spiritual level within an organization that service paradigms are changed. Once a genuine service principle has been identified as foundational, everyone knows that they come to work each day to do one thing—to serve somebody. And from this foundation, no one asks, "Should we refund this?" or "Should I give this to the customer?" or "Should I do that?" Everyone knows that the customer is exalted. No one has to think about what decision they should make, nor does anyone have to worry about how to behave or act. Service simply exists in all things, in all ways, and at all times.

In order for service to be steeped within the organization's basic philosophies, the organization must be evolving from their old paradigms into new paradigms. The new market doesn't care about yesterday's ways or rules. Just because that's the way you've done it in the past means nothing to the customer unless it works best for them today.

The evolution of paradigms

What got me where I am won't get me where I'm going.
Michael Lebeouff

If dazzling service is dependent on the organization's foundational values, it needs to show up daily in the way the organization does business at the most basic level. No one expects this change to happen overnight. In fact, it can't happen overnight. Too many behaviors and policies have become habit from years and years of operating from a paradigm not founded on service. But if your organization is serious about service, you need to be somewhere along an evolutionary path that supports a service paradigm. To better understand where your organization is in its evolutionary process, ask yourself where your organization, or department, falls on this evolutionary scale:

OLD PARADIGM .... NEW PARADIGM

1	2	3	4	5	6	7	8	9	10

Control...Empowerment
Problems... ....Causes
Strategy... ....Vision
Policies...Values
Manager...Leader
Cost...Investment
Top-down...System-wide

If your organization scores 1s, 2s, and 3s on most areas of this scale, you will have a tough time integrating genuine service into your organization's everyday performance. If you are scoring an occasional 4 but mostly 5s, 6s, and 7s, you are well on your way to becoming a customer-driven organization. And if you scored mostly 8s, 9s, and 10s, congratulations on the wonderful contribution you are making to your customers, employees, stockholders, and community.

Changing the paradigm

Is it easy to change an organization's service paradigm? No. But there is one paradigm that no one can afford to resist—that business is dependent on customers for mere survival. If everything on earth isn't being done to secure customers' life-long commitment to you, then you're kidding yourself about being a contender in the future.

Although it can take time and considerable effort for an organization to change its paradigm, an individual's paradigm can change in a heartbeat. There are no systems, no forms, no group-think to change. A person can simply choose to be better every day in every moment.

Conclusion

The cornerstones of genuineness, attitude, congruence, and paradigm are at the core of all great service. If nothing more than these four cornerstones become the center of your service philosophy, you will thrive.

4

Change

Knowing why service is important and what service means will not establish an organization's service image. In order for service to have any real value, it must be part of everyday operations. And in most organizations that means there is a critical need for change. Forler Massnick, consultant and author, claims that a number of companies *talk* customer service but few are actually providing it on a consistent basis. In other words, nothing's changing. One of the reasons for this, as we discussed in chapter one, is that front-line workers are not buying in. Why? Because nothing has changed in the way they are treated or in the systems and polices that create their work foundation. Workers today look at service and quality initiatives simply as ploys to get fewer people to do more work with fewer resources. If service is going to be a foundational principle within an organization, that organization must transform or change so that all aspects of its existence are based on service principles.

Change is an interesting process with which all humans are faced. According to material presented by consultant Mary Jo Paloranta, within the decade between1985 and 1995:

• Half of all U.S. companies were restructured.
• Eighty thousand firms were acquired or merged.

- Several hundred thousand companies were downsized.
- At least 700,000 companies sought bankruptcy.
- More than 450,000 others went out of business.

In other words, these organizations faced incredible change. Although some of these changes were chosen, more often change was imposed. Either way, everyone within these organizations was affected by change one way or another. Some people find it difficult to endure the process of change, even more find it hard to embrace. Although change is an inevitable part of life, it affects people in a number of ways. Since it takes energy to change, many find it draining. Others find it exciting. Then there are those who do anything to avoid change all together.

Those who will do anything to avoid change avoid it even if the change might prove to be better for them in the long run. This was brought to life in the response to the question: What's the difference between a human and a mouse? The answer: If a mouse is put into a maze with a piece of cheese at one end, it will run through the maze, grab the cheese, eat it, return to the starting point and repeat the process. However, if one day no cheese is put at the end of the maze, the mouse will run through the maze, go back, start again, run through the maze, go back, start again, run through the maze, go back, start again, and again, and again, and again. But one day the mouse will stop running back to look for the cheese. Human beings, on the other hand, never seem to get the message. No matter how poor the results might be or how obviously hopeless the situation, some people seem to repeat the same behaviors day after day, year after year, until they die. Unless they choose to step out of their comfort zone and establish new behaviors, the fear of change will keep them stuck in a maze where there is no reward. People who are willing to change accept and appropriately respond to the messages they're given. Not because they have no fear. They simply proceed in spite of their fear.

Change, in and of itself, is neither good nor bad. Change simply is. What we do know is that things can change for the better or they can change for the worse. Which actually occurs largely depends on our reaction to change. Organizations must change right down to their core. Why? Because people are changing. Expectations and demands are changing. Political climates are changing. Organizations that ignore these changes will not only lose but will find themselves completely out of the race.

The ill effects of change

Why does change create so much anxiety? It's usually not the change itself that creates anxiety, but the uncertainty that comes with change. When people know exactly what will happen in the process of change, there is some apprehension. But when there is ambiguity, as there usually is with change, there is anxiety and stress. The changes organizations face today are filled with uncertainty and ambiguity and are creating enormous amounts of anxiety and stress. (We will discuss remedies to stress in chapter sixteen). Right-sizing. Re-engineering. Down-sizing. No matter how many different ways it's said, these changes often mean someone is going to lose their job and some manager needs to decide who that will be. Anxiety? There's a world filled with it.

Some leaders choose not to implement necessary changes because they assume that people don't like change. That isn't necessarily true. People can be exhilarated by change if they perceive there is opportunity for improvement as a result. For people to proceed without fear, leaders must provide accurate, timely information, and be open to honest communication along the way.

The ramifications of change

Because all change involves self-change, everyone within an organization needs to stop and ask:
- What does this change mean to me?
- What do I have to learn to implement these changes?
- How will I best use my skills?
- How can I contribute to this change's success?

If part of the organization's new directive is to become customer-driven, people will need to unlearn old ways and learn new and innovative methods that will stop customers in their tracks with delight.

In addition, everyone must ask:
- What is my role in this change?
- What does this change ultimately mean to the organization's success?

In today's unbelievably fast-paced world, the ability to change may be equal to an organization's ability to survive.

Organizations that make the changes necessary to compete often find themselves at the head of the pack. Tom Peters tells how the Swiss watch industry was revitalized by the creation of the Swatch. The Swatch signaled to the world that telling time was no longer the most important part of the watch. It was now about fun and jewelry. The Swiss, stung by the loss of market share while stuck in their watch-making paradigm, learned their lesson and chose to use this change in the watch industry to their advantage.

Making change a success

Because change is participatory in nature, when change is eminent, this question must be asked, "What needs to be done to make this change a success?" Following are several conditions that must be present in order for change to be successful.

Patience

People working within organizations that have historically been top-down or hierarchical are anxiously waiting for things to change. They hear their leaders talking about "empowerment" and "putting customers first," yet the business is operating in the same old authoritative, top-down manner. "When is it going to change?"

Change takes time, and patience is born over time. In many organizations, fundamental change can take years. The culture—norms (policies, procedures, and rules), traditions, values, and beliefs—needs to catch up with the new paradigm. Most of the time, the culture reflects the old paradigm. It takes time for the new culture and the structure to be established.

As was stated before, one of the most powerful realizations is that even though the organization's ability to change its paradigm might take time, an individual's paradigm, yours, can change in a heartbeat. The commitment to service can be made in an instant. "I'm going to serve the customer from the heart *in spite* of our organization's structure." True winners don't wait for the organization to take the first step. They recoil from the whining, "Well, my manager hasn't changed. Nothing has changed in the organization. Why should I break my neck to give good service when no one else is?" And winners, not whiners, blaze through that dead-end thinking with, "I don't care what anyone else does. This is about me and me doing what's right for myself and for my customer."

Be patient with the changes your organization must go through while becoming customer-driven. And in the process, be a champion of service. Not because the people around you deserve it, but because you are a person who consistently chooses to do the right thing.

Commitment

In addition to patience, change also requires commitment. How many times have you tried to do something and failed? No matter how important it was to you, or how deeply you promised yourself you would succeed, you failed. Maybe it was your commitment to quit smoking or lose weight. Most of us have tried, at one time or another, to achieve some goal in our life and have failed. But we don't fail because we are bad people or because we don't really want to succeed. We often fail because our degree of commitment wanes as time moves on.

For many people who try to quit smoking, the experience unfolds something like this: On day one, when commitment is strongest, all kinds of temptations are overcome. "This isn't too bad. I don't miss it at all. I can do this!" Day two: "There's a lot going on at work, imagine how good a cigarette would taste. I never noticed before that everyone I work with is so irritating." Day three: "It's getting harder.

Everyone smokes. There's smoke all around me. I've got to go outside and hang out with my smoking pals and breathe in some of their air." Day four: "I can't stand it any longer. I can't do it. I've got to take one tiny, little puff off of someone's cigarette just to calm my nerves (which doesn't count since it's just a puff)." Day five: "All of my friends are outside. I've gotta go outside, I miss them. And as long as I'm here I'll bum a cigarette (this doesn't count either because I didn't buy it)." Day six: "I'll stop at Quik Stop on the way to work and buy cigarettes." The craving outlasted the commitment.

There are all kinds of good people everywhere with the best of intentions. They are going to stop smoking, start to eat right and exercise, go back to school, or whatever. And many people fail in these most noble of intentions. The same is true with service. There will be days when the weather is bad, you don't feel well, the customer is in an ugly mood, or the stars are not properly aligned, and you will be called upon to serve someone. At that moment, the only power you have is within yourself. You can choose to do the right thing and reaffirm your commitment to service, or you can resort to behaviors that might feel good at the moment but ultimately get you nowhere. The commitment to service is strengthened in the daily affirmation: Today, in spite of whatever else might get in my way, I recommit myself to serve those around me.

Trust

Along with patience and commitment, trust is important, both during change and as a foundational value within the organization. Mutual trust is a foundational element of all effective working relationships. According to Lynda C. McDermott, author of *Caught in the Middle*, trust is an "assured reliance on the character, ability, strength, or truth of someone in whom we have placed our confidence." It is a critical ingredient for an effective team and is essential throughout the process of change. Trust comes from open, supportive communication. With open, supportive communication, uncertainty is lessened and acceptance easier. In almost all instances where trust is low, communication is lost and uncertainty and blame emerge.

An environment of change and uncertainty leads to insecurity, creating a tendency for people to become self-absorbed, filled with anxiety and, sometimes, full of suspicion. The result is a lack of trust. This leads to cynicism and blaming which destroy relationships. We are dependent on our relationships at work to achieve the goals set before us. Yet many times, people have no trust in the people upon whom they depend within the organization. Compare how we trust people with whom we work to people we don't even know. Don't we trust the people who made the brakes for our cars, put the elements in the red light, and welded the legs on our desk chair? We never even stop to think about who these people are or what their capabilities might be. We just trust them. And yet, we often don't trust people with whom we sit in meetings, share an office, or maybe even have lunch. How can we transform our organizations and make the changes necessary for service if we don't trust the people who are standing by our side in the process?

Trust: the bedrock of relationships
When the question is asked, "What elements make a relationship work well?" the three most common responses are: **communication, respect,** and **trust.** And how important is trust? Of these three, trust lays the foundation for both of the others. It is doubtful that there would be good communication in a relationship where there is little or no trust. And if a person or organization can't be trusted, chances are good that they are not respected. Trust is vital to all relationships. Animals need to trust their masters, children need to trust their parents, friends need to trust their friends, and partners need to trust their partners. Whether in business or in love, trust plays a significant part in the quality of a relationship.

There are people who no longer trust the people for whom they work. This is terribly destructive for everyone involved and there is only one piece of advice to give these folks—quit. Whether the relationship is personal or professional, if there is zero trust, its time to pack up and move on. As hard as this is to do, you really have no other choice. Being in a relationship of any kind where there is no trust is dismal and should not be endured. The absence of trust within organizations breeds indifference and destroys the spirit, eventually spreading to other workers and, ultimately, to the customer. Zero trust has no place in an environment that is dependent on cooperation at its most basic level.

It is hard for many workers to trust their leaders when they talk all the right talk but are not doing the walk—they talk about service, yet they don't serve their employees. This is one example where the trickle-down theory actually works. Unfortunately, the wrong things are trickling down. With trust absent, the changes necessary for organizations to focus their cultures on service are impossible.

Although there are some front-line workers who may not want to believe it, most leaders truly want to walk the service talk. Many just don't know how to do it. They have boards of directors and shareholders hounding them about dividends and year-end earnings. They have acquisitions versus cut-backs and down-sizing versus growth. They are often steeped in a culture that has taken years to evolve and is now difficult to change. They, too, have been part of a culture filled with policies, rules, and procedures that, for all intents and purposes, seemed to work just fine in the past. Why should we change this? What do we change? What do we eliminate? What do we keep? How do we hang together in the process? Leaders must answer these and many other questions before change takes place. Change simply for change's sake rarely makes sense.

If you work within an organization where you feel only a sliver of trust— a morsel, a hair—focus on that, because trust plays such an important part in genuine service. Trust whatever you can, no matter how small, and cling to it. But remember, if all trust has vanished, for the sake of the customer, your co-workers, and yourself, find the courage to turn in your resignation and move on.

Laying the foundation of trust

Although trust is a requisite for an organization to achieve true success, it can not be imposed or mandated. No leader can walk into a room and say, "Trust me." Nor can any worker look a leader in the eye and say, "Trust me." Trust grows from consistent performance and behavior. Trust is inspired. Trust is the reward for honesty, decency, and consistency.

Trust lays the foundation for true service

The diagram above shows the flow or cycle of trust and its effect on an organization's performance. At the top is the leader's values and integrity. The leader's behavior (what is done not what is said) reflect those values and integrity, and ultimately affect the staff's willingness to perform and serve. This willingness to perform shows up in the face of the customer who purchases more frequently and in greater volume which, in turn, results in increased sales and more money and, in the end, happy leaders.

The lack of leaders' integrity and values has an extraordinarily negative impact on trust, fostering one of the most destructive forces in an organization—issues that are driven underground and treated as secrets. The known secrets that are not to be discussed grow into insidious barriers that make people spiritually ill. Whether it's the manager's drinking problem or a leader's habit of lying, burying the issue under the boardroom table brings most organizations to the apex of dysfunction.

Employee loyalty and commitment depend on trust and telling the truth, not on retreating from the truth. Trust begins with the leader's values and integrity. Values and integrity cannot be pronounced, announced, or plotted like a marketing ploy. They are observed in every business deal, every conversation, every behavior, and every decision. Values and integrity are shown in observable behavior. This behavior is witnessed consistently by the front-line workers. Not just when the leader is in the mood or in the spotlight, but on an on-going, daily basis. Behavior that is consistent and positive breeds trust. Productive, quality work comes from a work force inspired by trust. And an inspired work force usually results in satisfied customers. Satisfied customers buy more often and in greater volume, increasing sales. This, in turn, reinforces the leader to remain dedicated and committed to her/his values and integrity. Stephen Covey calls this the "dance of energy and power moving in unison with goodness and decency. Anything moving in this manner moves toward life and away from destruction." An organization that moves toward trust, values, and integrity and away from power, greed, and deception, will move consistently and deliberately towards life and all the rewards that come with it.

A lot of organizations are focusing on humor in the workplace and having fun on the job. These things are vital to our work life experience. But as important as they are, they can't be taught. Although talented consultants travel the country doing training seminars on humor and fun in the workplace, enjoying one's work environment ultimately depends on the organization's culture and people's level of trust. Humor is natural to human beings. When people feel safe, it becomes part of the workplace culture. Without the safety inspired by trust, people can wear clown noses and honk party horns until they turn blue, but the smiles and laughter will only be at the surface. Real humor and joy are born out of the comfort of being one's self, and being one's self is dependent on the level of trust we have in those around us.

Building Trust

To build trust, managers and leaders must be accessible, listen openly to people at all levels and, under all circumstances, provide accurate, open information.

According to authors Robert E. Staub and Lynda C. McDermott, there are principles of trust that must be foundational if leaders and managers are serious about creating an open and honest work environment. Those principles are:

- Demonstrate integrity;
- Keep your word;
- Do what you say you will do;
- Model your values;
- Courageously face reality;
- Tell the truth;
- Offer a meaningful structure to work together;
- Provide clear guidelines to honor each person's contribution to the process;
- Communicate openly and consistently—no mixed messages;
- Put the welfare of others above your agenda;
- Treat all people as knowledgeable, skilled, and competent associates.

Creating customers' trust

In order for customers to be loyal and committed to an organization, there must be a foundation of trust. As Lynda McDermott teaches, "trust is at the heart of why a customer, employee, or fan will maintain his or her allegiance, fidelity, or commitment." No banners on the wall, slogans, or peppy jingles will create one element of trust with your customers. Just like money, trust comes the hard way—it must be earned.

To earn the trust of the customer, you must

1. Solve the customer's problem, not yours. It's not the customer's problem that you bought 1,000 pairs of those snappy red shoes for your spring collection. The customer wants pink and your behavior should not be influenced by your need to unload that abundance of red shoes. Listen to your customers, then solve their problem, not yours.

2. Respond to phone calls and other customer issues within the time frame to which you committed. If you said you would call back with the information on Tuesday, call back on Tuesday, even if you

don't have the information. Be committed to the tenet that your word is your promise. Don't break your promises, and you will be rewarded with trust.

3. Know your products and services *and* the products and services of your key competitors. Although this can be a lot of work, it always pays off in the end. For instance, if you are looking at new cars and have narrowed your choice down to three models, imagine the difference between a dealer who knows the other two cars and one who does not. At the dealership where the salesperson knows little about your two other choices, you would probably hear, "Well I don't know much about those other cars, but I do know our car is really good." The salesperson who has taken the time to know his or her competitor's products will be able to say, "Let me tell you how our XYZ compares to the ABC and the CBS. Here are the similarities between the cars and here are the differences. And here are the reasons why I believe you would be more satisfied with our car." Knowing about the options customers have and doing an honest comparison builds trust. Put-downs and unfair remarks regarding the competitor's products or services win no fans, and the customer loses faith that you will be straightforward with them in solving their problem.

4. Everyone within the organization must be able to live up to the organization's slogans. If your slogans can't pass the customer's "snicker test," don't hang them on the wall. Imagine visiting a shop where a sign saying, "Service is the boss" is hanging on the wall. You walk up to the counter and find the salesperson writing up a previous sales order. The employee looks up at you, then in a dead voice drones, "I'll get to you in a minute." You notice that this employee is having problems with the calculator and becomes distracted. I doubt that you believe that service is really this person's boss. When you don't live up to your slogans, trust is destroyed.

Digging deep into change

If there is no transformation inside each of us, all the structural change in the world will have no impact on our institutions. The moment we think we get the point, and others don't, it all goes back to square one.

Peter Block

We know that change is inevitable and that patience, commitment, and trust are all part of successful change. It is also true that in most organizations, change is something that occurs on the surface. In other words, we focus on things that are visible and measurable such as structure, roles, responsibilities, systems, strategies, and management. But these kinds of change are as shallow as a person changing their wardrobe and imagining they are changed at the core. Although change in structure, roles, responsibilities, systems, strategies, and management are important, they are not enough. Real change must take place inside of us. This is also true of organizations. Without significant change inside the people within the organization, all the structural change in the world will have no impact.

For example, if an organization announces that it will be calling all employees "associates," but still demands that everyone punch a time clock, there is no real change. A number of companies now call their managers coaches or team leaders, but these new titles are meaningless if they still operate from control and authority and there is no change in behavior.

Conclusion

Change is a natural part of life and is necessary for organizations to move into the future. Although many people resist and avoid change, those who are successful are able to turn on a dime to effectively respond to its challenges. In order for participants of change to more easily merge into their new world, there must be patience, commitment, and trust. Without these, change can reek havoc with the basic fiber of the organization and, instead of the success effective change can bring, relationships are lost in a maze of cynicism and despair.

5

Culture

*A strong culture is sort of an anchor for letting
people loose to create a lot of change, not to impede it.*

Rosabeth Moss Kanter

For many, the changes that will most significantly affect the process of becoming customer-driven will be in the organization's culture. In order for service to be part of an organization's everyday landscape, it must have a culture that enhances, supports and sustains it. In an article written by John Case for *Inc.* magazine, he states that, "Companies with clever, highly involved cultures have an advantage precisely because of the particular challenges of the current marketplace. Culture helps companies compete."

As important as an organization's culture is, it is difficult to define. One way to look at it is through the eyes of the Total Quality Management (TQM) movement. Here customers are the *why* and culture is the *how*.

Another way to view it is through the eyes of comic-strip writer Scott Adams. He believes that culture is made up of all of the "little stuff." He should know. In creating his cartoon series and books on "Dilbert," Adams receives up to 300 e-mail messages a day from people from all around the country. Here is Adam's conclusion on culture from those thousands of messages: "Culture is defined by stuff like how you handle your office supplies. Or popcorn. A lot of companies are putting a ban on popcorn, not the popcorn itself, or the eating of it, but the smell of it. Companies are now saying there are only certain hours you can make microwave popcorn or not make it at all."

When Scott Adams weaves these conclusions into one of Dilbert's many corporate observations, it gets lots of laughs. But it's not so funny when you are working in an organization where the culture seems to be devoid of joy. But does joy really have anything to do with culture?

Defining culture

Culture within an organization is very much like culture within a country or any contained group of people. Anytime people are gathered together, there will be norms, traditions, values, and beliefs which ultimately create the group's culture. To one degree or another, the group recognizes these as part of their common experience. Not all members always practice the group's collective beliefs, or observe its traditions, or live by its values. Yet, most people within the group agree that they exist.

In most instances, the culture is formed by the group's history, leaders, and members. Each of these secondary groups contributes to the culture and each is deeply affected by it. Culture affects people so deeply that, as author Michael LeBeouff says, "People pretty much behave the way the system (culture) teaches them to behave."

Culture is introduced into an organization at its conception. No matter how large today, most companies started with someone's big idea. From that idea a business was started and, at that moment, the business' norms, traditions, values, and beliefs were those of the originator. The culture of that new business remained intact until someone else, such as a secretary, receptionist, or associate was hired. The moment that new person was introduced into the company, his or her norms, traditions, values, and beliefs were introduced into the culture as well. And from that day on, even with only two people, the culture was forever changed. Over time, every new employee's norms, traditions, values, and beliefs will, to some degree, affect the organization's culture. However, no matter how many others enter the picture, history and common sense tell us that the people with the most power will have the greatest impact on the organization's culture.

Communicating the culture

Employees are not moved by balloons in the atrium, but rather by making meaningful contributions to others through their work.
William George

Culture is communicated throughout the organization one person at a time. As new people enter the realm, the culture is communicated to them. This happens in the way people talk to each other, the way they behave, the degree to which they exhibit integrity and character, how often others are included in decision making, how errors and conflicts are handled, and by hundreds of other nuances and cues. Possibly the greatest indicator of culture is the degree to which people trust each other at all levels of the organization.

Culture affects service the same way that people talking to each other and acting with dignity and character affect any relationship. A service culture is one in which everyone within the organization (1) talks to each another with respect and openness, (2) interacts with dignity and character, and (3) works in harmony with a willingness to cooperate.

Culture Conflict

It takes happy employees to make happy customers.
J. Willard Marriott, Sr.

As new people begin to infiltrate the culture and bring their own norms, traditions, values, and beliefs, conflict begins to develop. This is a natural evolution of groups, and often happens without malice or intent. Let's imagine this scenario where the most powerful person brings the following to the group: "I want to tell you that in our organization...

"Everyone dresses in business suits or proper business attire." (norms)

"Only flowers should be sent on secretary's day." (traditions)

"The longer hours one works the more things get done." (values)

"Men make better executives than women." (beliefs)

Unless the rest of the group buys into these elements of the corporate culture, there will be conflict. That conflict will only be resolved by (1) modifying the current culture, (2) accepting the culture, or (3) ending the relationship with the group. An employee's experience with the organization will be either positive or negative depending on their attitude regarding the culture and their willingness to modify, accept, or leave.

Once conflict enters into the culture, leaders begin to write policies, procedures, rules, and handbooks like crazy. The decision makers and people in power want to insure that the governing tools (policies, procedures, systems, and so on) closely resemble their own norms, traditions, values, and beliefs. And the degree to which leaders fight to protect their view of the culture will continuously reinvent it in the process.

A culture committed to service

The culture of an organization reflects either (a) its commitment to service or (b) its commitment to self-interest. To find which is reflected in the culture of your organization, there are two questions that must be answered, "Why are we here, and what is our motive for being here?" In organizations known for their impeccable service, the answer is rarely, "For the money," "To stroke our egos," or "To show the world how smart we are." There is a higher intent. A more noble value moves them. That higher intent is to achieve success by placing service squarely at the center of all of the organization's norms, traditions, values, and beliefs.

In his *Minneapolis Star Tribune* column, "For Executives Only," Harvey MacKay shares these insights on culture from retailer Marshall Field. In this story, MacKay tells how Field inspired his work force through "sound values that deeply affected the work culture." The values he fostered made it possible for people to perform in a "sensible" way. To create a culture where people could work well together, Marshall Field introduced these values and beliefs to the people in his organization:
- Understand the limitations of everyone's time;
- Persevere and it will breed success;

- Know the pleasure of working;
- Be a person of character;
- Be kind;
- Influence others by example;
- Respect the obligation of duty;
- Be wise about economy—don't waste;
- Know the virtue of patience;
- Continually work to improve talent;
- Experience the joy of originating.

When service is at the center of a culture, it is friendly, supportive, and fun. A lot of work gets done, and people are happy. Managers and leaders don't spend time in meetings discussing the best hours to make popcorn. They talk about things that honestly matter to customers and employees. Be honest. How many customers have you lost because of the smell of popcorn (except maybe if you work in a clinic or hospital), by letting a secretary choose what he or she wants for Secretaries Day, or by selecting the best person—female or male, black, brown, white or blue—for an executive position? The culture—norms, traditions, values and beliefs —that tells us popcorn-making must be controlled, all secretaries should get flowers, and men make better executives, is at best self-serving, narrow, and leads to a dead end. At worst, it destroys people's spirits and, ultimately, the spirit of the organization itself.

Conclusion

Culture is foundational. For an organization to be driven by service, its norms, traditions, values, and beliefs must all be service-based. Culture has an enormous impact on all of the contributors within an organization. It can either enhance and strengthen it or diminish and destroy it. If service truly is the goal, the customer and front-line worker will be exalted. If it is only lip service, people at the top will continue to create a culture that ultimately exalts power and greed.

6

Hierarchies and Service

We are going to win and the industrial West is going to lose out; there's not much you can do about it because the reasons for your failure are within yourselves. Your firms are built on the Taylor model. Even worse, so are your heads. With your bosses doing the thinking while the workers wield the screwdrivers, you're convinced deep down that this is the right way to run a business. For you, the essence of management is getting the ideas out of the heads of the bosses and into the hands of labor. We are beyond your mindset. Business, we know, is now so complex and difficult, the survival of firms so hazardous in an environment increasingly unpredictable, competitive and fraught with danger, that their continued existence depends on the day-to-day mobilization of every ounce of intelligence.

Konosuke Matsushita, 1982

Most organizations' cultures have been created inside of hierarchical structures. Within those structures, someone is at the top, a few more are in the middle, and a lot more are at the bottom. Throughout time, people in organizations have learned that the higher up in the structure they are, the more important they are, the more valuable they are, and the more they are rewarded.

So what's the problem with this? Isn't this our successful, capitalistic system at its best? For some, yes. But for most, no. In a system where the people in power are first in line for service, the customer is usually last. In our traditional model, we have leaders at the top, middle managers in between, and front-line workers at the bottom. Even below those front-line employees are the customers.

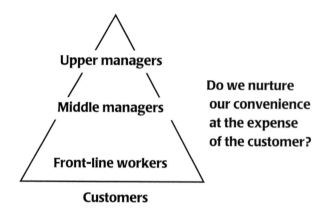

For many organizations, this is not simply a flow chart of authority. It is also a flow chart of importance and service. It tells us, when push comes to shove, who is most important and whom to serve first. For example, in this model, if someone at the top of the triangle called a 1:30 meeting for the front-line workers and a customer with a problem walked in at 1:25, what do you think that front-line worker would do? In most instances, that worker would say, "Could you come back a little later? I have a meeting to get to," or they would make it obvious through their body language and tone of voice that they were in a hurry. The last thing a customer with a problem wants is to be put off. But the front-line worker is in a bind. Who should be served first, the boss or the customer? In a hierarchy, the employee knows the answer is the boss, and if they get this answer wrong, they may have to start looking for a new job.

An example of this folly was experienced at a shop specializing in wildlife art. A woman interested in purchasing a pair of carvings for her husband's birthday visited the shop at an upscale Minneapolis mall. Somewhat confused, she brought two identical carvings to the checkout counter. One price tag read $300 and the other $400.

"Which is the right price?" she asked, "$300 or $400?" The clerk at the counter entered the item numbers into the computer. "Oh, dear," she responded, "I think there's been a mistake. They both should be marked $400." The customer replied, "I'll pay $300 and $400, but I'm not going to pay $400 for both." Torn between her need to either please the customer or the owner of the shop, the employee replied, "I'm sorry. They're both $400." With that, the customer put both carvings back on the counter and walked out. She was angry, the friends with her were angry, and several other people in the store witnessed the interaction.

What really happened was that the clerk was caught in the middle. She was going to make someone mad. She believed that if she sold the carvings for $300 and $400, she would make the owner mad, and if she didn't, the customer would be mad. When push came to shove, she chose to make the customer mad. But was it really worth it? A customer's anger has direct as well as indirect implications on a business. In this instance, the direct implication was that she probably lost that customer. But indirectly, she may have lost the goodwill of the friends who were with the customer and dimmed the reputation of the store in the eyes of the other customers in the store at that time. In addition, if you remember the statistics stated earlier, this unhappy customer may tell from 14 to 20 other people about her experience as well.

Chances are, if the owner had been in the store that day, those carvings would have been sold for $300 and $400. Or maybe this owner, knowing the value of a loyal customer, would have been willing to sell both for $300. That day, by saving $100, the clerk thought she was saving the store. But imagine the residual and long-term loss.

Another example of a system serving itself occurred at a bank. There an elderly gentleman went to meet with a personal banker to help straighten out his checking account. His life had been in a turmoil. His wife had just died and he, too, had recently been diagnosed with a serious illness. In the middle of everything, he had inadvertently let his finances go. This was not his usual behavior and he now wanted to put things back in order. He made an appointment with his bank. Once he arrived, the banker informed him that she only had nine minutes to work with him. That was the amount of time the bank's management had set for personal bankers to spend helping people with menial tasks such as balancing personal checking accounts. ("There's work to be done and reports to generate, for Pete's sake.") But this gentleman, unable to deal with her apparent lack of concern, got flustered and left the bank without getting anything resolved. He was so upset by her lack of concern that he inadvertently left without his checkbook. Fortunately this story has a happy ending. He went to another branch of this banking system and met with a banker who took his situation into account spending the necessary time to resolve the man's questions and concerns. In other words, this banker put the customer, the man ultimately paying her salary, before the self-serving system.

The top is served by serving the bottom

Uninformed leaders and managers might believe that they are being well served when employees jump through hoops to please them and bestow all kinds of attention on their every need. But in the end, the only way the investor, leader, or owner wins is when customers are willing to continue spending bundles of money with them. And whenever the customer must be sacrificed for the sake of the leader or system, the organization will eventually lose. In fact, service is a paradox: the front-line worker ultimately serves the leader/investor through serving the customer. Happy, satisfied customers are more loyal, spend more money, and tell others. All of these things enhance the bottom line, which ultimately rewards the people at the top. This is not to minimize the importance of leaders within an organization. The role of an organization's leaders is significant. They create a stable framework and roots that give the organization nourishment and life. How important are strong roots to an organization? The Chinese bamboo tree doesn't grow at all during its first four years of life. In the fifth year, it grows eighty feet. Before it can grow tall, it has to grow deep. The same is true with service-bound organizations.

The chasm of hierarchy

Brains and talent are merely the entry fee for the race.
To win, you have to know the secret: Do unto others as
you would have them do unto you.

Burt Manning

In the model that serves the top first and the bottom last, there are lots of rules, policies, and procedures, and they are seldom made with the bottom two levels of the pyramid in mind. In fact within hierarchical organizations, the last question asked when rules, policies, and procedures are being imposed is: How will this affect the customer? The second to the last question is: How will this affect the front-line worker? When these are the last questions asked, we find customers and employees chaffing at the mandated policies, procedures, and rules. Employees become disheartened and customers walk away irritated. In the end, with these two groups basically rejecting the imposed decisions, the leader and investor will not succeed. Disheartened employees produce low-quality work, high absenteeism, low morale, high turnover, and uncooperative attitudes. All of these rear their ugly heads in the face of irritated customers who walk away, leaving a trail of lost opportunities in their wake.

The model of hierarchy also puts a chasm between the leader and the front-line worker. There are a number of people who believe that the only reason managers exist is to be buffers between the "idea people" and the "doers." In many instances, there has been such animosity between the top and the bottom groups that they have historically not spoken to each other. Many workers say that their leaders don't communicate with them to help them comprehend their ideas. In fact, according to Louis Harris, two-thirds of people in the work force have no idea as to the values or vision or ultimate goals of their leadership. Nor, they say, do they have any idea what really matters to their leaders. They claim that the leaders' goals and visions change daily and that there is little direction or commitment to anything of apparent value.

With middle managers acting as buffers between people at the top and the bottom of the hierarchical structure, some leaders believe that they can bluff their way through difficult topics and issues. For instance, with middle managers protecting them, leaders don't have to answer employees when they ask, "Why do you make six zillion dollars a year when twenty of my friends just got laid off and they're talking about closing the plant?" Who would want to answer that question? Most leaders don't. They sit in meetings with their managers and blah blah about things and then the managers go to the workers and try to make sense of it all. The trouble is, the workers don't buy it, the chasm is widened, and the rift between the people at the top and the bottom becomes more contentious.

General Colin Powell said, in a speech before employees at US West, that one of the most powerful lessons he learned during his time in the service, and one that all leaders, in all organizations, at all levels, need to learn, is that you "never snow the privates." You can snow the other generals or people at the top or people working right below you, but you can never snow the privates. Why? Because they can see through it. They live with the truth every day and know exactly what's going on. And they cling to the truth because their lives depend on it.

Front-line workers are the same way. They know the truth. They feel the embarrassment when people are being snowed. Tellers in a bank see unhappy customers waiting in lines ten to twelve people deep. Standing next to the lines is a rack where a questionnaire with the picture of the CEO asks, "How are we doing? How is our service? Let us know how we can better serve you." "Well," customers are thinking, "you can get rid of these bloody lines for starters!" The truth is that these long lines are due, in part, to the fact that that same CEO has laid off tellers to save money and increase stock value. And, yet, his (and you've got to admit it still is his) salary is in the millions and going up. Don't snow the privates with your "tell us how we're doing" questionnaires. The privates know pretty clearly that as long as the bank's stock is healthy and the people at the top are making tons of money, it doesn't really matter whether the customer is happy or not.

Inverting the pyramid

The organizations who perform well year-in and year-out were not marked with strategic genius or legendary leadership. Mostly they were outfits that paid obsessive attention to the front-line folks who did the work and the customers who bought the product or service.

Tom Peters

If a foundation based on service is to be effectively laid, the service hierarchy must be inverted. Leaders and top managers must know that service focused on themselves instead of customers will ultimately create the loss of customers. Instead of putting everything aside to impress the boss, the front-line worker needs to pull out all the stops to impress the customer. If a manager calls a 1:30 meeting and a customer walks in or calls at 1:25, there can be no question in that employee's mind what to do—serve the customer. When the front-line worker arrives late for the meeting, the person in charge has every right to ask, "Why are you late?" But once the employee responds, "I needed to deal with a customer," the next words out of that leader's mouth should be, "Did everything get taken care of?" The front-line worker's affirmative response should bring a smile and a nod as the meeting continues.

In Peter Block's excellent book, *Stewardship: Choosing Service Over Self-Interest,* he contends that the creed for many organizations unfortunately goes: "We believe in compliance (which means don't express yourself freely, public assembly might be dangerous, and due process is important—it controls insubordination). Watching is better than doing. (In other words those with wealth, power, and privilege monitor those who do the work. Those at the top watch...those at the bottom do). And finally, when things get tough—try harder (usually at compliance)."

Organizations begin to change when the creed is about mission, vision, and doing the right thing. As shown on the models of service diagrams on page 102, to create an organization based on true values and vision, the leader moves to the bottom of the pyramid and becomes a steward.

model 1

Leaders	Managers	Front-line workers	Customers

model 2

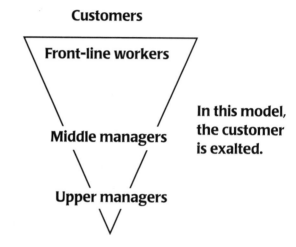

In this model, the customer is exalted.

model 3

Stewardship means to hold something in trust for another. Organizations in which leaders genuinely want to create a culture that exalts the customer begin by equalizing the balance of power. By flattening (model 1) or inverting the pyramid (model 2) or using a circular model (model 3) and then living by it, people begin to see changes that translate into a culture that puts customers on top and front-line workers by their side.

Equalized power is dependent on truth

One way to equalize power is to tell everyone in the organization the truth. This is part of the theory of open-book management. In his book, *The Great Game of Business: The Only Sensible Way to Run a Company*, author Jack Stack argues that leaders no longer have to be closed-mouthed or closed-minded to maintain order. Historically, information has been used to intimidate and control. But this method of management has also maintained the wall between the leader and those being led. In addition, it has closed most of the stakeholders (who are many times those most affected by a decision) out of the decision-making process. Today, in what is an ever-increasing global market, everyone must be trusted with the facts and be given the information needed to make the best decisions.

A wonderful example of this came out of RTW, Inc. a successful workers' compensation insurance and management company based in Bloomington, Minnesota. RTW stuck to its participatory-management guns and gained a competitive edge during a difficult transition. Facing a financially draining expansion, the leadership team decided that a temporary reduction in staff would be necessary to maintain sufficient capital. Committed to a strong participatory management philosophy, the leadership team resisted the temptation to make decisions behind closed doors and then impose them on an unsuspecting staff. Instead, RTW leaders pulled their sixty-seven employees together, gave them the company's financial information and all of the data and information necessary to make an informed decision. The group was then sent into a room and told to find a satisfactory solution to the problem.

After a number of hours, some dissension, and even a few tears, the group came back with a decision more effective and financially favorable to the company than the leadership team would have imposed. Even more incredible, no one lost her or his job. Instead of laying off six or seven people, several employees decided to take time off without pay. Others chose to job share temporarily. Once the expansion was complete, everything went back to normal. Today, RTW enjoys a success that most companies would envy.

It would have been easy for the leaders of RTW to have reverted to typical management practices when the decisions got difficult and the stakes high. But by choosing, instead, to maintain openness and encourage employee participation, they reinforced the foundation of trust that RTW founder, David Prosser, believes has contributed to the company's strong niche in the workers' compensation insurance market.

Building a new foundation

If an organization's leadership is serious about service and willing to create it from the inside out, the basic structure will be built on a new foundation. To build this new foundation and help heal the chasm that has been created by a hierarchical structure, cross-functional, multi-level groups will create all rules, policies, and procedures. No rule, policy or procedure will be introduced until the group has answered these questions: How will this policy, rule or procedure (1) affect the customer? and (2) How will it affect the front-line employee? Then, nothing is put into action until those questions have been satisfactorily answered. Policies, rules, and procedures must be connected to the external and internal customer's needs. Honest answers to these questions will connect the real expectations of customers to the work at hand. If those questions aren't addressed, the policies, rules, and procedures may be simply layered one on top of the other with no ultimate value to anyone.

To help reinforce service-based policies, rules, and procedures, everyone needs to remember that the most valuable asset inside or outside of the organization is the customer. The most valuable asset is not the buildings, machines, accounts, inventory, tools, instruments, knowledge, image, or investments. It is always the customer. The organization's second most valuable asset is the front-line-closest-to-the-product-or-customer employee. Organizations in which these truths are lived to the fullest are guaranteed to be in the winner's circle long before the other contenders have crossed the finish line.

Employees and their value to the organization have been the theme of several articles written by Marjorie Kelly in the *Minneapolis Star Tribune* column "Business Ethics." The articulate and insightful Kelly asks, "What is the company if it is not its employees?" Machines are useless unless someone knows how to operate them. Computers generate no information on their own. Processes don't unfold without people on the line. What good is anything without someone who knows what to do throughout the process? Companies must ask themselves, "Do our buildings, equipment, tools, engines, history, or even our potential make us great?" In most service organizations the answer to the question has to be no. Instead it is the employee, the person with the know-how and skill, that gives an organization its greatness. Does your organization base its day-to-day operations on that reality?

Hierarchy and rewards

One of the most difficult issues for any organization to address is the discrepancy between the salaries of the people at the top of the pyramid and those at the bottom. Dr. W. Edwards Deming preached that to maintain the morale of the worker, no one should be paid more than twenty times more than the lowest-paid person in the organization. How can it be honestly justified that anyone's idea is 50, 100, or 223 times more important or valuable than the hands or minds that bring that idea to life? As unbelievable as it seems to anyone with a morsel of common sense, executive compensation rose in 1995 by 23 percent even while those same companies laid off thousands of workers. This continued practice in American business and industry has created a spiritual ghetto on the loading docks, at the assembly lines, and in offices throughout the country. It is manifested in the depreciated self-esteem of the everyday work hero who makes someone else's dreams come true. We must make sure that an organization's entire constituency—the employees, stockholders, leaders, community, customers, and environment—is treated fairly and with equal degrees of respect. If any one of these stakeholders is sacrificed for the benefit of any of the others, the organization is headed for spiritual and financial bankruptcy.

There was a day when communities sensed the importance of keeping its citizens employed. In the movie, *Pretty Woman*, the character played by Richard Gere is confronted with the dilemma of a hostile corporate takeover. He wonders, "Do I make my money at the expense of these other people?" In the end his answer is no. And the American public, long tired of this type of privileged gluttony, cheers his decision.

According to columnist Kelly, there are some organizations today that seem to be getting the picture of the importance of treating all stakeholders fairly. For instance, in 1996 United Airline's employee owners voted down a lucrative acquisition because it would have meant layoffs. And at Kodak, the CEO tied part of his own compensation to measures of stakeholder satisfaction, including a survey of employee opinion.

Cutting the pie into more equitable slices

In some hierarchies, there is an unwritten rule that people's successes and achievements shouldn't be acknowledged so that they don't expect too much in return. If we applaud their good work, what would they want next? Cars? Money? Stocks? It's important in *hierarchical* structures to keep everyone at the lowest level possible and remind them of how grateful they should be that they have a job. Keeping people at this level might help organizations control some pittance of spending, but keeping people down breaks spirits.

Any progressive, forward-thinking company knows that people are the most important asset within their organization. Employees and customers drive every mile of the journey. When organizations lose sight of this and treat people as expenses to be controlled, people's spirits begin to break. And in this brokenness is a black hole where trust has been replaced with bitterness, despair, and a diminished sense of self. Compounding distrust and frustration even further is the power and privilege that remains solely at the top. The imbalance of power and privilege has dispirited America's work force. "Why," they ask, "should we break our backs and get so little, when you, on the other hand, do so little and gain so much?"

Not only is the pie being sliced inequitably within organizations, but it is also being sliced disproportionately within whole industries. With the consolidation and takeover of so many organizations, fewer and fewer entities are owning major pieces of specific industries. Take banking for instance. Every week we hear about small banks merging with other banks or larger bank takeovers. As the takeovers occur, jobs are lost, branches are closed, and customers, as well as employees, have fewer options. When competition is diminished, the motivation to reward both the customer and employee diminishes as well. If you want to work at a bank or put your money into a bank, your choice of banks will be fewer and fewer. What seems to become more apparent is that these pies are being sliced into pieces designed to feed CEOs and shareholders while the front-line workers and customers are getting the leftovers.

Removing levels of authority

Equalizing rewards and exalting the customer are two important benefits of inverting the pyramid. In addition is the need to reduce the levels of authority. Changing the service hierarchy does not mean that organizations no longer have people in positions of authority. Somewhere, at sometime, on some day, someone or some people have to make decisions. Organizations need authority, whether that authority lies in an individual, the majority, or a team. There must be a process that resolves disputes and makes decisions. But this process can no longer flow from the people at the top to those in the middle (the messenger) to the people on the front line. This creates too many channels that make the process cumbersome and the message diluted.

Today, as often as possible, information should go from the idea maker directly to the idea implementer. In other words, the person at the top interacts with the person doing the job. In this process, there are no middle people or buffers to work as go-betweens. Walls will come down, pedestals will be toppled, and a variety of issues that are service detractors will be eliminated. Some of those detractors are:

Misunderstanding. The order or request comes straight from the horse's mouth.

Time delays. From the time the decision is made to the time the request is given, there is little waste or delay of time. In the old way of doing business, the initiator tells the middle person, then the middle person has to get organized, then the middle person meets with the front-line workers to explain the idea, then if the front-line workers have questions, the middle person has to meet again with the initiator and on it goes. In the old process, significant time, time that no organization can afford in today's fast-as-a-speeding-bullet marketplace, was wasted.

Unanswered questions. Questions and concerns no longer have to creep back up formal communication lines. They are asked on the spot in real time.

Detachment. Once the information trickles down to the implementers, the passion or vision surrounding the idea is gone. In zero response time management, the person who created and developed the concept or idea can bring the passion she/he experienced to the implementers.

Resentment. Often workers feel imposed upon or dumped on. By having the initiator introduce and explain the new process or product, a sense of partnership can be established. Instead of the separated worlds that top-down management implies, this is a singular world of concept and creation, where neither is better or more important than the other, but both are essential for success.

Conclusion

Logically we know that no one on earth is really any more important than any one else. Americans scoff at the notion of royalty and we know that our heroes usually come from the rank and file. But

American organizations have created internal caste systems that rival any in the world. If leaders and people at the top continue to be treated as the most important members of the work team, even more important than the customers, any attempt to provide genuine service will fail. In the new-world order that revolutionary companies are creating, customers and front-line workers are exalted.

7

Systems and Policies

Our systems sometime cast shadows that keep people from shining.
Dan Hanson

If the hierarchical organization is to change, so must its systems and policies. Systems are the least colorful and dramatic part of an organization, but they are the foundation on which significant aspects of service performance depend. Organizations ought never minimize the importance of the effect of systems and policies on the service process.

For organizations to become customer driven, they must be genuinely committed to both employees and customers. One practical way to express this commitment is by creating systems, policies, and procedures that are simple and friendly. In addition, the organizational structure must be free from the layers and encumbered processes that create barriers to good service. Layers have to do with power and hierarchical thinking. Power and hierarchy are rarely foundational elements of extraordinary service. Customers and employees find it frustrating when they have to go through different people, or layers, to get answers. And they find it equally frustrating if the process is encumbered. When businesses are saddled with complex layers and encumbered processes, customers will do anything to escape the maze. Who needs to actually go out and pay someone to add more hassle to their already stressful lives? If the process gets in the way of customer satisfaction, the process must be changed. Some companies argue that standardized processes are in place to guarantee customers a consistent experience with the company. This may be true. But should companies strive for a standardization and consistency that provides no room for exceptions?

Tom Peters didn't think so when he needed to check into a Washington, D.C., hotel early one afternoon. The seemingly well-trained reservation clerk noted that he would first have to check into a "day" room and then later a "night" room. He was told to check with the front desk because the night room was "handled by a different department." Supposedly these departments had been assigned separate tasks to keep each efficient, effective, and consistent. However, when an *exception* entered the equation in the form of Tom Peters, everything collapsed. His preference would have been that the reservationist's primary concern was to make him happy. Peters said he wanted her to "stop acting like a reservation clerk and, instead, start acting like the CEO in charge of customer care." Many organizations achieve this is by adopting a "mom and pop" mentality even within a structured environment. As difficult as this might be, it's essential if service is your business.

SYSTEMS

Three companies that continually strive to achieve operational excellence are Federal Express, American Airlines, and Walmart. These organizations have worked hard to create systems that are easy to work with for both their internal and external customers. In fact, because of the ease of their systems, any employee of these three companies could transfer to any one of the others and quickly feel at home.

As customers play a more important part in the conscious decisions of the organization, it follows that the systems need to suit the needs of customers as well. Systems which have been designed with the end-user in mind are almost invisible. In most organizations, systems include equipment, facilities, communication processes, policies, rules, and procedures.

Equipment

If an organization really wants to drive its customers crazy, it should conduct its business with equipment that is ineffective, antiquated, or unreliable. Many times equipment is ineffective because the people using it are not properly trained. This often occurs in organizations where there is excessive turnover, or one that utilizes a number of part time or temporary employees. New employees or employees not familiar with the equipment never seem to be sure how this gizmo works. In order to prevent disruption of the service process, be certain that whoever is providing service that is dependent on equipment has been properly trained before being dispatched to the work site.

Antiquated equipment fails to provide what the customer needs within the time frame that they need it. Often antiquated equipment is a budget issue. But other times, it is the result of short-sightedness. The decision makers just didn't see the change in technology coming and now their organization's equipment is behind the curve and out-dated. Stay on top of technology. This doesn't mean you need to buy everything that comes down the line, but you cannot let your equipment cease to be the service enhancer it is actually meant to be.

Unreliable equipment might be the biggest irritant of all for customers. Machines that always seem to be down frustrate everyone. From copiers to computers, the excuse customers hear is: We can't give you that information now because our equipment isn't working. To avoid this, make certain you have quality equipment at the time of purchase and never nickel and dime maintenance contracts. Be demanding and unrelenting in your requirement for quality equipment maintenance, even if it is more expensive.

Facilities

The facilities aspect of systems may affect the internal customer more than the external. Although external customers want to do business in places that are convenient, clean, well-maintained, and functional, internal customers *live* in these places and are deeply affected by the environment.

For facilities to provide the environment in which people choose to serve, they must support the service process. This means that the facility is convenient. Work stations make sense. There is a reasonable flow of work. Departments that interact most frequently with one another are close in proximity. Break rooms and rest rooms are easily accessible.

Facilities also must be clean. One of the most dismaying comments I hear when I ask to use an organization's restroom is, "Oh, don't use that restroom. That's the employees' and it's not in the best condition." What? Do you mean that you allow your staff to be treated like second-class citizens? Any company that does not put adequate money into maintaining a clean work environment for its staff should be ashamed.

A well-maintained facility is one in which everything works as it should all of the time. As frustrated as customers get when machines or systems are down, they pale in comparison to the frustration that employees feel when they are forced to work with shoddy equipment and machines. Equipment and machine breakdowns are the chief cause of employee blaming. As they face the frustrated, angry customer with their own frustration and anger, their most common response is, "I'm sorry, but our systems are down again and it's making me crazy, too." Although this might be true, saying so doesn't shed the best light on the organization. An enlightened customer may think: It sounds like this happens a lot. Maybe I should get this service elsewhere.

Finally, the facility must be functional. Not only does the equipment need to work, but the equipment necessary to do the job effectively and efficiently must be available. Some of the functional aspects of the workplace are basic. For instance, electrical outlet strips for multiple equipment power use are a relatively minor purchase. With them, a job can be made easy. Without them the same job can be encumbered and frustrating. But many employees work with substandard functional job enhancers and, ultimately, this impacts the customers' service experience as well.

Communication processes

Employees often ask, "What comes first, answering the phone or taking care of customers in the store?" Answer: The customers in the store. "But what should we do with the ringing phones?" The answer to that question is that the system must support the communication process of the organization and there must be an effective process to handle incoming calls. In order to serve all customers equally, there must be a system in place where calls are handled quickly and efficiently. This can be done either with an answering station that dedicates all of its time to answering calls or an automated option telling customers they can hold for a certain period of time or leave a number where they can be reached later. However, in order for this to be effective, the employees must actually call the customer back as quickly as possible. If customers come to trust that they will, indeed, receive a returned call, this system works well.

> *We never started out to become 1,000 percent better at anything.*
> *Just one percent better at the thousand different things that are*
> *important to the customer. And it worked.*
>
> Jan Carlzen

W. Edwards Deming, the godfather of the modern-day quality initiative, believed that 6 percent of all quality problems are due to special causes—something done, not done or incorrectly done—by a worker. The other quality problems, or 94 percent, are caused by systems, work processes, procedures, and machines. A number of experts believe those figures are closer to 15 percent for special causes or those caused by employees, and that system-causes are closer to 85 percent of today's work problems. Regardless of which expert's numbers are correct, the real issue is the huge gap between special (employee) causes and system (management) causes. Most experts agree that the real problems in quality today, whether in service or manufacturing, come from the systems, work processes, procedures, machines, or tools with which employees are forced to work. And all of these are the direct products of the systems and decisions that have been created by management and leadership.

RULES AND POLICIES

There is a difference between an organization's policies and its rules. Policies are guides to follow, while rules are non-negotiable mandates. Many organizations use these terms interchangeably—the reason why so many customers resent them. Policies or guides should be in place to streamline, enhance, and support the service process. If under certain circumstances, the policy is encumbering and not enhancing the service process, it should be ignored and the empowered employee should do whatever is best for that specific situation. Rules, on the other hand, are created for safety, privacy, protection, or to uphold a law and must be followed at all times. If they are not, real damage can occur.

Many organizations use policies as if they were rules. Perhaps it's because the word rule seems so harsh and unfriendly that service providers soften the message with "it's our policy." Because of this, the word policy has become negative to many customers. Because of the negative response to rules and policies, organizations need to ask: Is this rule or policy necessary? If it is a rule, they must ask: Does it still apply? If it is a policy, organizations must ask: Do we really need it? Would anything awful happen if we eliminated it? Was it written with the majority of our customers in mind? If the answer to these questions is no, you might want to get rid of the policy or rule. It is probably more aggravation than it's worth. However, if the answer is that we do need this policy or rule, then ask if it can be written in such a way that it sounds like a benefit instead of a barrier.

For example, on-site managers in many apartment communities don't take cash. From a practical standpoint, this is a rule. There is obviously a huge safety risk when managers store significant amounts of cash in their offices. Because of this, the practice of not taking cash is a reasonable rule and should be non-negotiable. But what about a retailer's policy that states that there can be no return of merchandise after thirty days? What's that about? What if the customer only started using the product twenty-nine days after purchase and just discovered it doesn't do the job? This policy is saying: We don't really care that you're not happy. We can't be bothered with the inconvenience of returned merchandise especially if we no longer stock the item. Now it's your problem. What a wonderful experience it is for customers when the policy instead says: If you are ever unhappy with our products or services, we will do everything in our power to make it right or we will cheerfully refund your money. This policy says we're a no-risk company; customer satisfaction is our business.

The same is true for the policies and rules written for internal customers. A Nordstrom rule for employees is to "simply use your good judgment in all situations." This kind of rule is one that most people find easy to embrace.

Because not all customers are going to be fair and honest, rules and policies are often created for those few, bad apples. These policies and rules often sound unfriendly and rigid and many times do more harm than good. The majority of customers are good people who are offended by negative sounding mandates. "No refunds without sales slip," "No checks," or "We have the right to refuse service to anyone!" Yikes! Who wants to develop a long-term relationship with these people?

Rules and policies should be written with the good customers in mind, not the bad. When bad customers are encountered, they should be dealt with on an as-needed basis. This is sometimes difficult because companies fear being accused of discrimination. But if companies truly don't discriminate, they will be able to defend their position. If they do unfairly discriminate, they deserve what they get.

One way to discover whether or not your policies and procedures are barriers is to ask, "Who are they written for and at whose expense?" Whenever an organization is instituting new policies or procedures, they must ask, "How will these affect the customer? How will they affect the front-line worker?" If the answers to these questions indicate that they will have an adverse effect, then they should not be instituted. We have to ask the ultimate policy question, "Is our convenience at the customer's expense?"

Stupid rule stories

When organizations set their jaws and inflexibly enact policies and rules regardless of their implications or repercussions, there are bound to be *stupid* stories. For instance, a bungee jumping business in Michigan had a sign hanging next to the cashier that read, "No Refunds." One day, much to the horror of those watching, a young man jumped, the cable broke, and he fell. Fortunately, he survived with just a broken ankle. As he was being carried away by friends, in pain and terrified, he stopped by the booth and asked for his money back. The rule-abiding employee dutifully pointed and said, "Read the sign. No refunds." Perhaps under the circumstances, it would have been a little smarter to have said, "Of course I'll refund your money and, by the way, do you want me to call an ambulance?"

Another example included the late Rudy Perpich who was then governor of Minnesota. He went into a small bait shop to buy a fishing license but didn't have his driver's license. (He had a driver at the time and didn't need one.) The rule-bound clerk behind the counter refused to sell him the license. Yes, he knew he was the governor and yes, his was the same signature as that on the fishing license, but the rule is you've got to have your driver's license or some other form of ID or no fishing license.

This stupid rule story took place at a bank. A man went in to use the ATM (automated teller machine). On his way out, he stopped at the teller's window and asked if she would validate his parking ticket. In a functionally robotic I-know-the-rules voice she responded, "No, I'm sorry, sir, we only validate if there has been a transaction with the bank."

"But," he protested, "I just used your ATM."

"I'm sorry, sir," she countered, "but we don't consider that a transaction."

With that, the man pulled a piece of paper out of his pocket and wrote down two account numbers. Then he handed the piece of paper to the teller. "I'd like you to pull up these two account numbers on your computer screen." She did. "Now I'd like you to transfer the money in those two accounts to the bank down the street."

That afternoon, she transferred 1.4 million dollars to a competitor's bank. Then he responded, "Now was that a transaction?" She assured him it was. "Well, then stamp my ticket." She did.

Conclusion

The nicest, most effective people in the world will have a tough time giving great service in an environment that is governed by rules, policies, procedures, and systems that encumber them. Good systems are invisible. All the customer knows is that doing business with the organization is easy, pleasurable, and pain free. When organizations work from systems that are inflexible and filled with layers, customers cringe and retreat. Organizations that create systems with the internal and external customer in mind create systems that not only enhance the process but return joy to the relationship.

8

Mission and Vision

Vision without action is merely a dream. Action without vision just passes time. Vision with action can change the world.

Joel Barker

Just as systems and policies are written to reflect the structure of service, mission and vision must be written to move the spirit of service. Though the terms often are used interchangeably, there are powerful differences among mission, purpose, vision, and strategy. For our purposes, these critical issues will be defined this way:

MISSION: I'm going to build a house. (Intention)
PURPOSE: To provide a place to live. (Practical application)
VISION: The house will look like this. (Artist's rendering)
STRATEGY: These are the plans by which I will build the house. (Blueprints)

Further defined, mission answers the question: What is our function and whom do we serve? Vision answers: Who will we become, what will we do, and where will we be tomorrow?

Mission statements

Because mission is the most common of theses terms, we'll begin by looking at people's understanding of the function and purpose of mission statements. A whole lot of flutter and flurry has gone on over the past few years as everyone has climbed aboard the mission-statement bandwagon. But the truth is that most people either don't have a clue as to what their organization's mission statement is or, if they do, they think it's just more corporate jargon. For many workers, a mission statement is just another irritation imposed on them by managers who had nothing better to do then go to a hotel, eat donuts, and come up with a saying that hangs on the wall. Not only in most organizations does no one know what the mission statement says, but in many instances, they don't care. They don't care because their organization's mission statement has no real meaning. A lot of organizations have spent good money for a fancy mission statement, hung it on the wall, and not spent one day living up to it. When that happens, it has no real meaning or value. For real meaning and value, a mission statement must be crafted with all of the organization's constituents included and rewarded. Those constituents include, but are not limited to customers, employees, suppliers, shareholders, the environment, and the community.

A good mission statement is something that is written for people's hearts. It's an invisible lifeline that runs through the very soul of the organization where it binds everything and everyone to its core. An effective mission statement should be no more than one sentence in length. Every time people hear it, they also should feel it. It touches people and moves them to action. It tells the world what is unique about the organization. A good mission statement also drives the decisions and direction of the organization. Every decision made is based on whether or not it supports the mission. Every time the organization changes direction and moves toward new goals, the question is asked: Does this new direction work in light of our mission?

In 1981, my college roommate, Mary Nygaard, then an employee of Northwestern Bell, was instrumental in bringing the 911 Emergency Response System to Minnesota. Few, if any, organizations were talking mission at that time. I know I hadn't heard the term used before, and I remember that when she said they were creating a mission for 911, I thought they were planning to serve soup to the homeless. Because 911 was a new concept and it was important that it be presented to the public in the best light, the team creating the mission statement worked hard to capture the very essence of

911. Although the task was long and tedious, in the end they created a mission statement that read:

> The mission of 911 is to provide to the people of Minnesota safety and security.

Thinking they had achieved their mission statement goal, the organization began training operators, creating marketing campaigns, and further developing the 911 concept. But in the process of putting their plans into action, they discovered that the mission statement wasn't working. People were not moved to perform. The group which had created the mission statement went back to the drawing board and reworked it until they had crafted the statement which read instead:

> The mission of 911 is to provide to the people of Minnesota with peace of mind.

Was this just a game of word-smithing and semantics? Maybe. But about six years ago in northern Minnesota, a family's large dog dragged their three-year-old son outside in the middle of winter. The dog tore off the boy's clothes and left him lying in the snow in 20-degree temperatures. Several hours later, the boy's father came home, found his son, and thought he was dead. The father bent down, scooped his son into his arms, ran into the house, and dialed 911. He was hysterical. The 911 operator knew that her mission was to restore this father's peace of mind. She first talked to the father and calmed him down. Then she was able to tell him what he needed to do to help his son until the emergency workers arrived. Although it was close, his young son survived. Had the operator's mission been safety and security, as it was first written, chances are that her first call to action would have been to get the ambulance to the house. But she was moved by her mission of reassuring a father who, in turn, restored life to his son.

This is an example of how a mission statement that is clear and understood inspires performance and drives behavior. Federal Express is another wonderful example of an organization driven by mission. Through excellent advertising and even better performance, many people know that Federal Express' mission is "overnight delivery—guaranteed." This isn't the mission only for drivers or the people loading packages on planes. It is everyone's mission. Whether an employee is a receptionist or a maintenance person, if there is a package to be delivered, everything else becomes secondary, and all effort is focused on getting that one job done. Everyone's behavior and every action is subjugated to the mission.

Mission and business focus

How and what the mission statement claims not only establishes behavior for the moment but creates a basis for business focus. My friend and long-time fitness guru, Lonna Mosow, for years had been focusing her fitness business on people's bodies. People came to her to get fit and trim and she accommodated their wishes. However, after twenty years of working with bodies she asked, "What am I really doing? What is the real purpose of my work?" She worked with a business consultant and went through the laborious process of discovering her true mission. At the end of their work together, they had created a mission statement that stated: "The mission of Lonna Mosow's fitness centers is to 'Shape people's lives.'" From that moment, the focus for her business broadened and changed. She brought a nutritionist on board, added yoga for stress, introduced Joseph Pilates' mind/body approach to well-being, and began to address a number of components that ultimately affect the totality of a person's life. From that one, simple mission statement, she changed the focus of her entire organization.

Identifying the core business

Before an organization seriously discusses mission, there is another question that needs to be answered, "What do we really do?" Put another way, "What business are we really in?"

To answer this question, organizations need to focus on and analyze their core work. In the apartment industry, most owners and property managers would probably respond that their business is renting and managing apartments. No one would argue with that. But there may be a deeper purpose for their work that is not as obvious. Some might conclude that they are really in the business of providing quality housing at reasonable prices or providing a home. Others may say that they create space in which people live out their hopes and dreams, or yet others may argue that they provide a place were people can return to find sanctuary from the world. If property management companies really believed any of these was their real mission, would their relationship with their residents be different? I think it would be.

Departmental mission statements

Larger organizations will often create mission statements that are too sweeping and broad to be motivational to each individual department. One hospital's mission statement said, in essence, that it would provide the "most ethical and sound medical intervention based on state of the art medical practices, information, technology..." For obvious reasons, the hospital's hospice unit wasn't moved by this. So they created their own mission statement, "Our mission is to enhance the quality of our patient's life." This was a statement that they could feel and it moved them to perform and act. Because of this, hospice employees know every day, when they come to work, that they're not there to cure someone's illness or change the course of someone's life. Instead they focus on making someone's life just a little better or brighter each day.

An important element to be considered when a department creates its own mission statement (and I support this being done as often as possible) is that it reflect the values and philosophy of the parent mission statement. In other words, it must be compatible with and related to the mission statement of the organization.

The power of mission

Luck is not chance—it's toil. Fortune's expensive smile is earned.

Emily Dickinson

Marjorie Kelly, newspaper columnist and publisher of *Business Ethics* magazine, writes that when employees of Medtronic Inc. gathered to meet with recipients of the company's pacemakers, they were reminded that their ultimate product was not the appliance but life itself. They were reminded of the mission of Medtronic, which is "To restore people to full lives."

Earl Bakken, retired CEO of Medtronic, has inspired hundreds of others to fulfill that mission since he formed the company in 1959. Even though he considers himself retired, he still meets with each individual employee (and Medtronic has thousands) and gives them a medallion on which the mission statement is inscribed. He tells them, "Keep this where you can look at it—this is what we're about." Medtronic's mission-driven organization has paid off handsomely. Sales are in the billions and, for a number of years running, return on equity has exceeded 25 percent.

In contrast, Dow Corning, based in Midland, Michigan, seems like a company in search of a mission. They, too, make medical devices that are placed inside people's bodies—silicone breast implants. Although their revenues at in the billions, are close to Medtronic's, at this time their return on equity is far below Medtronic's 25 percent. They are, in fact, near bankruptcy due to the law suits claiming that their implants have harmed thousands of women. If Dow Corning has a mission statement, it doesn't seem to have driven the decisions or the direction of the organization. (That is unless their mission reads, "To make a profit at any cost.") When the customer is in jeopardy and the organization making the product runs from its responsibility, the company always loses. Making a profit at customers' expense will eventually bring any organization to its knees.

We are also seeing this in the war between many Americans and the tobacco industry. In the near future, tobacco companies will be held accountable for their part in the destruction of people's lives. This will be the end of an industry that got rich while their customers became sick and died.

The power of vision

Businessman John O. Alexander defines vision this way, "To be able to see what's on the other side of the hill." Setting one's sights properly and reading the terrain is a tremendous skill and extraordinarily beneficial to any organization. Another way that vision can be defined is as a vivid picture of a future state that, in the customer's eyes, is better than the current state. The ideal vision is clear, memorable, in line with company values, connected to the customer's needs, and seen as difficult but not impossible. It is both an inspiration and a guide for decision-making

A vital and significant vision will always precede success of any kind. This includes anything from envisioning yourself lying on the beach on your vacation to the color of your new house. Those visions must be in place before the travel agent is called or the house plans have been sketched on the drawing board.

Stephen Covey has suggested that not having a vision is like putting a puzzle together without a clue as to what the intended outcome should look like. Imagine having a thousand-piece jigsaw puzzle with all of the pieces lying helter-skelter on the table ready to be transformed into a magnificent image. Almost always, before the first piece is put into place, everyone involved wants to take a look at the picture on the front of the box. Before anything begins, people want to see what they are creating to help them focus on what they need to do. Imagine putting a puzzle together where there is no picture. It can be done. But certainly there will be more frustration, and probably more chances of putting the wrong piece into the wrong place. Or worse, imagine putting a puzzle together with the wrong picture on the box.

The same thing happens in organizations where there is the wrong vision. Unfortunately, the results are the same as putting a puzzle together. There is frustration, arguing, dissension, abandonment (I often quit after I get only the border of a jigsaw puzzle completed) and, ultimately, failure.

Every individual in the organization must be able to see the corporate vision and assimilate it into their everyday performance. Federal Express, one of those organizations driven by vision, has gone so far as to deliver one single small package by Lear jet simply to keep a promise to a customer.

Bringing vision to life: strategy

Vision is nothing if it is not brought to life. Because the idea people are the ones with the vision, it's up to them to bring their visions of service to the consciousness of others so, collectively, the picture becomes action. This is done by 1) communicating clearly and often what is envisioned and how it will look, 2) laying foundations that will support the vision's reality, 3) allowing others the privilege of bringing their own ideas to the vision, and finally, 4) staying the course every day until the vision becomes reality. If you must make a mistake in planning your vision, have it be too great rather than too small.

No vision will ever become a reality without having a strategy or plan of action. Imagine taking a trip to a city for the first time. Before you leave, you envision the city and the trip. But if you're serious about getting there, you will look at a map before you leave. Just envisioning the outcome doesn't make it happen. The same is true with the vision of an organization. Once the vision is clear, you need a plan to make the vision come to life. If you leave on your trip without a map, will you make it to your destination? Probably some day. But how much time and money for gas, food, and lodging would have been wasted along the way? Even worse, what if your map led you to another destination. Imagine getting around New York City with a map of Washington, D.C.

Creating strategies to make dreams come true works as well for individuals as for organizations. Writing down goals is a master skill and part of building a strategy to achieve your dreams. In 1953 a group of Yale students was asked if they had goals. Many raised their hands, then shared their goals and how they were going to achieve them. However, only three percent of those with goals wrote them down. Twenty years later, the same class of Yale students was tracked down for an update. It was discovered that those in the group who had written goals had more net worth than the other ninety-seven percent combined. Organizations can't have a vision of providing extraordinary service without a plan. And like those Yale students, a plan that has been thought through and then committed to in writing has greater power than those which have not. Anything that is written holds greater power. Just look at the enforceability of a written contract versus an oral contract. Even though both are equally binding, the written contract is far more enforceable. It holds more power.

Building a bridge between today and the future

Peter Senge, author and consultant, teaches that an organization must be clear on two things: (1)Where we are today, or our current reality and (2)where we want to go, or our vision. Once these disparate points are clarified, the challenge is to close the gap between them. Too often, when organizations face challenges and obstacles, they bear down on their vision. They spend their energy looking ahead. Instead, according to Senge, organizations would be further along if they focus on their current reality. If organizations aren't willing to focus on their reality, mistakes are repeated and lessons are lost. Sometimes a mistake is only an opportunity which has not yet been turned into an advantage. When organizations are constantly future focused, much of what is happening today is lost from sight.

When the vision is first created and communicated, tension may surface within the organization, tension which is both appropriate and necessary. This comes from the energy that moves people to perform. Part of the tension comes from realizing the distance between the organization's current reality and its vision. "Here's where our service quality is today, and look how far we have to go to get it where we want it to be tomorrow!" To help alleviate some of the anxiety that accompanies this initial snapshot, organizations must be certain they have an accurate picture. According to Senge, "The vision for the future and the view of current reality must be both accurate and clear. As destructive to the future of the organization as not having a vision, is not knowing your real current reality." Organizations may climb the soap box and proclaim that they are going be *customer driven* (the vision) but knowing what the customer thinks about them right now is equally as important. This is one of the reasons measurement is so important. It helps answer the question: Where are we today?

Fitting into the vision

Vision is drawn from the organization's spirit. The same questions that organizations need to ask also need to be asked by individuals: Who am I? Where am I going? What is my purpose within this organization? How do I fit into their bigger picture? How can I affect an outcome that has value in that bigger picture? Many of today's workers say that they do not know the vision or values of their leaders. They say they don't get clear directions and seldom, if ever, are inspired to perform. In fact, many argue that the people in charge just *get in the way* of getting the job done.

A story circulated some time ago that further defines the need for leaders with vision. A group of people were working their way through a dense forest. They were chopping every tree and bush in their path and each of them was working very, very hard. Someone in the group decided to get a better look at the situation so she climbed a tree. All of a sudden, she yelled down to the others, "Stop. We're going the wrong way!" To which the person in charge responded, "Who cares? We're making progress!"

Vision based on values

> *A value is a deeply held and enduring view of what we believe is worthwhile.*
>
> Jesse Stoner

Values need to be a part of vision. One can not exist without the other. As long as the values on which the organization was founded are clear, the vision has a foundation upon which it can be built. Without values, vision is created on shaky ground.

Johnson & Johnson's values are clearly stated in their motto: Our first responsibility is to our doctors, nurses, patients, mothers, and all others who use our products and services. This motto was put to the test in 1982 when cyanide was found in capsules of the Johnson & Johnson product, Tylenol. When this tragedy occurred, Johnson & Johnson could have said, "This isn't our problem and certainly not our fault. It is obviously the work of a very disturbed person and the problem of the suppliers of Tylenol." Instead, they stood firmly on their motto. They pulled all of the Tylenol bottles from the shelves of their distributors nation-wide. They obviously lost a great deal of money in the short term. But in the long term, they saved something more important to them—the public's trust. During the middle of the crisis, a Johnson & Johnson spokesperson kept the public informed every day and sometimes every hour as to what was being done. It was clear to everyone that they were more public-minded than profit-minded. They responded with a long-term safety measure, the tamper-resistant bottle, that bolstered the public's assurance that in the future the product would be safe. The speed at which they came forth to own the problem, their openness with the public, their willingness to lose a lot of money for people's safety, and their long-term solution to avert another tragedy helped Johnson & Johnson regain most of its 35 percent market share.

Audi, on the other hand, took a different position. In 1987 they faced accusations that sudden acceleration had caused seven deaths and 400 injuries. Although drivers reported a much different version of the story, Audi insisted it was all due to driver error. They believed that the drivers, especially short women, were stepping on the accelerator instead of the brake. If this was true, technically Audi was no more at fault than Johnson & Johnson. But its refusal to own and solve the problem caused sales to drop from 74,000 cars in 1985 to 26,000 in 1987. Even parking lot attendants refused to park the Audi. Customers felt insulted and betrayed. Finally under pressure from the government, Audi redesigned and modified the foot controls and the sudden acceleration incidents stopped—even for short women!

Johnson & Johnson had been willing to sacrifice with short term loss, but Audi chose to protect its pocketbook. In the end, while Audi saw its position in the United States destroyed, Johnson & Johnson's humanitarian position kept the company strong and competitive. According to Johnson & Johnson's values, they could not fail on their public promise during the Tylenol crisis. They had built their reputation and their relationship with the public—public relations is not just a image gimmick—on the following creed: Permanent success is possible only when modern industry realizes that

- service to its customers comes first;
- service to is employees and management comes second;
- service to the community comes third;
- service to its stockholders last.

This creed was put into place over forty years ago by Johnson & Johnson's president, Robert Wood Johnson. He probably never imagined an ordeal like the one the company faced from the deaths of the two people who had ingested the tainted Tylenol capsules. But Johnson & Johnson upheld the spirit of that creed in its handling of that crisis. In the short term, stockholders may have lost some value of stock holdings when more than 31million bottles where pulled from the shelves. But in the long run, the company's commitment to its customers sustained the long-term relationships.

Bringing vision to life

One of the keys to the success of an organization's vision is that it is shared openly and frequently with all stakeholders. Consultant and author Sajeela Moskowitz Ramsey teaches that "shared vision fosters risk-taking and experimentation at all levels of the organization." People need to believe that it is safe to bring the vision to life and contribute to it by their own methods. A worthy vision inspires commitment, personal vision, ethics, standards, and values. For clarity and consistency, the shared vision must include the organization's fundamental purpose and mission as well. Creating a vision filled with purpose and mission is ultimately a group process. Someone initially has a vision or dream. That dream is then effectively shared with the people who can help make it come true. Those people, in turn, weave their own vision into the process. When woven together, this vision is more powerful and attainable than a vision any one person could have created alone.

Conclusion

In order for organizations to provide impeccable service, they need to lay their foundation with service in mind. Service will be evident in their mission, vision, purpose and strategies. For vision to have real meaning, it must also include the organization's values. Those values must remain in place even during difficult and challenging times.

9

Making a Commitment to Service

Good is the enemy of the best.
Stephen Covey

Service commitment statements

Once the hierarchy has been refigured, the rules and policies changed, and the mission and vision established, the commitment to serve must be entrenched in every customer transaction. This depends on the depth and the degree to which an organization is willing to stand behind its products and services. To assure customers that the organization is serious about service, many put their reputations on the line through service commitment statements. A *Harvard Business Review* article titled, "Keeping Customers," argues that if organizations are truly serious about putting customers at the heart of their business, they must manage their business from the customers' point of view. Designing a credible service commitment statement is the beginning of that process.

A service commitment statement is a public declaration regarding an organization's dedication to perform at a level that will satisfy their customers' service requirements. In practical terms, it is a displayed, written promise that commits everyone to certain behaviors that customers can count on every time they do business with the organization.

Consistently living up to a commitment to serve is a difficult task. But this is what the service commitment statement is about.

You are saying: Customer, you can count on this behavior absolutely every time you come in contact with us. We promise we will never let you down. Of course, this is risky. Once you have proclaimed this promise, there is potential for a problem whenever it's not met. Several large chain stores have put up signs that declare: "If there are ever more than three people waiting in a checkout lane, we will open another." This represents good customer service until you are the fifth customer in line and there is no indication that another lane is being opened. Without the service commitment statement, you probably wouldn't have paid much attention to how many people were waiting in line before you. But once the commitment was made and the organization failed to live up to it, you become an unhappy customer.

The bottom line is this: Whatever you put on your wall must be guaranteed to happen all of the time. No matter what! No matter who is working, how busy the day, or how stressed the staff, that promise hanging on the wall must be lived up to. If you're not certain it can happen all of the time, don't write it down or hang it on the wall.

Creating an effective service commitment statement

As with most decisions within an organization, a service commitment statement created by the entire staff will be most effective. For best results, create a cross-functional, multi-level team to identify the behavior(s) that are important to the customers. The best way to discover those behaviors is simply to ask customers what genuinely matters to them. Next have the team identify which of those behaviors they can live up to all of the time. Review these behaviors with the entire staff. Ask them: Can you live with this? Are you willing to commit to this promise? Once everyone is on board, write the commitment statement, have everyone sign it, then hang it in a prominent place for the world to see.

To further ensure an effective commitment statement, be sure that it is not just a slogan. It must be action oriented and move people to perform. It also should be a concept that both the customers and service providers can understand and embrace. Be certain your statement really means something to the customer. If your service commitment statement says, "Our staff will always wear blue," I think most customers would respond, "Who cares?"

A good service commitment statement will do four things: 1) create a clear image of what your customers can expect from you; 2) limit the customer's perception of the risk in doing business with you; 3) help employees at all levels focus on service behavior(s); and 4) lay a foundation for continuous improvement.

Create a clear image

When customers first enter your business, their senses respond automatically to your surroundings. This automatic response creates the customer's first impression which, in turn, introduces them to your business in either a positive or negative light. One of the questions that customers want answered is: How am I going to be treated here? The service commitment statement helps answer that question. If your statement reads, "We will always make you feel welcome and treat you as a member of our family," the customer gets an impression of how to expect to be treated by you. And if your statement is your promise, then everyone within the organization is obligated to welcome customers and make certain they're treated like members of the family every time they walk through the door.

Limit the perception of risk

There is no question about it, every time we walk into a shop or business of any kind, we take some kind of risk. Even though those risks are subtle and most often not life-threatening, businesses have the option to make our first visit comfortable or uncomfortable. We subconsciously wonder if they care whether we give them our business or not. We worry about the possibility of rejection or some other unpleasant behavior. But when there is a clear service commitment statement that proclaims the promise of how we will be valued and treated, it helps lessen some of the perception of risk.

Puts focus on service behavior

In most organizations, people are hired, quickly trained, and sent out to perform on the job. There is little, if any, on-going training, and the training that does occur is often either technical or basic. One of the elements lacking in most training programs is the reiteration of the organization's core identity. This is who we are! This is what we do. We are here to serve and put customers at the center of our universe. This is the message that must resound throughout all organizations serious about customer service.

The service commitment statement keeps everyone focused on the critically important core identity of service. In other words, the service commitment statement is not just for the external customer but is for the stakeholders within the organization as well. Everyone needs to be reminded that when work is bogging them down with details and with day-to-day frustrations, they need to refer to the message on the wall and get back to the real heart of their job—serving the customer.

Continuous improvement

Many good organizations that want to deliver extraordinary service simply don't know where to start. A service commitment statement is an excellent beginning. It can be the foundation from which you build other goals and commitments. Once everyone is on board and actually doing whatever has been promised, you can move on to the next level. As this evolves, it may be necessary to redo your service commitment statement so it incorporates this new behavior. Often organizations bite off more than they can chew at one time. The best advice is to become good at one thing, and then grow from there. Find that one thing that can be done all of the time, by all of your staff, for all of your customers.

In the movie *City Slickers*, Curley, the trail boss, announced that what mattered most in life was that "one thing." "What one thing?" he's asked. His response: "That's up to you. Everybody has to find out what matters most." The same is true for your organization. Find out what matters most to your customers, write a service commitment statement that supports it, and then be sure that everyone within the organization lives up to that *one thing* everyday.

Service guarantees

Christopher W. L. Hart writes in the July 1988 issue of *Harvard Business Review* that service organizations need to "look at the possibilities, challenges, and rewards of guaranteeing service to customers." For a number of years, the manufacturing industry has bolstered our buying confidence by guaranteeing the products we purchase. Some have lifetime guarantees, others, such as automobiles, have guarantees for a specific number of years or miles, and still others might be guaranteed for a certain period of time from the date of purchase. Why do so many manufacturing companies include guarantees as part of the purchasing process? In short, to reduce the customers' perception of the risk factor. The less risk the customer perceives associated with the purchase, the greater the probability of purchase.

Until now, few service organizations have offered guarantees on the services they offer to their customers. It has seemed impossible and out of the question. "How can we guarantee our work when we can't control our people?" But maybe it's time to consider some forms of service guarantees. Maybe it's time that the risk of doing business with you is eliminated altogether. One of the reasons this is important is that continued transactions from the same customer are conditional events. They depend on the customer's satisfaction with the previous transaction. In other words, in the customer's eyes, you're as good as your last interaction.

Although most service organizations are aware of the need for customers to be assured that the services, and the products they purchase, are flawless, most don't know how to make guarantees a reality. Can you imagine a doctor saying, "If that leg still hurts next week, come back and we'll take care of it for free?" Or an attorney saying, "If you go to jail, I go to jail." Hardly. But whatever an organization can do to take the risk out of doing business with customers will create a solid foundation for the relationship.

A number of organizations have tried to offer service guarantees, but they include so many hoops to jump through and exceptions to the rule that people say, "Forget it. It's not worth the hassle." To make service guarantees work well, you can't stack the deck in your favor to lessen the impact of the guarantee on you while maximizing its marketing punch. People in the service industry need to learn from the lessons of those in manufacturing and take some advice on how to offer a truly valuable service guarantee. Christopher W. L. Hart believes that in order for a service guarantee to be truly valuable, it should:

• Be unconditional and independent from anything else. In other words it should say, "If you're not satisfied in any way..."

• Be easy to understand. Complicated caveats only irritate the customer.

• Be easy to communicate. The customer *gets it* in one sentence.

• Be meaningful to the customer. How do you know if something is meaningful to the customer? Ask.

• Be easy to invoke. For example: "Put the box on your porch and we'll pick it up." Not, "We need it post-marked in five days. You'll have to send it Fed-Ex, wrapped in the original wrapper, blah, blah, blah."

Unconditional service guarantees

If the customer doesn't win, you lose.

Petra Marquart

With so many variables throughout the service process, from people's performance to what customers expect, can any organization absolutely guarantee dazzling service? Maybe they can. This example offered by Christopher W.L. Hart tells how one company is staking its reputation on unconditional service guarantees.

BBBK, or "Bugs" Burger Bug Killers, is a Miami-based pest extermination company headed by a CEO with the unlikely name of "Bugs" Burger. As in many metropolitan areas, there are a number of companies that do what BBBK does. But what makes BBBK different from the rest is that the other companies simply reduce pests to an *acceptable* level (I'm not sure what would quality as an acceptable level of pests) while BBBK guarantees to eliminate them entirely.

According to Hart, this is what BBBK guarantees to its hotel and restaurant customers:

- You don't owe a penny until all pests are gone.
- If a guest spots a pest, BBBK will pay for the guest's meal or room, send a letter of apology, and pay for a future meal or stay.
- If your facility is closed down because of roaches or rodents, BBBK will pay all fines, all lost profits, and $5,000.
- If you are ever dissatisfied, you will receive a refund of up to twelve month's service and payment for an exterminator of your choice for up to one year.

Sound outlandish? Here's what this service guarantee has meant to BBBK. Although BBBK charges ten times more than its next competitor, it has an extraordinarily high share of the market. And because BBBK does good work, it rarely has to pay out on its promises. For instance, in one year, BBBK paid out $120,000 on sales of $33 million.

In part, the service guarantee has been so successful because Al "Bugs" Burger started out with an unconditional guarantee and built the company around it. He didn't build a business and then, as a marketing gimmick, add an unconditional guarantee. He knew whatever business he went into that he would work to make it the best in the world; and the surest way to be the best in the world was to offer an unconditional guarantee of quality in both work and service.

Would your organization be able to guarantee 100 percent satisfaction to your customers? Before you decide to create a guarantee of customer satisfaction for your company, be aware that living up to this promise must be a foundational commitment. As Hart states, "If you are afraid of it or don't trust your customers, don't do it." Or, if the only way you are willing to provide the guarantee is by placing all kinds of controls on the process, you will do more damage than good. Service guarantees lose their power in direct proportion to the number of conditions and caveats they contain.

Why service guarantees work

Christopher Hart's work has shown that service guarantees offer specific advantages to organizations willing to make the requisite commitments. Some of the advantages of service guarantees are:

- Everyone focuses on the customer—you must know what the customer wants.
- They set clear standards—they define who you are and what you do, e.g.: BBBK eliminates pests, Fed Ex delivers absolutely at a specific time.
- They generate feedback. They give customers an incentive to complain. Remember that 96 percent of customers will not complain when dissatisfied. Hart says, "Less information on mistakes means fewer opportunities to improve."
- They cause you to understand why you fail. More often than not the cause is process related but we usually blame people. If it is people, we need to know what needs to be changed, from hiring to training to firing. And if it's the process, we change it.
- They build marketing muscle. Doing business with you loses its risk.

When guarantees don't work

Although in most instances, service guarantees create a competitive advantage, they don't work equally well for all organizations for the following reasons.

1) Guarantees may not work as well for organizations already perceived as being quality leaders in an industry. If an organization's reputation for service is impeccable, the risk factor for customers is already a non-issue.

2) Service guarantees may not work well in organizations where employees are already service-driven. Organizations rarely need to worry about focusing on customer service in this situation.

3) Another circumstance that eliminates an organization from service guarantees is when employees are truly empowered to do whatever it takes. Since extraordinary service is created in the moment and on the spot, empowered employees are already consistently serving their customers.

4) And finally an organization where service guarantees may not be necessary is where there are few errors.

Many companies fear the effort and cost of living up to a service guarantee and, consequently, won't offer one. But in the midst of that fear, they should ask, "Which costs more, living up to a service guarantee or replacing a customer?" In most cases, once they do the math, they'll discover that the cost of living up to a service guarantee dims in comparison to the cost of losing a customer.

Another fear of offering a service guarantee is that customers will cheat you out of something. But research has shown that only about one percent of customers cheat. The other ninety-nine percent are good, decent people who will appreciate the fact that you trust them and who will reward that trust with continued patronage.

Conclusion

If your organization is serious about providing extraordinary service, put it in writing. The service commitment statement is one way of letting customers know your intentions and how you would like to see your relationship with them unfold. If you are willing to take this even further, guarantee your customers that your service will be without flaw. And if there are mistakes or problems, they will receive something in return. Do this without reservations, red tape or fear. If you are afraid to stand behind the service you're providing, why should anyone take the risk of doing business with you?

10

"Moments of Truth"

...anytime a customer comes in contact with
any aspect of your organization...

Jan Carlzen

W. Edwards Deming claimed that there is really no such thing as a fact. All, instead, is a "matter of what we observe and believe to be true." What we believe is usually based on our perceptions, and our perceptions come from our impressions. All impressions that customers have of your organization can be summed up in one phrase— moments of truth. According to Jan Carlzen, author of *Moments of Truth*, a moment of truth is experienced "anytime a customer comes in contact with any aspect of your organization—the systems, the people, the policies, the rules, the facilities, the processes, the equipment, the products, and the services—and from those things, forms an impression of the quality of your service."

Moments of truth were at the foundation of the "miracle" story that came out of the immediate turn around of Scandinavian Airline Systems (SAS). It was then that 39-year-old Carlzen was called on to bring SAS out of its $20 million debt. With the struggle many airlines were having at that time, he seemed to have few easy options.

The first thing Carlzen did was go to the SAS work force and say, "Hi, my name is Jan Carlzen. I have been asked to bring SAS back to life, and I know I'm going to need your help." In addition, he reasoned that if customers experienced better service on SAS than with any other airline, they would choose to fly SAS whenever possible.

Because the airline was part of a regulated industry, a number of service issues were out of its control. But one thing that was within its control was the passengers' experience with the airline before, during, and after their flights. Almost all passengers came in contact with at least these five SAS positions—the baggage handlers at the curb, the ticket counter personnel, the boarding gate staff, the flight attendants, and the handlers at the baggage claim area. Carlzen believed that if every encounter with an SAS employee was dazzling, its ten million customers would have five memorable moments from which to draw an impression of the entire airline. Five moments times ten million customers per year translated into fifty million dazzling moments of truth. To that end, Carlzen commissioned 20,000 people to be trained over a two-month period in "drop dead, knock your socks off" service. And at the end of one year the payoff was unbelievable—SAS realized a profit of $80 million.

People: the most powerful moment of truth

Customers generalize from one experience to the entire company.

Linda Silverman Goldzimer

SAS was successful, in part, because it capitalized on an organization's most powerful asset in any moment of truth: its people. Do customers say, "I just love doing business with your organization," because you have fancy stationary, added an addition to the building, or painted the walls blue? Rarely. Although each of those items— paint, additions, and stationary—are moments of truth, none is as powerful as the people who interact with each and every customer.

Whether you like it or not, you are the company in your customers' eyes. If your organization has a bad reputation, it's not because you painted your walls a funny color or the building is ugly. Most of the time it's because a customer had a bad experience with someone in your organization. No matter how much you spend on advertising, marketing, or building improvements, in most customers' eyes, the organization is the people. More precisely, it is the front-line workers.

It's the little things that matter

Even though people are an organization's most powerful agent, everything else still contributes to the customer's experience. Our definition of moments of truth includes any aspect of the organization. This means that in addition to the policies, rules, facilities, and equipment, customers also judge an organization by any sight, sound, smell, action, or event. Any one of these can create an impression so powerful that it translates into an assumption that represents the quality of service of the entire organization.

I experienced this when I visited a relative at a suburban Minneapolis hospital. It was late in the day, around 7:30 PM, and mid-winter, so there had been a considerable amount of dirt and salt tracked into the hospital from the parking lot. As I entered the elevator, I noticed a grimy, grungy build-up of dirt and sand around the perimeter of the elevator's floor. When I pushed the button to the sixth floor, I saw that the number 6 had been written with black magic marker. Instantly, from the appearance of the floor and the marker on the panel (moments of truth), I questioned the quality of the medical care of the entire hospital. Fair? No. Real? Yes. How many times have you, tired and sleepy from a long trip, driven past the motel with a light out in the motel sign to the one next door with all of its lights working?

Somewhere in the back of your subconscious mind you were thinking: If they didn't change the light, maybe they didn't change the sheets.

Moment of truth truths

In your customer's experience, moments of truth
1. are usually subconscious
2. may not be fair, but are always real
3. include all of their senses: smell, touch, sight, sound and taste, and
4. distinguish you from your competitors. "Do I have a different impression of your firm than I do other firms offering the same service as yours?"

Why are moments of truth important to your service image? Because they become the criteria by which your customers judge you. Your moments of truth form the conclusions your customers draw about your entire organization, whether they are fair or not fair, real or not real. What customers perceive to be the real is what they believe is real. It is imperative that you know what your moments of truth are, so you can effectively and consistently manage them.

First impressions

Every job is a self-portrait of the person who did it.
Autograph your work with excellence.

[author unknown]

The minute we first meet someone, whether in person or over the phone, we react to them with an involuntary response or, in other words, we draw a first impression. First impressions can be wonderful or disastrous. How many times have you encountered someone and responded with immediate like or dislike? A first impression over the telephone is completed within six seconds of "Hello." In person, the first impression is made in twenty seconds. Clive Davis, founder and CEO of Arista Records, who also *discovered* such musical greats as Aretha Franklin, Bruce Springstein, and Whitney Houston, was asked, "How long does it take you before you know someone has star potential?" His response: "Twenty seconds." In order for an organization to effectively compete, those first few seconds with a customer, whether in person or over the phone, must create a strong, positive first impression.

How customers judge us

First impressions are created, to a certain degree, by answers to subconscious questions customers ask about us. According to a study for Minnesota-based Wilson Learning by Dr. Brad and Dr. Velma Lashbrook, customers make twenty-six judgments about us within the first four minutes of their first encounter with us. Those judgments are based on three subconscious questions:

1. Are you technically competent?
2. Do you understand me?
3. Do you really want to help me?

Technically competent

The question, "Are you technically competent?" is answered by exuding **confidence.** Not arrogance, but assurance and confidence about what you do. Dale Dauten, in an article for the *Minneapolis Star Tribune*, defined the difference between confidence and arrogance this way: "Confidence is feeling that you have something to say; arrogance is feeling that you have nothing to hear." People who have a healthy sense of self-esteem stay educated and up-to-date in their field are people with an easily recognized sense of confidence.

Confidence in what you do and who you are is essential in order for customers to put their trust in you. Can you imagine walking into your heart-transplant surgeon's office and asking, "Do you think the operation's going to go okay tomorrow, Doc?" The surgeon looks nervously at you, looks down at his shoes, and tentatively responds, "I...I think so." The question, "Are you technically competent?" certainly would not have been answered satisfactorily for me, and I'd probably start looking for a second opinion. I don't know about you, but I want my heart-transplant surgeon, as well as anyone else I depend on for their expertise, to be filled with confidence regarding their capabilities and skills.

Understand me

"Do you understand me?" or "How much like me are you?" are answered by the degree to which we **care.** Dale Carnegie said, "People don't care how much you know, until they know how much you care." We all want people to understand us and know what we need. Charles Swindoll, pastor and author, has said that one of the greatest pains in life is being misunderstood. Remember the elderly widow and her interaction with the nurse as she had her blood pressure taken? Even though the nurse wasn't elderly or a widow, she knew what it felt like to be alone, deeply sad, and afraid. She also knew that she needed to find those feelings so she could help her patient get through her feelings. At that moment, the customer needed her nurse to care about her, to say, "This must be very hard for you. I understand. Is there anything I can do to help you?"

Help me

Finally, we answer the customer's question, "Do you really want to help me?" by being **creative.** Have you ever walked into a shop needing an antiquated part to repair some old appliance? Filled with hope, you walk up to the counter, dig the antiquated part out of your pocket, hold it up to the counter person, and ask, "Do you have this gizmo?" To which the counter person grumbles, "Nah, we quit carrying that thing years ago." Your heart slips into a skid. This was the only place in town that might have had the part, and now all hope is gone.

Or, you may have walked into a shop, held up the gizmo, and asked, "Do you carry this?" only to have the counter person grunt and say, "No, we don't. But I think my brother knows a guy........." during which he starts digging through phone books and looking up numbers. Or the counter person says: "No, we don't. But, I think if we tie this what-cha-ma-call-it to the end of this widget, we can replace your gizmo with our newly-designed thing-a-ma-job." At that moment, when the counter person could have just said no and walked away, he became creative. By his willingness to go out of his way, it was crystal clear that he truly wanted to solve your problem.

I remember a time when someone's willingness to be creative solved a huge problem for me. I bought a used car from a friend and had only had it for a week. I loved this car, so I was depressed when I heard a serious grumbling sound coming from the rear end. I took it to the dealership and the car soon disappeared into the fix-it room. Not long after, the service manager came into the waiting area with a "You've got a real problem on your hands, lady" look on his face and said, "You've got a real problem on your hands, lady." The problem on my hands came to the tune of $1,200. I panicked. The car had cost only $5,000 one week before, and I couldn't imagine putting another $1,200 into it. I began calling around to other repair shops and finally reached Eddie at Imported Car Repair. Eddie told me to have the dealership leave the car disassembled as they would charge to reassemble it, and that he would send his tow truck right over to pick it up. Eddie spent the next day looking over my car and, when he found the problem, he called and said he thought he could fix it for $500. Once I agreed, he had my car repaired within hours. Instead of $1,200, I got my car fixed for $500, for which my friend reimbursed me. Do you think I would take my car anyplace else? Never! Why? Because when I needed him most, Eddie got creative, solved my problem, and earned my undying loyalty.

Conclusion

There is no reality, only perception. You need to ask what reality customers experience when they do business with you. Whether it is perceived to be positive or negative will depend on a series of impressions called moments of truth. Because moments of truth are the measurement by which customers judge you and your organization, it is critical that you know what they are so you can manage them effectively. The most powerful agent in any moment of truth with any organization is its people. A first impression can make or break you. In order to be successful within those first few moments, be confident, caring, and creative.

11

Hiring and Training

Companies can improve the attitude and service of their employees by making sure they hire caring people who want to help others. The basic trait of liking people and wanting to help them cannot be taught.

Tom Gegax

If the most powerful moment of truth within any organization is its people, it would be prudent and wise for organizations to spend considerable time and resources hiring the right people and training them well. Barbara Trimarco Gulbranson writes in *Executive Excellence*, "Winning is dependent on how well you link business strategy with people strategy." Building a strong people strategy begins with designing an employee base built on well-formulated criteria and developing that base through effective, productive education. If an organization is serious about service, it is essential that its human resource philosophy reflect it. And as Trimarco Gulbranson believes, organizations serious about service will live by the law that

Human resources are a valuable asset; and

Human resources drive the organization.

Creating a people strategy

Of the elements necessary for integrating people strategy into organization strategy, none is more important than the ability to recruit the right people and train them well. World-class companies hire right and train well. Southwest Airlines is so committed to this philosophy that they occasionally ask their frequent flyer customers to be a part of the job interview process for flight attendants. Their thinking is that if the applicant doesn't *Wow* the customer, why bother. In addition, ongoing training to enhance skills, re-enforce thinking, and gain new knowledge must be a core value of the successful organization.

Most people experience a company or organization based on four encounters: with its people, with its products, with its promotion, or with its presentation (how it looks).

Of these, as we discussed regarding moments of truth, the most influential item in creating an impression in the customer's mind is always and forever, the people.

Hiring

In the past, a variety of criteria have been used in selecting the right people for the right job. Some low-paying, low-tech jobs, where the only requirement is showing up for work, need very little selection criteria. Other jobs require people who are technically capable and able to complete specific tasks. Companies serious about competing are looking for an additional element in the people they hire—to get along with others. For too long, people who are impossible to get along with have been hired and allowed to keep their jobs. Some are so difficult to work with that co-workers are afraid to confront them regarding even the smallest issues. Supervisors steer clear of them to avoid a blow-up.

A bad temper is not the only negative behavior with which people have to deal. There are some employees who erode the spirit of the organization with their constant cynicism or sarcasm. We all have bad days or find ourselves in a bad mood once in a while. That's usually not the kind of destructive behavior that does damage. The behavior that we find so destructive is that which is chronic. If service is an inside-out job, the organization that allows an employee to maintain negative behavior has set a precedent that almost always proves destructive at some level. Ultimately, that level often ends up in the face of the external customer.

How does an organization avoid this kind of problem? The

answer is simple. Hire people who are intrinsically nice. That sounds so simple and naive. But it is what organizations are doing today at record speed. Hire nice. Train well. Many companies are learning that most technical skills can be trained. But the basic ability to work well with others has to come from within. We know from experience that most people are hired for their technical skills but fired for their people skills. The people who lose their jobs often lose them, in part, because they are *a pain* to be around. They don't seem to care about what they do or how their actions effect others. Tom Gegax, head coach of Tires Plus, says, "We can always teach someone how to improve their communication skills. But we can't teach them to care about other people."

Today you need to hire people who, to some degree, like people. That doesn't mean that everyone has the same interpersonal skills, but it does mean that the people you hire can adapt, interact, and communicate with others. Too many breakdowns between people or departments have stemmed from people's refusal to work well with others. And these breakdowns almost always show up in the form of bad service to the external customer.

Hiring the right people

Most of us have jobs that are too small for our spirits.

Studs Terkel

One of the reasons that hiring is a key component to service success is that being hired for the right job and being the right person for the job help make people satisfied with the work they do. Being hired for the job best suited to their skills allows people the freedom to grow and expand those skills and, ultimately, to find job satisfaction.

Because of its attention to its employees and their well-being, Southwest Airlines is one of the ten best places to work according to the book *The 100 Best Companies to Work for in America*. One trait that Southwest looks for in new hires is a sense of humor—an attitude that includes listening, caring, the ability to look friendly, the willingness to thank and praise, and a sense of personal warmth.

Not all organizations would establish sense of humor as a criterion for hiring. For instance, I don't care if the medical professionals in the emergency room get *a kick* out of the way I broke my arm or not. But there are certain criteria that would matter to me. In addition to knowing how to set a broken bone, I would appreciate their ability to be compassionate and comforting. Organizations need to establish what is valued by customers and then put those criteria high on the requirement list before hiring.

Interviewing

To be certain that an applicant is the best fit for your organization and the job, it is important to go through a thorough process before making an offer. That process is called interviewing. The companies that have been successful in service have put a premium on hiring the right people. To that end, they have established effective interview processes to assure that the right candidate is selected for the job.

One of the most successful customer-focused companies around today is Nordstrom. "How do they get their staff to give such good customer service so consistently?" people ask. Part of the answer comes from the fact that Nordstrom candidates are thoroughly screened before they are hired. Nordstrom applicants often go through as many as three interviews. To make this work, Nordstrom profiles the person they are seeking—possibly based on employees who are succeeding within the organization. Next, they stick to that profile while interviewing. In other words, the interviewers have a clear picture of the attributes the best candidates will possess. Finally, they conduct an interview which reveals behaviors based on real-life customer situations from the past. For example, they may ask, "In the instance where a customer does this, how would you handle the situation?"

Another leader in customer service today is Saturn. Part of their success in delivering fabulous customer service is in their process of hiring employees. The following is an excerpt from a customer service quiz given to Saturn candidates.

A woman brings a blouse she just had laundered back to the cleaners, pointing to a tear. What would you say if you were the clerk?

1. "I'm sorry, but that tear must have been there before, because our employees always mark the mistakes they make."
2. "We will be glad to partially reimburse you for the blouse."
3. "I am sorry. Would you like me to get the manager?"
4. "I am sorry. What can I do to make it right for you?"

Even though Saturn is not in the laundry business, the answer to this question can be translated to almost any service situation. And the answer may mean the difference between losing or keeping a customer.

To make the interview as successful as possible, be clear about the core values and vision of your organization. These are at the center of all that you do and are immutable. Through discussion and questioning, find out if the candidate fits with the values and vision. If there is any doubt, this is not the right candidate for the job. Values can rarely be taught, they are found at the core of character. Following is an example of a *character* question and responses.

Question: "What would you do if a customer rudely and inappropriately blamed you for something?"

Candidate 1: "I'd be ticked off. I'd tell them I didn't do it. It's not fair to be blamed for something that wasn't my fault."

Candidate 2: "I'd feel bad, but I would listen and then try to solve the problem. I think if I handle it well the customer might realize it really wasn't my fault. Even if they still did, I'd try to do the right thing and make them happy."

Additionally, to make the interview as successful as possible, be sure to know if you are looking for technical skills or interpersonal skills. Although the ability to work well with people is essential, there may be skills that are absolutely critical to the job. For instance, if you are looking for someone who can do geometric dimensioning, you will want to know the extent of the candidate's abilities in this area. If, however, you need someone at the reception desk, you may pay more attention to quality of voice and the ability to deal with multiple priorities.

To be successful, the interview must be thorough. The right questions need to be asked and the responses listened to carefully.

Ask how the person would handle situations that may be difficult. Look more for the approach to the response than the details.

If being service-driven is a key element for the job, ask the candidate what her/his values are regarding service. "What does *dazzling service* mean to you?" Better yet, role play a potential customer interaction with the applicant. "I'm going to be a customer who is really unhappy with our product and you are the first person I talk to." Once again, be more conscious of the candidate's approach than the specific solution.

In addition to situational responses, some good questions to ask in an interview might be:

> What do you enjoy most about your work?
> What would you consider your greatest strength?
> What part of any job do you dislike the most?
> How do you like to be managed?
> What rewards matter most to you?
> Would you prefer designing a structure, building a structure, or managing a structure?
> What do your friends say about you when you're not around?
> What kinds of things do you contribute to your community, civic group, or place of worship?
> Do you think customers frequently take advantage of companies?
> How do you exhibit anger?
> If someone questioned your integrity, how would you respond?
> What job did you enjoy most in the past and why?
> If you had all the money in world, what would you do with your life?
> Do you prefer clearly defined job descriptions or do you like to do whatever it takes to get the job done?

There are no right or wrong answers to most of these questions, but they shine a light on what the applicants value and how they may approach their work with you.

If you are looking for a person with strong interpersonal skills, you may want to interview in a group interview format. For this to work best, simply set up questions or situations for the group to discuss, then sit back, observe and listen. The person who does most of the talking and listens very little probably doesn't care much about what others have to say. Unfortunately, those *others* could someday be your customers.

Finally, before you make an offer to anyone, be certain that you check references. If you neglect this aspect of the hiring process, you may regret it down the road. As often as possible, try to talk with someone who has been in a supervisory position with the candidate. Although many organizations have strict guidelines on what kind and how much information they will share, ask the questions that you need answered. If you are not able to get pertinent questions answered, ask what process you need to follow in order to get more detailed information regarding the candidate. This might include having the candidate sign a release statement that asks that the information be sent directly to her or him. In some cases, you may simply ask the previous employer to verify the information you have and relieve them of the responsibility of offering other comments regarding the quality of the candidate's work.

If you are serious about hiring people who are customer-focused and friendly, do the following exercise before you hire. Write down the attributes and behaviors that are most likely viewed as dazzling by the customer. Then ask yourself, "Does this person possess those attributes and behaviors?" If not, can these attributes and behaviors be taught or are they a part of a person's basic attitude or character? If the behaviors can be taught, you may choose to give the applicant a chance. If not, ask yourself whether you can afford to have people on your staff who lack this particular service skill.

Introductory training

Once people are hired, the next important step is to be certain that they are effectively and properly trained. Some people chafe at the use of the word *training*. As contributing columnist for the *Minneapolis Star Tribune*, Dale Dauten writes in "Corporate Curmudgeon," his February 12, 1997, column, "Dogs and seals are trained; not people." But by definition, training simply means "to form by instruction, discipline, or drill; to teach so as to be fitted, qualified, or proficient; to make prepared." Unless Webster's definition of training is obsolete, it's clear that most people still need to be trained to one degree or another for the work they do. Introductory training is in addition to the on-going education of your work force. If this training is presented properly, new employees can begin their work with confidence and a sense of security.

A good example of this is the successful Disney organization. How do they get both long-term and short-term employees to share in Disney's image? For starters, all employees at Disney, from the street sweepers to the vice presidents, have a minimum of four days of customer service training before they start working. Disney knows it can't justify bad service to a customer by saying, "That employee is only part time. You don't expect her to give the same service as the others." Oh yes I do!

Create a quality training process

In the past, the work force was considered a cost to be controlled. In the New Economy, it must be considered an asset to be developed.

American Society for Training and Development

A good training process begins day one. It is disheartening for a new employee to come to work the first day and find no process in place for his/her entry. The new employee often sits at an empty desk for hours wondering what to do first or spends time with someone in a similar position to *learn the ropes*. This is uncomfortable for both the new employee as well as the person being *watched*.

Instead, advise the new employee of the introductory process at the time the offer is accepted. "I will meet you Monday, June 1st, in the third-floor lobby at 8:00 AM, and we will walk together to your introductory training." As an aside, it is vital for you to show up for this training on time and be ready to conduct the training session. This establishes the impression that people within the organization stick to their word and respect one another's commitments and time.

To expedite the introductory training process, have forms, policies, employee handbooks, and other pertinent information sent to the new employee prior to this session so that the employee can bring any questions or concerns to the first meeting.

The initial, introductory training should include, but not be limited to the following:

The organization's
   history,
   vision/purpose/mission,
   values,
   structure (who does what);
The new employee's role in
   the structure, and
   the vision;
What is expected of the employee
   how she or he will be measured,
   how to use basic equipment (copier, fax, voice mail, etc.),
   the logistics (lunchroom, restroom, etc.),
   how to handle concerns or complaints she or he might have,
   any rules, laws governing the business,
   vacation time, holiday, personal time, sick time processes, etc.

Continuing education

Effective training meets the needs of the customers: the trainees.
                                                    Marshall Saskin

There is a paradox facing many organizations today. As jobs have become more high-tech, there has been a decline in workers' relevant job skills. This is a significant factor supporting on-going education. But even in this high-tech environment, service reigns as a critical element in an organization's basic relationship with the customer. All too often, in organizations where service is the product, training teaches employees how to process customers, not how to please them. Even in retail stores where service is king, we hear that many stores, including Macy's and Bloomingdale's, use take-home videos to train new employees on technical skills such as how to run the cash register or process returns; yet they don't train on how to satisfy the customer.

Competitive organizations are also learning organizations. How important is it to U.S. business and industry to stay educated? Consider the following. If you could wave a magic wand over America's school systems and have high school students graduate as fully competent, capable employees, it would still take thirty-three years to favorably impact America's work force.

According to the American Society for Training and Development, within the next ten years 75 percent of the current work force will need training. Over the next decade, 65 percent of jobs will require some education beyond high school, 50 million workers will need retraining just to do their current jobs, and the narrowing distinction between management and labor will require a greater need for knowledge and skill across a broader cross-section of the work force.

• In 1992, the life-span of work force skills was ten to fifteen years. In 2000, work force skills were obsolete in two to three years. In 2010, it will be less than two years. Why is this happening? Because of the incredible speed of changing technology.

• In the mid-1990s, the U.S. Department of Education discovered that 50 percent of the nation's work force was functionally illiterate. Chances are that has not significantly changed today.

• Seventy-five percent of the people who will be working in the year 2010 are in the work force right now.

• The face of business in America is changing: 80 to 85 percent of the people entering the work force in the 21st century are going to be minorities, women, or immigrants.

• According to Carnevale and Villet in an article in *Training in America*, formal training has been found to be four to five times more productive than informal training, and three times more productive when done in-house. Unfortunately, only about $30 billion, or one to two percent of the payroll is currently spent on formal training.

• Almost 90 percent of American employees never get formal training that is provided and paid for by their employers.

• Sixty percent of German youth receive three years of formal apprenticeship training in the workplace.

• U.S. business spends $30 billion on training each year, $20 billion of which is spent on people who have university degrees.

• According to the American Society of Training and Development, France, Ireland, Sweden, Korea, Japan and others all have national workplace training incentives.

• Japanese auto workers get three and a half times as much training as U.S. auto workers.

• Only one half of one percent of companies do 90 percent of the training in this country today.

• A survey of executives at thirty-five insurance companies found that they received an average of two years in-house training upon being hired in the 1960s and 1970s. None of those companies has formal training programs today.

Training preparation

According to training consultant Roger Major, there are five basic questions that must be asked prior to training in order for training to be effective. Those questions are:

1. Do workers know what they're supposed to do? What is their role in the mission?

2. Do workers know the tasks that need to be accomplished to achieve that mission?

3. Do workers have the skills to perform those tasks? (If the answer is no to these questions, training should solve the problem.)

4. Do workers have the resources to do the job? (If the answer is no, training will not help. It is a resource problem.)

5. Are workers not doing the job, but could if their life depended on it? (If the answer is yes, there is an attitude problem and training will probably not solve the problem.)

If training is the solution to the situations your organization is facing, Kateri Schmerler, president of Arrow Associates, has these suggestions on how to turn the expense of training into a money-in-the-bank investment:

- Choose training wisely. Make sure it matches the real needs of the work force.
- Prepare for it. Let participants know:
    a. The reason for the training.
    b. Their responsibility to the training, i.e.: take notes, give feedback, participate.

- Debrief and evaluate:
   a. What was learned?
   b. How can it be applied?
   c. Who else might benefit?
- Share it through a written summary or short presentation.
- Reinforce it. Ask for measurable changes participants intend to implement after the training.
- Measure it. Monitor the progress.
- Recognize it. Talk about it and keep the training alive in the organization.
- Reward it. The new behavior should be rewarded in salary increases, bonuses, promotions, time off, etc. Promote the message that learning, changing and doing are expected.
- Encourage it.

Training methods

There are a number of different training methods and options to choose from. Gone are the days of an overhead projector and screen as the only source of education. Minneapolis-based Bl Performance Services has established this list of training methods and their most effective use:

INTERACTIVE MULTIMEDIA TRAINING
Provide just-in-time training for real-time issues.
Update information frequently at a reasonable cost.
Convey ideas and simulations in an engaging and active format.
PRINT MATERIALS
Communicate policies, procedures, warranties or standards.
Communicate complex ideas through pictures/graphics.
Keep frequently used information accessible at arm's reach.

VIDEO PRODUCTION
Spotlight leaders expressing important messages.
Convey energy and emotion.
Address an audience with variable levels of literacy.
CLASSROOM INSTRUCTION
Enhance learning, expressing important messages.
Address real-time issues through discussion and feedback.

Communicate organizational change or other sensitive issues enhanced with two-way communication.

EXPERIENTIAL LEARNING
Promote a shift in attitude or energy.
Provide a setting for personal development and/or team building for commitment to groups.
Create clarity among issues using experiential metaphors.

DISTANCE LEARNING
Transmit information quickly to people in different locations at the same time, for example during product launch.
Promote participation and interaction across the country or world.
Spotlight leaders communicating important messages.

As time goes on, these options will alter and change as technology alters and changes. Used wisely, any one of these methods has the potential to play a significant role in the education of your work force.

Support and encourage the learning process

Adult education of any kind is about change. If nothing has changed at the end of an educational experience, the effort was a waste of time and money. Yet, many organizations spend hundreds of hours and thousands of dollars on training, only to have everything remain the same. This is most likely to occur if nothing has changed for employees once they return to the work site. Training is meaningless if it is not supported once the employees return to their jobs. In fact, one reason that training often doesn't work well is that once employees return from the training, the managers they work for never use what was learned. So it simply dies.

New behaviors need intermittent reinforcement. This can be done through newsletter articles, tying rewards to the new behavior, or, most importantly, by the manager deliberately modeling the behavior in everyday situations. To further experience success with training, encourage and reward employees who continually come up with new ways to use and implement the new behaviors. In addition, be sure your organization's policies and procedures are written with the new ideals in mind.

Resource learning centers

Another method of learning that re-enforces training comes from internal resource centers. According to Vicki Perri, president of People Coach, these resource centers need to be stocked with books, tapes, movies, and any other materials that support four types of knowledge:

- Business operations—how the organization works, history, policies, etc.
- Product knowledge—the organization's products, history and future.
- Customer knowledge—trade magazines, newsletters, anything written about your customers (best if the information is not more than 90 days old).
- Interpersonal/customer service knowledge—any interpersonal skills.

Resource centers can be used as clearinghouses where all employees can discover information regarding the organization's current reality and past history. Any article that someone finds interesting or pertinent can be posted, and reading lists that help ground the entire staff in the latest business thinking can be made available as well.

Training to support the process of change

Most companies eliminate training first in hard times—just when good training is most important. Scandinavian Airlines trained 20,000 people in two months when they were already $20 million in debt. Doesn't that sound foolish? Training would have been the first thing to go in most organizations with a $20 million deficit. But SAS did the right thing, and it paid off handsomely.

Changes such as down-sizing, right-sizing, or re-engineering require leaders to re-focus and recommit to the *surviving* employees. Many times those survivors don't have the experience, skills, or knowledge to handle the new responsibilities and challenges they face. They often don't know how to deal with the added stress new responsibility brings, or perhaps how to prioritize multiple tasks. It is imperative that those employees who remain are willing to do the work required to be successful. They must be skillfully prepared to achieve that success.

According to Martha M. Hamilton in an article for *The Washington Post*, surveys have found that "in most cases layoffs didn't result in increased profits or productivity." What they did find was, "Companies that followed layoffs with increased training budgets were twice as likely to show increased profits and productivity as firms that cut back on workers and training."

One of the most important elements while realigning the work force is training. When Drake, Beam, Morin, an international executive placement and consulting firm, asked leaders from some of the country's largest organizations, "What do you need most in assuring your continued success?" they heard, "To accurately assess the needs and abilities of our current work force." This is an honest and heartfelt response. They are saying, "We simply don't know what our people can do and in what areas they still need help." Many companies are spending thousands of dollars in employee training, and there is a good chance that they have no idea whether that training is appropriate to the employees' real needs or not.

The solution to this dilemma is to have quality assessment tools available that properly match the needs of the organization with the skills of the staff. There are a number of excellent tools available today that make this process effective and efficient. One such tool is the Career Architect®. Career Architect® is a valuable assessment to analyze the skills of managers and leaders throughout the organization. A baseline template is established with the first assessment, then each person is assessed in relation to that template. The instrument itself offers suggestions on how to remedy areas that are weak or challenging. Those suggestions include specific classes to take, books to read, and mentors who consistently model the behaviors that the employee finds challenging.

When training isn't the answer

When people within organizations feel pain, or when productivity is down, the manager of the department often calls in a consultant or trainer to solve the problem. Often the conversation the consultant has with the manager reveals that the employees are not working well together or not doing the job, and concludes with a request that the consultant work with them to improve the situation. So, the consultant brings in a kit filled with How to Improve Communication Skills or Building Good Work Teams or Empowerment, and takes the group through some type of intervention process. What's wrong with this picture? Often the intervention has little to do with the real issues keeping the employees or teams from being successful. In many situations, the manager doesn't want to face the real issues, and certainly doesn't want anyone to talk about them. It's much easier for managers to go to their supervisor or CEO and say, "We're working on communication with a consultant and I'm certain that's going to straighten things out," instead of, "The real issue is that I don't give good feedback and I've let them down as a manager. They are frustrated and angry because I am not clear on our priorities. They feel that they have not been recognized for their contributions and that their ideas are always ignored. I think I need some help on how I can improve my skills."

There are few managers who would have the courage to say that, though this reality may be closer to the truth. Millions of dollars are being spent on training to improve the quality of people's work, but the real issues are not being addressed. This is part of that silent deception that keeps organizations sick. Everyone knows the truth, but no one, except for a few crazies, will ever speak the truth out loud in a place or time where it counts. In addition, everyone knows that the person who points out that the emperor has no clothes has a chance of being demoted, diminished, or demoralized all the way to the unemployment office.

Training: an expense or an investment?

If you're allotting less than 3 percent of gross revenues to training, you're joking about competitiveness.

Tom Peters

Does investing in training pay off for companies? According to an Associated Press article in the "Workplace" column on June 6, 1995, in the *Minneapolis Star Tribune*, it does indeed. "Companies that invest in people through training programs, and treat employees as valuable assets are more profitable." This comes from a study conducted by Ernst & Young LLP for the U.S. Labor Department. Here are the most compelling findings of this study:

- Economic benefits were most substantial when innovations in management and technology were integrated with employee training and empowerment.
- Companies that invest in employee development enjoy higher market values than their competitors.
- Companies that actually implemented new management practices reaped the largest rewards.

Motorola estimates that it earns about $30 for every $1 invested in training. When organizations invest in their people, the employee has a greater sense of partnership and, usually, a deeper commitment to the organization's goals. In addition, an educated staff is more likely to have good self-esteem which is at the center of desirable behavior, especially within service organizations.

Does that mean that every employee who goes through training will suddenly become a committed player? No. There are some people who by virtue of their own insecurities or personalities will never get on board. Does it mean that workers will never leave and will serve with an indebtedness simply because you have invested training dollars in them? No. Some will leave. In fact, in some cases, you may train your competitor's best worker. Today there's a smirking underhandedness in the way some companies thrive on poaching other companies' best-trained, most-skilled employees. It probably makes sense that the people most likely to jump ship are also the best swimmers. But those are the risks organizations must take. Companies that say: We'll train you or we'll send you to school but you've got to stay here for 'X' months or years if we do, are missing the point. Sure, some people will leave after you've just invested hundreds of dollars in them. But, if they are treated well and paid fairly, most will not. Most will respond positively if they are respected and valued, allowed to perform with some autonomy, paid fairly, and given a chance to move up within your organization. But no organization can expect that just because training dollars have been spent on employees that they will stay if their working conditions or relationships are less than desirable.

Converting knowing into doing

Jim Belasco, author of *Teaching the Elephant to Dance* and *Flight of the Buffalo*, told this story to a group of GIS/AT&T workers: "There was a young man who thought he could learn anything by studying. He studied the stars and he became an astrologer. He studied history and became a historian. He studied swimming and he drowned."

It doesn't matter how much an organization knows about service. All that matters is that it performs service. When an organization decides to take on the initiative of service, and plans to train its entire staff in new service ideals, the organization must first ask: Are we really going to support the necessary changes and do all of the things being taught, or are we simply going through the motion for appearances sake? In other words: Do we have the commitment to real change or are we on the service bandwagon simply because everyone else is?

There isn't an organization in the world that will have service success because people know a lot. Good service isn't a head thing. It is about doing things—no matter how small or large—that you know are going to make the customer happy. Service starts in the heart and is created in the moment, and all of the knowledge in the world can't change that. It happens when people choose to do the right thing.

Diversity

Each culture has a different set of expectations. What we must offer is consistent quality while incorporating those cultural nuances.

Dorothy Riddle

Many people are uncomfortable with people who are different from themselves. That discomfort often turns into fear and, when people are afraid, they find it harder to be open to all of the possibilities needed to maintain the relationship and to make the best decisions. But the ability to overcome fear or prejudice must be a priority in order for organizations to avoid financial suicide. According to information presented by

Professional Development Group, Inc., in the United States in the 1990s, African Americans, Asians, and Hispanics together spent about $424 billion. That number was projected to reach $650 billion in this century. Older Americans control more than 50 percent of all discretionary income and spend more than $800 billion annually. Doesn't your business want to be assured of its piece of this pie?

Our customers come in all kinds of packages. Unfortunately, customers sometimes receive different service based on the color or physical appearance of their package. If we have a bias that one group of people should be treated differently than another, we have a problem with the core meaning of service. With a bias for or against certain groups of people, service will not be a sincere gesture of the heart, but instead a forced behavior. In fact, three of the four cornerstones of dazzling service will be challenged. Service won't be **genuine** when it comes from a biased **attitude** or a misguided **paradigm.**

It's a different world

Let's take a look at some of the diverse realities that exist in our customer base. Our customers are often different from us in color, job status, economic status, communication ability, marital status, education, national origin, disability, race, sexual orientation, size, political beliefs, gender, religion, attractiveness, financial status, personality, self-esteem, and age.

This list in no way exhausts all of the differences that separate us from others. Any one of these can be a barrier to service for someone who has a bias against it. If we could learn to perceive people by their actions and not their being, we would live in an entirely different world. We would not only live by the Golden Rule: Do unto others as you would have them do unto you, but by the Platinum Rule: Treat people the way they want to be treated, not the way you want to be treated.

Why the Platinum Rule? Because not all people want the same things in life. For instance, I sat next to a woman on an airplane who told me she divorced her husband because he never gave her a birthday party. Although I was quite certain there was more to the story, she said she had asked all of their married life that he throw a big birthday party for her. And throughout all of their married life, he asked that she not even mention his birthday. You know what he got every year for his birthday? A big party. You know what she got? Nothing. What's important in all relationships, whether professional or personal, is to find out what genuinely matters to the other person and then make it part of your life's work to give whatever that is to them.

For some people this might not be easy. But part of being in a relationship sometimes includes sacrifice. This does not mean that people should ever live with abuse or demean their values for someone else's pleasure. What it does mean is that they are willing to step outside of their comfort zone on occasion for the benefit of someone else. A good example of this was shared by an elderly woman when I asked her, "How do you let your husband know that you love him?" Her answer, "I cook for him and I iron his shirts." I then asked, "What do you think he really wants from you?" And she answered, "That I talk to him and watch television with him." But she was not comfortable spending time sitting around chatting or watching TV. She was more comfortable staying busy and doing something constructive. But those things really didn't matter to her husband. Consequently, even though their marriage has survived for a number of years, it has never really thrived. Relationships that are void of sacrifice never thrive and, in many instances, neither do they survive.

Building a diverse work force

Keep in mind that just as employees may be comfortable doing business with customers just like them, customers also want to do business with people like themselves. Because it is not always possible to hire a work force that includes all categories of diversity, it is important that your work force understand the need to be diverse in communicating their desire to serve to all people.

The right behavior communicated to customers is demonstrated as respect and as a desire to satisfy the customer's needs. To make certain this happens all of the time, and to all of their customers, employees must be trained in culturally sensitive service delivery. For instance:

- Handshakes. Some people shake hands, others nod. Firmness varies as well.

- Eye contact. Some customers want direct eye contact. Some want employees to look down or away. Europeans seem to maintain long periods of eye contact without a break. Americans, on the other hand, need to gaze away periodically.
- Distance. Europeans are not comfortable with being closer than an arm's length. Others need to be closer, and still others need to be farther away, to feel comfortable. Let the customer take the lead and don't try to compromise their comfort for yours.
- Degree of formality. Some customers expect an air of formality. "How may I help you, sir?" Others expect a more friendly, "How're you doing today?" The best, first approach is friendly formality. Then, depending on the customer, adjust up (more formal) or down (less formal) as the customer opens up and becomes easier to read.

There are a number of other issues that matter in differing degrees to people. The important piece in working with others is to care about what matters most to them. Even though you may not always know what matters to them, be open to their suggestions or comments, take the time to learn about different cultures and diversity issues, and put their genuine happiness at the center of your behavior.

The importance of a diverse work force

It is important that organizations hire people from all walks and experiences in life. Resisting or resenting diversity can have a deeply negative impact, not only on the success of your organization, but on its very spirit. Stephen Covey writes in *Executive Excellence* that "not embracing diversity or differences can create negative dynamics in work relationships which in turn can kill creative potential." How can you possibly stand out or be recognized for your contribution if everyone else is just like you? A diverse team can bring a variety of options to the table and stretch our ability to solve problems and create unique solutions.

Making everyone in the group as much like us as possible at first makes us feel secure and, in a way, validated. Everything runs smoothly and it's easy to get uniformity as well as conformity. But tomorrow's successful companies won't get ahead by doing things the same way things were done in the past. Narrow thinking kills success. A diverse team stimulates synergy, unity, and creativity. We need to realize that sameness is not oneness, and uniformity is not unity. And, as the adage goes, when two people agree, it's pretty clear that one of them is not needed.

As Covey concludes, "Although personal security may be threatened when differences between people abound, if our personal security is grounded in shared vision, common purpose, and integrity, we can use those differences to move the process far beyond the usual *group think* results. What we need to share with others is philosophy, purpose, value system, and perception. Not race, religion, gender, or nationality."

Conclusion

A service-focused work force is not a product of luck. It is, instead, the product of skilled hiring and training, and motivating people to perform. Organizations bent on providing incomparable service view their work force as an asset to be nurtured and developed, not an expense to be controlled. Because our world is filled with people who come in all different shapes, colors, sizes, and traditions, we need to be open to all of those differences. Diversity is a good thing. Can you imagine having only robins, perch, pine trees, the color red, Buick Skylarks, Coca Cola, poodles, and Tuesdays? What makes our world wonderful is that we all are different from one another yet cut from the same cloth and on the same journey.

12

Recognition and Reward

The deepest principle in human nature is the craving to be appreciated.
William James

RECOGNITION

Once a well-trained work force is in place, an organization must seriously address the issue of reward and recognition. One of the most powerful human motivators is to be recognized for one's contributions to a business, society, home, or relationship. However, genuine recognition within many organizations is often rare. When asked if they could accurately and effectively recognize the contributions their staff has made to their organization, many managers sheepishly admit they cannot. Some managers don't know what their staff is doing, let alone what they are doing well. Nor do they know how employees spend their time, the significant challenges they face, or their needs for training and improvement. If there are numbers to collect or goals to reach, managers can lose sight of the day-to-day performance of employees. They simply sit in their offices and read reports, many times with the door closed.

Several years ago, Tom Peters coined a phrase that still applies today: "management by wandering around." Not spying or looking over people's shoulders for mistakes, but simply being visible and available. The most common reasons managers give for not being available to wander around is that they are at a meeting or out of the office. It's impossible for someone to be effectively and fairly recognized or rewarded if the people in charge don't have any idea what's really going on. And people who are not recognized for the contributions they make typically become less apt to contribute over time. Consequently, it is vital that leaders and managers give the recognition they need and deserve to those within their span of influence. Recognition that motivates and energizes people is (1) timely, (2) sincere, and (3) specific.

Timely

When managers and supervisors are absent during the work day, they can't grasp the extent of the contributions their staff is making to the organization. Usually managers hear about an employee's effort or success long after the contribution has been made. By the time it's acknowledged, the person being acknowledged has often moved on to something new and recognition has lost its value. In order for recognition to have real meaning, it must take place in a timely manner while details of the event are clear and the energy surrounding the contribution is still present.

Sincere

Nothing rankles people more than positive feedback that is perceived to be insincere or manipulative. In fact, if there is any chance that someone might perceive recognition to be insincere or manipulative, don't do it. It always does more damage than good.

To be effective, gratitude and recognition for a job well done must be from the heart. Nothing fancy, no big deal. Just honest and sincere. As external customers expect service to be genuine, so internal customers expect recognition to be free from pretense and hypocrisy as well.

Specific

"You do a good job, Mary. A doggone good job." There's nothing wrong with congratulating a hard-working employee this way, but does Mary have any idea what part of her job is doggone good? We all know that our on-the-job performance is not perfect. No matter how well we do our job or how hard we try, there are always things that we could do a little better. When we hear we've done a good job, we wonder what part of the job is being referred to. You do a good job is a one-size-fits-all statement that really has little impact on us.

On the other hand, if Mary's boss says, "Do you remember this morning when the customer from X-Mark called regarding the problem with their stabilizer? I happened to overhear your conversation with them. I know how angry they were and I want to tell you what a good job you did handling a really difficult situation. This, by the way, is one of the reasons I really appreciate having you on our team. You have a wonderful ability to handle people even when they're at their worst. Thanks for the good work." This is a response that has been custom-designed for Mary, and Mary can wear it with the same pride people have when wearing a suit of clothes that has been tailor-made for them. Mary will feel special because something was said with only her in mind.

Praise and attention

> *The deepest hunger of the human soul is to be recognized, valued, appreciated, and understood.*
>
> Stephen R. Covey

Joseph L. Mancusi, Ph.D. from the Center of Organizational Excellence, tells how trainers work with killer whales at Sea World. As the training begins, the whale is in the pool with a rope stretched across the bottom. As the whale swims over the rope, the trainers celebrate and praise the animal. In time, the rope is raised and the whale has the option to swim over or under the rope. When the whale swims over the rope, the trainers praise and encourage it to continue the action. When the whale swims under the rope, the trainers simply ignore it. The mammal is acutely aware of the responses of its trainers and responds to them in subsequent performances. This pattern is followed until the rope is lifted ten feet out of the water. Each time the whale jumps over the rope, it is praised. And each time it swims under the rope, it is ignored. How do they teach the whale to twist and turn as it jumps over the rope? They don't. The whale is such an intelligent animal that it simply gets bored and expands its movement to amuse itself. However, once the whale introduces this new behavior into its jumping routine, the trainers go wild and praise the animal profusely.

If whales respond so positively, wouldn't it make sense that the human animal would respond positively as well? Most service providers or employees want to be good performers and relish the genuine recognition of a job well done. And yet, as was mentioned earlier, many managers have no idea what their staff is contributing to the organization, let alone encourage them with significant attention and praise. Being with their employees, knowing what is being accomplished—not controlling or monitoring—and giving good, timely, honest, specific praise and feedback is what the work force is starving to receive.

Appreciation

Dean Spitzer writes in an article for the May 1996 *American Management Association* titled, "Rewards that Really Motivate," that when workers were polled as to what they valued most in recognition for their work, the number one answer was "appreciation for a job well done." Managers, on the other hand, rated that at number eight on a scale from one to ten. Is there any wonder that many employees feel unappreciated?

During a recent holiday weekend, several employees from a toy manufacturing company were working late into the evening. During a radio interview, the employees were asked, "Why are you working on this holiday weekend?" Their response: "Because there's work that needs to be done." Many employees work hard and long hours simply because there is work to be done. Many, not all, get paid overtime for their extra work; but this is not the sole reason for their willingness to work. Most are committed to doing their job and doing it well. What do they want in return? Appreciation. People just want to be appreciated for their effort and commitment to the organization. They want a genuine, honest thank you; and they want to believe that their contribution is appreciated.

Appreciation for and attention to employees' contributions can be shown in a number of different ways. In a story for *Executive Excellence*, Bob Nelson shares a study by Gerald Graham showing that of 1,500 employees from across the country, 67 percent most valued a personal thank you or congratulations from the manager. The second most valued form of praise was a written note or letter. Recognition and appreciation are valued most when they come from people who are available, present, and able to assess the true contribution of others and their impact on the success of the organization.

REWARD

Most "rewards" are as bad as punishments—they single out behaviors and people—they don't focus on the total.

W. Edwards Deming

According to consultant Dean R. Spitzer, "Creating a meaningful cost-effect reward system is one of the most important challenges facing any organization today." But whom does this system need to reward? Stephen Covey talks not only about customer satisfaction but stakeholder satisfaction as well. There are three levels of stakeholders that organizations must take into consideration when discussing rewards:

- Customers need to be rewarded with superior products and services.
- The company needs to be rewarded with profits and growth.
- Employees need to be rewarded with
  a. Fair pay;
  b. Opportunities to advance and grow;
  c. An environment that recognizes their contribution with genuine praise and feedback.

In order for an organization to thrive, none of the above can be rewarded at the expense of any of the others.

Customer rewards

Customers, who are at the center of your business and the only reason your business exists, must believe that doing business with you is, in and of itself, a reward. They experience this through a combination of competent, caring, consistent service and quality products.

In order to have value, customer rewards must also have meaning to the customer. If the reward has no meaning to the customer, it has no valuable effect on the relationship. Even if you reward customers with discounts or other promotional ideas, you must be certain these are the things that have real meaning to the customer.

Don Peppers and Martha Rogers write in *The One to One Future*: "You need to customize your relationship with your customers in order to be competitive. This will also include their rewards for doing business with you. If your organization offers a one-time trial offer on a new product to all long-term customers, are you sure the trial offer is something they will value? Maybe they already know they want the new product and what would be more valuable to them would be an early-bird price discount." At the center of reward is a term we hear time and time again in customer service and satisfaction: communication. The best way to know what customers truly want and what rewards they value is to ask.

Company rewards

We also know that the organization must be rewarded. Why go through the effort and all of the work if the organization gets nothing in return? Organizational rewards come in the forms of income, increased organizational value, good will and reputation, and the satisfaction of providing a good product or service to the community. In addition, if an organization chooses to be rewarded at the spiritual level, or that level that sustains all else, it will return a portion of its profits to those in need and protect and support the earth and its environment in the process.

Employee rewards

Act in such a way that you always treat humanity...
never simply as a means, but always at the same time an end.

Immanuel Kant

In addition to customer and company rewards, employees at all levels of the organization must be rewarded. Employees need to be rewarded in order to feel that they have received a return on their investments of time and energy, just as the stockholders need to be rewarded for the money they have invested. Not all organizations believe that the employees' investment of time and energy has any meaningful value. Columnist Marjorie Kelly writes, "In too many corporations today, employees are being treated as tools, not greatly different from equipment. They're something that has no intrinsic worth, only an instrumental value—something to be used to create wealth for others, and to be discarded when no longer useful." Any organization that remotely believes this is true need not even attempt to achieve a quality service reputation. Since their service philosophy is built on a house of cards, the smallest breeze is guaranteed to blow them away.

The flavor of the month programs

How are employees rewarded? One method of reward comes in the form of a contest or program that singles certain individuals out for special recognition and praise. Some of these programs have even been given catchy names like Star Performer, Today's Soaring Eagle, Tiger Sales Performer, Tomorrow's Answer, to name a few. On the surface, there is nothing inherently wrong with any of these. But at the core, they rarely promote the desired behaviors, nor do they reward the right things at the right time.

In addition to rewarding and encouraging the wrong behaviors, contests also often make people's span of work too narrow. Whatever is being rewarded in the contest is what matters...nothing else. For instance, one credit agency was rewarding its agents for the number of calls they took during any given day. The more calls, the more points they received. What did the agents focus on? Not service nor taking care of problems, but getting the caller off of the phone as quickly as possible to move on to the next call.

Regardless of their popularity, most organizations would be better off by eliminating contest-type reward programs. As Deming said, some methods of reward are as bad as punishment. Criteria used to measure results are usually vague and often subjective. Consequently, people are never really clear as to what they need to do in order to achieve the reward or, in other words, how they should perform in order to win. This also brings to the fore another down-side of contest programs. If there are winners, then there also have to be losers. Losers usually include everyone who did not win. Even when used with the best of intentions, these methods of recognition often pit one person against another.

Let them decide

Some organizations have become aware that contests bring on negative morale. To avoid this, instead of having managers choose the contest winners, they have employees nominate one another for the reward. These contests usually go something like this:

A set of criteria for performance is established. Employees are informed of the details regarding these criteria and told if they observe any of their co-workers exhibiting any of these behaviors, they should write that worker's name on the form provided and drop it in the Stellar Performers Name Barrel. At the end of each month, all of the names will be listed in a newsletter but one name will be drawn from the barrel and that person will get a $100 gift certificate to wherever. Let the games begin!

All of this sounds quite harmless. That is until you notice a co-worker exhibiting one of the behaviors from the list. You dutifully write that person's name on the form and drop it into the barrel. A couple of days later, you do something you think is pretty swell. You look around and notice that the person whose name you dropped into the barrel is watching. You wait, but this person makes no effort to write your name on the form. You can't believe it! You now spend every waking hour trying to figure out how to get that person's name out of the barrel. This method of reward pits one person against the other and often causes unnecessary conflict.

The reason most programs don't accomplish what is intended is that they are not personal. Somebody needs to get the reward! This has an entirely different effect than recognizing an employee's genuine contribution to the organization, acknowledging it in a way that truly matters to that individual and reacting in a manner that is sincere and straight from the heart.

Rewards must have value to employees and customers

According to author, Michael LeBeouff, more than 80 percent of the front-line employees' behavior is determined by the organization's reward system. If this is true, organizations must be careful and thoughtful as to the behavior they are rewarding.

If rewards are to have value, they must be tied to the long-term relationship with the customer. If they are not, rewards can defeat their purpose. A good example of this occurred when a bank in southern Minnesota heard that customers were unhappy with the waiting time it took to meet with a personal banker. The bank's leaders decided they would solve the problem by rewarding all bankers who met with their customers within three minutes of their appointment time. If they did, the banker would receive a $25 bonus per customer. This seemed like a reasonable method of rewarding a desired behavior.

Predictably, what happened was that the bankers stopped focusing on customers during meetings. Instead of satisfying the customers' needs, they were watching the clock. Customers were rushed out of offices, questions went unanswered, and sales opportunities were lost. In fact, many customers thought the bankers had lost their minds. Sitting in the lobby, they watched in amusement as relatively reserved financial people raced out of their offices at break-neck speed to greet their next appointment.

When bank leaders finally realized that this program was not doing what they had intended, they asked the customers for more information about their wait time. To their surprise, they found that customers were willing to wait for up to ten minutes without any adverse effect. They agreed that fifteen minutes was getting long and twenty minutes was, indeed, too long. They also found that customers wanted their banker to be apologetic about the wait, whether it was the banker's fault or not. Finally, the bank discovered that if coffee, tea, or some other kind of treats were available, the effects of the wait were diminished even further.

What do employees want anyway?

What gets rewarded, gets done.

Tom Peters

Intrinsic to the value of a reward is its meaning to the person being rewarded. A bright, capable, forward-thinking CEO of a major Midwestern hospital wondered why very few employees came to the celebrations the hospital held to reward and recognize each month's high-achieving contest winners. The answer: The celebrations meant nothing to the staff.

Organizations that reward and recognize people only at special celebrations, banquets, awards dinners, or year-end meetings are comparable to people telling their significant others that they care about them only in a card at the appropriate time once a year. The relationship certainly deserves better than that, whether personal or professional. People need to know on an on-going basis that they are valued, and their good work needs to be noticed consistently. The reason the hospital staff didn't attend the celebrations was that they saw little or no positive feedback on the job. In fact, they felt the environment they worked in was anything but positive. Consequently, the special celebrations held little meaning for them.

An organization needs to know what its employees truly value before rewarding them for a job well done. A well-meaning owner of a small company rewarded his staff for good work with tickets to the Minnesota Twins baseball games. The gesture was well-intended but for half of the staff it was no reward at all. They didn't care about baseball and consequently the reward held no value.

Managers need to know what each employee values. Because values vary, the best way to find out is to ask. An employee may value time off, a financial bonus, a gift package to a hotel for a weekend, or simply an extra long lunch once in a while. Zytec Corporation, a Baldrige-award-winning Minnesota company, rewards employees in ways from giving a day off to having an executive do their job for the day. When an organization knows what rewards are valued by their employees and they work to provide those rewards, people respond positively and feel motivated to continue to perform well.

According to author and businessman Frederick Reichheld, the issue that creates the greatest loyalty and commitment today is the organization's sensitivity to the employees' personal obligations. Personal obligations include issues from child care to elderly-parent care. Companies can respond to these issues in a number of ways with on-site day-care facilities, flexible hours, overtime conversions, to time off, and other employee-friendly policies.

Manager rewards

Good management is difficult and good managers should be rewarded for the good work they do. Managers, too, need to be recognized for their true contribution to the organization. If the organization is service-based, then managers should be judged by their ability to serve people within their span of influence. It makes sense for an organization to create a culture that rewards those who take responsible and moderate risks to satisfy customers and employees.

If managers are going to buy into their organization's service philosophy, their performance must be measured by service-based standards. A number of organizations are holding their managers accountable for the satisfaction of their customers. Managers' reviews at Taco Bell depend on customer feedback. In fact, at least 20 percent of their compensation is tied to customer satisfaction. It would make sense that everyone's salary and performance reviews be tied to internal and external customer satisfaction. But is that happening?

Not according to Jay Mathes in a story written for *The Washington Post*. He cites a study done by Rath & Strong Management Consultants that asked how 100 managers from Fortune 500 companies were compensated. They found that

- 87 percent believed that customer satisfaction was critical to their company's success (it would be interesting to hear what the other 13 percent believed about customer satisfaction);
- 20 percent tied compensation to customer satisfaction;
- 70 percent said performance was driven by internal measures, not customer measures.

This discrepancy is part of the reason why 75 percent of organizations that talk about service today are failing to provide it. If managers are not being rewarded and compensated based on the level of customer satisfaction, is it any wonder that service is failing? People, like many other animals, are programmed to do the things that provide recognition and reward. If there is no reward, then there is little reason to exert the effort. We have a limited amount of time and energy during any given day, and we will always place a high priority on those things that matter most to the people we want to impress. According to Tom Peters, "What gets rewarded, gets done." If service performance is not being rewarded at all levels of the organization, there's a good chance it's not getting done.

Money

Of all of the dreaded topics for many organizations to discuss with employees, money has to rank right at the top. However, we do know from a number of sources that money isn't the number-one rated reward for most employees. It ranks about four or five depending on the study. Being valued for your contribution, doing work you believe that you are destined to do, and having impact on the organization, all out-rank money. But because our society determines a person's value or worth according to the money she or he earns, it needs to be discussed under the topic of rewards.

First, we do know that people have to be paid fairly. As we discussed earlier, just as customers expect a fair dollar exchange for a product or service, employees expect a fair dollar exchange for their time and talent. But money doesn't motivate people to perform. According to Dean Spitzer, studies have shown that motivational impact of a raise is less than two weeks. Although salary is usually not a motivator, it can be a demotivator when people believe that they are not being treated fairly.

How do organizations know what and how to pay their staff fairly? One of the most important ways is to know the market-rate figures for comparable positions within the industry. Those numbers should work as baseline points from which salaries are formulated. Take into consideration any variables from one organization to another. If one organization pays $18 per hour plus all health-care benefits, profit sharing, and stock-options, another organization couldn't offer $18 an hour with none of those other options and call it parity.

Bonus rewards

Beyond a fair and equitable salary, unexpected bonuses or financial rewards given to those who have truly excelled seem to be more effective than competitive rewards. All employees excel at one thing or another at one time or another, and those things must be recognized and celebrated. One good way to celebrate is through spot awards or giving a monetary portion of the sale or gain. Knowing who played what role in the process, and who was responsible for what, is critical when giving financial bonuses. This is another reason that managers need to be continually aware of what employees accomplish.

A critical element in making these awards effective is making certain that they are given in a timely manner. Research shows that time delays of bonus rewards diminish their effectiveness. In an experiment done by one major corporation, it was discovered that when employees were offered $100 immediately or $500 over the course of a year, an overwhelming majority chose the $100.

Sharing the pie

Owning 1 percent of something is worth more than managing 100 percent of anything.

Harvey MacKay

Do people perform at a greater level and dedicate more energy to their jobs when they have a stake in the action? Most people believe the answer to that question is yes. People take better care of their homes when they own, children when they're theirs, cars when they're not leasing, and their work when they have something to gain.

Shares of the pie can be given in the form of ownership in the company, stock options, or portions of the sale or gain. When the financial gain is not immediately evident, the pie can be created by the organization itself. For instance, the organization may choose to put a certain amount of money into each employee's or team's *pot*. Money from that pot can be paid out to any customer who reports bad service. For example, if there was a $50 discount given to an unhappy customer because of bad service, that amount comes out of the pot. (This needs to be managed well. For instance, if a customer is unhappy about the product or something separate from service, that should not affect the money in the pot.)

To sweeten the pot and further encourage great service, the pot could be increased by $25 (or whatever) for every customer comment praising service. At the end of a predetermined time frame (90 days, six months), the money remaining in the pot would be given to the individual or divided by the team. We could assume that those who wind up with more money in their pots probably have given great service; those who have little or no money in their pot, probably have not. Because we know that loyal customers will spend more over time, it makes sense that those who have money left in their pot deserve a share of the financial rewards a loyal customer brings to the organization.

A remarkable story appeared in the January 17, 1996, edition of the *Minneapolis Star Tribune* about a surprise gift given by the previous owner of Rollerblade, the first maker of in-line skates. Robert Naegele and his wife Ellis had sold 50 percent of their share of the business in the fall of 1995 and had made a tidy profit. That Christmas, all of the workers at Rollerblade were surprised with checks personally delivered by the Naegeles for more than $150 for every month they had worked at Rollerblade. For some, that meant checks of over $20,000, or almost half of their annual salary. Naegeles reasoning for this generous action: "These people are what made the company the success it is today. We were a team when we were achieving our goals and, as a team, we need to share the rewards as well."

In a similar act of generous heroics at the end of 1996, David Sun and John Tu, owners of California-based Kingston Technology Corporation, sold 80 percent of their stock for a windfall $1.5 billion. They knew, as did the Naegeles, that their success had been due in part to the hard work and dedication of their employees. They said, "Our employees are the reason our company sits atop the fiercely competitive computer memory industry." With that, they set aside $100 million to divide among the 550 Kingston employees. For some, that meant bonuses as large as $300,000. The average bonus throughout the organization was $75,000.

Did Sun and Tu have to perform this grand gesture? No. They did it because it made them happy to do so. Sun declared at the announcement of the bonus to the employees, "To share our success with everybody is the greatest joy we can have." How would you like to work in an organization that felt that way about you?

These stories represent the generous acts that bring most employees to tears. In addition to the genuine appreciation of their employees, these acts created good will and public recognition that was invaluable. There is no marketing budget in the world that could have bought the kind of positive image the Naegeles or Sun and Tu inadvertently gained for themselves. Although that was not their intent, doing something wonderful for others often has that kind of residual effect.

The destructive nature of greed

In 1996, Darling International, Inc. was fined $4 million for dumping animal wastes into the Blue Earth River in south-central

Minnesota. The company pleaded guilty to five counts of discharging pollution and submitting false water-sample reports. One of the suspected effects of this illegal and immoral behavior is that a thirty-mile stretch of the river is completely devoid of aquatic life. Sources said that it was impossible to know the total damages caused by this action because so many company records had been destroyed or falsified. This is not simply thoughtlessness. This is the evil that comes from greed and the complete disregard for nature itself. Do you really think that the employees who work within organizations based on evil or greed have the stomach or heart to provide impeccable, relationship-grounding service?

Today, the environment and employees have most clearly felt the abuse that stems from greed and thoughtlessness. Granted, it is wise for organizations to do business as efficiently and effectively as possible. If there is fat that can be trimmed from certain expenses, trim it. If there are people who no longer contribute to the organization and should be replaced, do it. If there is technology that speeds up the process by increasing efficiency, buy it. But workers in hospitals, schools, telecommunication companies, banks, and many other organizations have said, You've cut us until we're bleeding. We don't have the staff to take care of our customers and their most basic needs. Companies have down-sized, right-sized, re-engineered and restructured until people can barely perform. Because of this, workers' spirits are broken and their worlds are suddenly and terribly insecure.

To add insult to injury, employees don't see the people at the top suffering through these same issues. The top managers and CEOs have golden parachutes and other protections built into their contracts. Leaders are often paid for increased stock value or shareholder activity. The problem is that many of the decisions that increase stock value and make shareholders happy are not only short-sighted, but are made at other people's (the employees') expense. Yes, that's capitalism. That's how it works. But there is also the problem of killing the goose laying the golden eggs. The success of the product or service depends on all stakeholders—the people investing the money to create the product, the people with the ideas, the people who bring the ideas to life, the community that provides the workers, the environment and world within which the work is done, and the customers who purchase the product or service. There is not one aspect of this formula that is more important than the other. But in practice today, the rewards, training, growth opportunities, and job loyalty imply that the people who build the product or provide the service are not as valuable or important as the investors or people at the top. This painful message has left workers angry and bitter. How they show their frustration, whether deliberate or not, is at the expense of customer satisfaction. Ultimately, everyone involved loses.

Organizational environments

For many if not most employees, the environment within which they perform their work is as important as pay. There are all kinds of horror stories from top-notch, high-profile companies around the country detailing demeaning and spirit-breaking policies and behaviors. Marjorie Kelly chronicled some of these behaviors in her "Business Ethics" column for the *Minneapolis Star Tribune*:

"Deluxe Corporation in Shorewood, Minnesota, installed new carpeting in the front entrance of their building. How will they best maintain their extraordinary investment? They asked their employees to enter the building from the rear entrance."

"An executive at Edina-based National Car Rental System made an employee leap onto a table. Why? For no better reason than to show who was boss."

"The Bell Helicopter division of Textron Inc. in Texas allows no coffee makers in the building. Employees who would like coffee must purchase it from the coffee machine. There is one exception to this, however, the CEO has a coffee maker in his office."

"Amoco Oil Co. checked an employee's credit card records to see if he had 'abused' his sick leave." ("If you were sick, what were you doing in that restaurant?")

These are only a few of the millions of stories that create environments that are hostile to any service philosophy. In order to inspire people to perform, environments must not be only friendly, but psychologically safe. In environments where insanity and abuse prevail, risk-taking is minimal, spirits retreat, and the organization's customers sense that a subtle darkness exists. To avoid any association with that darkness, they will seek their products and services in places filled with light.

At Kingston Technology Corp., owners not only share the pie financially, but they make the environment a joy as well. According to an Associated Press story, "At Kingston, sodas and coffee are free every day. Lunch is free on Fridays. Some employees are rewarded with time off at resorts in places such as Cancun, Mexico, at the company's expense. And to further reinforce a sense of community spirit and team work, founders John Tu and David Sun sit in cubicles like everyone else. What do these perks breed in employee behavior? Greed? Entitlement mentality? Far from it. According to marketing director, Tricia Rodewald, "Everyone here would take a bullet for John and David." How many organizations can say that about their leaders today?

Salaries at the top

Another painful topic within many organizations is the inequity between the top people's pay and the pay of the people at the bottom. From 1980 to 1990, worker pay rose 58 percent, corporate profits rose 78 percent, CEO pay rose 212 percent. In 1990, Chrysler's earnings dropped 79 percent while Iacocca's compensation increased 25 percent. How can a CEO's salary go up when profits go down? This is the insanity that tears at the relationships between the people at the top and the people at the bottom.

And people wonder why morale is low in America's work force? Workers are asking all over the country, "How is it that people get laid off all around me; I'm being asked to do more work with fewer resources for the same pay; and the guy at the top (and, sadly, at this time in history it usually is a *guy*) makes more money than ever?" This creates destructive emotions that range from anger to the complete lack of energy to perform. And in the end, in addition to the misused worker, the ultimate recipient of this incredible unfairness is always the unsuspecting customer.

This inequity tears at these relationships the same way it would in a family where one of the family members gets most of the food at the table. While the others are left hungry, one person feasts on all of the food—wolfing it down with little concern for anyone else's needs. Even though the family member eating all of the food may have paid for it, the other family members who prepared the meal, set the table, and cleaned up the mess will never be fully nourished or satisfied. So it is in many companies as well.

We hear in defense of this inequity that people at the top have unbelievable responsibilities and that one of their decisions could make or break a company. They deserve to be reimbursed for the wear and tear on their psyches. (Try the psyche of a skilled plant worker in 95-degree heat with the chronic din of machines in the background.) Others' justification for this scenario, like that of over-paid athletes, is that it is a competitive and free market, and anyone who can make the big salaries should take them. Maybe. Most fair-minded and reasonably smart people probably reason that if you really make that much of a difference to the organization and contribute that greatly to its success, you should be compensated. But that compensation should come through profit sharing, not a salary that is guaranteed no matter how poorly or marginally you do your job.

CEOs and other top leaders of companies should be paid a reasonable salary, then realize potential for wealth through specific rewards for growing the company and satisfying the needs of all of the stakeholders. If a person's efforts or expertise raised the value of the company, they should reap the rewards. If not, just like everyone else who tries but fails, they should take their lumps. The same is true with professional athletes. Instead of signing multi-year, guaranteed contracts, they should be paid by their contribution to the team's success. If they contribute big, they should win big. If they contribute squat, they should get squat. No one should simply be rewarded for aptitude or potential. Everyone, at all levels and in all jobs, should be rewarded for performance.

Conclusion

In order for organizations to thrive, the customers, the organization itself, and the employees must be rewarded. The most powerful rewards come from a heartfelt thank you and genuine recognition of a job well done offered in a sincere, specific, and timely manner. But people also need to receive their fair share of the success that good work breeds. This is done through fair pay and equal shares of the pie.

13

Empowerment

Democracy is a political system not designed for efficiency,
but as a hedge against the abuse of power. Empowerment
is our willingness to bring this value into the workplace.

Peter Block

Rewards have little impact on service if people are denied the right and power to perform as they see best. Fabulous service is created *on the spot* and *in the moment.* That means decisions have to be made on the spot, and on occasion there may need to be exceptions to the rules. But many organizations get so involved with the service process that they're not able to handle the exceptions—remember the story in chapter 7 in which Tom Peters needed an early hotel check-in. Exceptions, for the good of the customer, often force people into decision-making and rule breaking—exactly what employees are taught not to do. In service-based organizations, employees are as comfortable with the exceptions as they are with the rules. This happens only when organizations allow people to use their own power to perform in the best interest of the customer. The use of one's own power within an organization is called empowerment.

We hear the term used often today, but what exactly is empowerment? Karl Albrecht defines empowerment as "reasonable freedom." Peter Senge says it's "replacing external controls with internal self-discipline." And author Bob Waterman, in his book, *In Search of Excellence,* defines empowerment as "letting go of control to gain control."

Waterman's definition presents the real paradox of empowerment. Empowering others to perform is giving up control and, at the same time, gaining control. Consider the following:

What are most managers and leaders held accountable for?

Answer: The bottom line.

What is the best way to be accountable for the bottom line?

Answer: Control it.

How do you do that?

Answer: Control the people whose work impacts the bottom line.

But the next important question is:

How far can the people who are being controlled go?

Answer: As far as the mind and talents of the controller will allow them.

In other words, everyone is limited by that one manager's limitations.

David E. Bowen and Edward E. Lawler III, in an article for the 1995 summer edition of the *Sloan Management Review* entitled, "Empowering Service Employees," take the concept of empowerment to an even deeper level. They refer to empowerment as an "empowered state of mind." To insure this state of mind, organizations must "change their policies, practices, and structures to create and sustain empowerment." Empowerment can not function effectively in a hierarchical structure. In order for empowerment to be a reality instead of a platitude, there must be "a distribution of power, information, knowledge, and rewards throughout the organization."

Bowen and Lawler further add that "an empowered state of mind is evidenced when employees have (1) control over what happens on the job, (2) awareness of the context in which the job is performed, and (3) accountability for work output."

Why empower?

The challenge in managing empowered acts of recovery is setting reasonable boundaries for employee heroism.

David E. Bowen and Edward E. Lawler III

Thanks to ubiquitous and unrelenting realigning, downsizing, restructuring, or re-engineering, everyone is looking to do more with less. Even managers and leaders are being asked to do more. And if they are doing the jobs they so desperately need to do, they don't have the time to micro-manage and control. They must let go. Tasks that were compartmentalized in one area now are being completed at different stops throughout the process. People need the power to make the best decisions along the way.

In addition, we must empower people because customers' requirements and expectations are becoming more and more specialized. This means that many things need to be decided and handled *right now, on the spot*. Often these situations are when customers are unhappy. Why is handling unhappy customers on the spot so important? TARP has done research that suggests that only 88 percent of customers will return if a problem is solved after going through some kind of process or proper channels.

For example, in a restaurant, a customer is unhappy with her meal. She tells the server that she doesn't think that she should have to pay for it. He responds, "I'll check with the manager." Even if she gets exactly what she asked for, in this instance, her meal taken off the bill, most likely she will not be completely satisfied. She was turned off by (1) the time delay, (2) a response that didn't seem sincere, and (3) the idea of people discussing her situation behind closed doors.

If, on the other hand, you solve the customer's problem on the spot, more than 95 percent of your customers will return. Under these circumstances, when the unhappy customer says, "I don't think I should have to pay for this meal," the empowered, do-anything-to-make-you-happy waiter responds, "I couldn't agree more. I'll see that it is taken off your bill right away. Oh, by the way, we'd like you to enjoy a dessert on the house. It's our way of saying we're sorry that you didn't enjoy your meal. We hope that you come back and give us another chance."

Organizations can lose up to 7 percent of their customer base by forcing employees to ask permission before they can make their customers happy. Can you afford to lose 7 percent of your customers? This is one of the most powerful reasons why empowered employees make good economic sense.

The final reason we must embrace empowerment is that ownership and responsibility ground each individual in loyalty to the organization. As businessman Harvey MacKay said, "It is better to own 1 percent of something than to manage 100 percent of anything." When we are empowered, we begin to sense the ownership that is lacking when we are simply responding to someone else's agenda. When service is at the core of an organization's spirit, there is a passion that can be sensed the minute we walk through the door. And passion is tied to empowerment. People can't soar with passion while they are tethered to other people's methods, rules, or agendas. Dan Hanson, says, "Empowerment doesn't mean the same thing to everyone. Some people thrive on the idea of greater latitude and responsibility, others retreat. We also know that it is not a quick-fix to problems or something that can be imposed. All we know is that empowered employees see themselves as personally responsible for the people they serve, and that that personal responsibility enhances the service image of the organization."

The benefits of empowerment

Chances are, in your organization as in others, there are people who know a lot more about certain things than the person in charge. And if there is free association among contributors, groups of people achieve more than the person in charge even imagined possible. When managers and leaders let go and allow people to use their own talents, capabilities, and knowledge, those people together will go further than any one person could go alone. And when people are given the freedom to work to their full potential, there are two things that become healthy and grow—their self-esteem and the organization's bottom line.

Not only do you gain control by letting go, the people you've empowered have the opportunity to be responsible. Stephen Covey says, "You can't hold people responsible for results if you control their methods." By holding on to the strings that control people's methods of performance, those in charge deprive people of the privilege of success or failure. If managers and leaders are going to error in their management style, it is better that they error on the macro side and not on the micro-management side. Micro-management is demoralizing and, often, incapacitating. Micro-management is like a puppeteer holding on to all the strings of her/his creations. The puppets can only do what the puppeteer has the talent and skill to do. No more. But people are not made of wood and cloth. Everyone brings something to the job that she/he does better than the manager, and perhaps better than anyone else on staff. If the manager and employees all know what is important and what needs to be done, a good manager lets go and lets the employees do their jobs. And while people are busy using their talents and doing their jobs, good managers stand ready to offer their support and give constructive feedback to the process.

In their article, Bowen and Lawler revealed the results of a survey of Fortune 1000 companies regarding the effects of empowerment. They discovered that empowerment not only improved worker satisfaction and quality of work life, but half of the companies also reported that profitability and competitiveness had improved as well.

How an employee goes about accomplishing tasks and reaching goals must be up to the employee. As long as the employee is on target and within set boundaries, methods should not matter. In fact, process improvement is only possible in organizations where processes are challenged. If employees are only working toward compliance, nothing will ever get better. But in shops where employees are encouraged to try new methods as they see fit, new and better ways of doing things are a matter of course.

Empowerment is a birthright

People often refer to empowerment as something you can give or bestow upon someone. But power can't be given. In truth, we have all of the power we need right inside of us. All we need is an environment where we can make choices based on our talents, experience, and knowledge. Vicki Perri teaches that people are born with all of the power they need. Have you ever noticed a two-year-old in action? Talk about power! Then babies grow up and go to school where they are taught to color inside the lines and conform. With this, a little bit of their natural power is taken away.

"But I want to paint the sun blue!"

"You can't. The sun's yellow."

Then they get their first job.

"People here wear suits and ties, laugh at the boss's jokes, start early, and work late."

"But I work better in a flannel shirt and jeans, I think the boss is crude, and my family is more important to me than this job. But, I need the money, so...."

A little more power is snuffed out of the spirit, and on it goes throughout the course of a lifetime. Is it surprising that many people are balking at the idea of empowerment today? After all of these messages, over all of these years, they're now being told it's okay to go ahead, act out, take a chance, and color the sun blue. And these messages are coming from the same organizations that blocked the use of their natural power in the first place. No wonder people don't know what or who to believe!

Empowerment, not dominance, must be a foundational value

Because so many leaders are held accountable for the ultimate success or failure of an organization, many believe that they must control all aspects of the business to insure positive outcomes. But Peter Block teaches that at the core of control, as opposed to empowerment, is often dominance. When organizations preach empowerment but practice dominance, empowerment is simply a "cosmetic adjustment on the surface of an organization." It has no real or lasting benefit. When dominance or patriarchy continue, only under different labels, oppression is still at the core and any real power to perform is withheld.

Human beings seldom, if ever, want to be dominated. Dominating people oppress the spirit personally and professionally. Dominance is usually a side effect of power. People in powerful positions, those who are physically or psychologically stronger or who who hold the purse strings, are often in positions where the opportunity for dominance is great. But dominance is not always a residual effect of power. Eric Nordstrom, of Nordstrom Department Stores, is a good example of a person with power who puts his staff's power before his own. To make sure that service is at the center of every customer's experience, salespeople are empowered with the authority to do whatever they think is best to make their customers happy. He further encourages employees to act with an entrepreneurial spirit and to treat customers as they would want to be treated. In order to bestow that much freedom on employees, a leader must be devoid of dominance.

Laying the groundwork for empowerment

We are reluctant to let go of the belief that if I am
to care for something, I must control it.

Peter Block

A process that lays the groundwork for empowering people to function at the desired level of service includes these steps:

1. Set clear job descriptions and roles, and be clear about the type of character needed to accomplish the organization's goals.

2. Interview well. As we mentioned in a previous chapter, interviewing is essential to good hiring. Even though hiring can be a tedious process, a good interview can reveal the necessary information required to hire the right person. Remember, it's much easier to eliminate a questionable candidate in the interviewing process than it is to fire an unsatisfactory employee down the road.

3. Hire the right people. Be careful about giving someone a shot or a try. If there are doubts, don't.

4. Be dedicated to impeccable training. As we discussed earlier, training is more than: "Here are the keys, be here at 8:00, and bananas are on sale for $.55 a bunch. Any questions?"

5. Set guidelines and boundaries and establish goals. "Here's

where we want you to go," or "Here's what we expect you to accomplish," and "Here are the parameters of your authority in spending, making decisions and keeping time frames."

6. Let go. Allow the individual to fly away and perform. The leader's job is not to control, but to create a culture filled with trust, and to offer constructive feedback and appraisal along the way.

Empowered employees need authority

According to Marshall Saskin, co-author of *Putting Total Quality Management to Work*, employees must also be enabled for empowerment to have a positive effect. They must have the tools they need— knowledge and skill—to use their authority.

Johnsonville Sausage, Inc., is a perfect example of employees being empowered and enabled to perform. The company is located in Johnsonville, a small town in Wisconsin, where it specializes in meat production. Although it had been successful by most standards, their CEO and founder Ralph Stayer was disappointed at the company's performance. He knew it wasn't living up to its full potential and believed that perhaps, instead of leading them to greatness, he might actually be in the way. With that, Stayer decided it was time for a major change. He literally turned the company over to the employees. What a risk! But did they fall apart as some feared they would? To the contrary. Since the staff was empowered, a) sales have increased by 20 percent per year, b) productivity has increased by 50 percent in the past four years, and c) rejects went from 5 percent to less than $1/2$ percent. In addition to these bottom-line statistics, morale has increased among workers, turnover is down, and absenteeism is almost non-existent. All of this because one man took a risk and chose to let go and give people the authority to perform to the best of their capabilities.

Stewardship: a step beyond empowerment

As human beings, we unintentionally divide our lives into three categories: our personal life, our work life, and our spiritual life. In a manner of speaking, organizations can be compartmentalized into these same three categories. Most organizations have components that are either people-oriented (personal life), task-oriented (work life), or goal-oriented (spiritual life). Stewardship, according to Peter Block, is about aligning these three areas so there is balance in the distribution of power, purpose, and rewards. Block's definition of stewardship is to "hold something in trust for another with the intent of being of service and accountable without having to be in charge."

Block further views stewardship as one's willingness to be accountable for the well-being of the organization by operating in service, rather than in control, of others. It is accountability without control or compliance. Stewardship is the search for the means to experience partnership, empowerment, and service. It is a set of principles and practices. When stewardship is at the core of the organization, employees are treated with the same spirit of choice and service that they, in turn, offer to their customers.

Stewardship is at the center of genuine service when

1. there is balance of power. People need to act on their own choices. We do a disservice to people when we make decisions for them, even if we are right.
2. the primary commitment is to the larger community. Focusing constant attention on the individual or on teams breeds self-centeredness and entitlement.
3. each person joins in defining the purpose and culture of the organization.
4. there is a balanced and equitable distribution of rewards.

As a steward, you will serve the organization and be accountable without caretaking or being in control.

From stewardship to partnership

Partnership is a step even beyond stewardship. Service-based organizations must put control close to where the work is being done. In order to do this, those in authority must give up some power to those who must make on-the-spot decisions. Partnership strives to balance power between ourselves and those around us. When organizations partner at all levels, employees bring their specific skills and talents to the situation. Each person defines her or his perception of the purpose, values, and vision of the process. In addition, everyone has the right to say no. Even though one person may have 51percent of the power, no one loses their voice, even if they lose the vote. Partnerships create the position of joint responsibility. Each person is equally responsible for the outcome. Finally, there must be absolute honesty. Not telling the truth in a partnership is an act of betrayal.

The success of partnership within an organization depends greatly on the willingness of those in authority to let go of as much power and privilege as possible. As Block maintains, once a servant leader says, "I want you to share in the felt ownership of this franchise. I plan to share with you the power and privileges of ownership, as long as it is used in service of the larger unit. This is the partnership agreement that I want to manage by," that leader will begin to see powerful unions of talent at all levels, and organizations brimming with ideas and energy.

Spheres of influence

Not all power within organizations is clearly defined. Leaders aren't always clear as to what decisions can be made with or without permission. People talk about empowerment, yet often employees aren't comfortable taking risks and making decisions. This forces us to break down the components of empowerment even further than partnership and stewardship. David Hultgren, a training specialist with Prism Performance in Detroit, developed a model representing the three Spheres of Influence that have significant impact on our life and the lives of others.

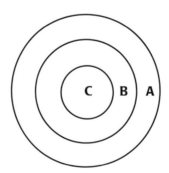

Spheres of influence

These spheres represent a view of your world from the inside out. The outer circle (A) represents those things in life you can not control. Such things as the weather, business trends, the location of your building, traffic, and the hundreds of other influences that are pretty much out of your control. In the inner circle (B) are those things that you can not control but you can influence. Some of these things might include, but are not limited to, other people, policies, procedures, laws, governments, and so on. And, finally, in the center circle (C) are those things that you can control. And what does that include? Only you. What you think, how you act, what you say, and all that you are.

Despite the implications of this model, where do you think many people spend their time and energy? In the two outer circles. "If the manager did this," and "If only she would do this," or "Did you hear what he said," and "blah, blah, blah..." And what does spending all of this time and energy on everyone and everything else accomplish? Nothing. Instead of worrying about the things they can't control or complaining about the behaviors of others, people must focus their time, energy, and attention inside the center circle. Instead of blaming and accusing, people must instead ask: What can I do to make this better? What is my role in this whole mess? Who can I call to influence a change in this policy? How can I act, in spite of how others are acting? What can I do to be certain the customer walks away happy? Once we start worrying more about our behavior than other people's, we will begin to change the world.

Putting customer complaints in the proper sphere

When interacting with customers, it is helpful to keep the spheres of influence in mind. This is especially true when dealing with customer complaints. For instance, if a customer complains how terrible the traffic was on the way to your facility or about the nasty weather, in which circle does this belong? The outer circle. Once you realize this, you can listen attentively and then let it go. The weather and traffic are pretty much out of your control. If there is a route with less traffic or a place to enter the store that is more convenient in bad weather, let the customer know. But in most instances, you'll simply need to listen to their complaint, unhook from it emotionally, and then let it go. In these situations, most people just want someone to listen to them blow off steam. However, if the customer is telling you that no one ever returns phone calls, a record of an invoice that was promised never arrived, or there are a lot of mistakes on a billing, you need to ask yourself: For what part of this complaint am I responsible? Those things for which you are responsible go into the center circle and you need to make a plan. Those things that are remedial, but out of your control, go into the second circle where your influence may be necessary for change.

Knowing into which circle an issue belongs helps you solve the customer's problem. If their complaint falls within the center circle, you can tell them what you are going to do to resolve it. You own it. You can do whatever it takes to make it right. If, on the other hand, their complaint is a result of rules, decisions, or behaviors of other people, you need to inform them of the process you will follow to get the information or their concern to the right people. "John, here's what I am going to do. I'm going to write a memo to the head of the accounting department and explain what you have told me. If someone from that department hasn't contacted you by Friday, I'd like you to call me at............." The point is that you have the power to do something to help the customer. If everyone within your organization does whatever they are able to do to satisfy the customer, service will soon become your crowning glory.

Our personal responsibility to service

We are the sum total of our choices.

Deepak Chopra

Can the actions of one person change an organization's landscape? Loren Eiseley writes in his work, "The Star Thrower," of a young man standing on the beach throwing starfish back into the ocean. A man walking along the shore walks up to the young man and asks, "Why are you doing this? The sun's up, the tide's going out, and there are thousands of starfish on the shore. What difference can you possibly make?" The young man picked up a starfish and threw it back into the ocean. "It made a difference to that one."

Doing whatever you can to make things better for one person at a time is at the center of extraordinary service.

It is about personal responsibility. Personal responsibility is not without difficulty. We find that people whose behaviors have created pain or disappointment for themselves and others often blame it on something or someone else. Dealing with an out-of-wed-lock pregnancy, beating up or battering someone less powerful, being stuck in a poor paying job, losing a job, having chronic financial problems, continuing to fall into the downward spiral of substance abuse, or maintaining violent and empty relationships are often situations blamed on someone or something else. People refuse to stand up and say, "These things happened because of my choices. These are the results of what I chose to do in that moment. Even if there was a gun to my head, it was always and ultimately up to me. It was always my choice. I am responsible."

Judge Ted Poe, a proponent of personal responsibility, requires that those convicted in his court take responsibility for their actions. Because he believes that remorse is at the core of atonement, they must write a letter to their victims, dead or alive, and apologize. Then they must stand up and say, "I am responsible."

I would guess that if we honestly look back over our lives at the circumstances which caused us the greatest pain or joy, we would probably find our choices at the center of both. We've had the opportunity to choose one thing or another and whatever we've chosen has created our current reality. For instance, some people complain that they can't get ahead, or that they only get hired for poor-paying jobs. As you further discuss their options, they will often remark that they just didn't get any breaks, or someone else always got the good jobs, or somebody had it in for them. It is never their fault. But if you talk about things such as education that can change their circumstances, the replies might go like this: "Nah, that's too hard and I never liked school anyway. Everything they teach is stuff I already know. It's just a waste of time." They choose not to do what is necessary to grow and change and because of this, will never get a better paying job. And instead of saying, "I blew it. When I had the opportunity to study and learn, I did other stuff that seemed more important, so I didn't try and now I have to pay the price," they say, "Ain't it awful. Life's been unfair to me and now I have nothing." The blame game is alive and well in America. In fact, it is probably at the center of a great deal of discontent and disillusionment. It's easier to sit back and take pot shots at the world than to ask: What can I do to make my life better in spite of my circumstances?

The same thing is true with individuals providing great customer service. Yes, there are organizations that are terrible to work for. They are hierarchical. They preach one thing and live another. There is greed at the top and few incentives for anyone else. But still, each person within these organizations has a choice as to what they will do and how they will act. They can turn terrorist and make every moment at work a nightmare for all with whom they come in contact. Or they can exert the energy it requires to find another job and, in the meantime, treat the people in their world well. Most likely, customers and co-workers are not the reason for their unhappy situation, so why take it out on them? Remember, in all circumstances and at all times you have the opportunity to choose how to act and what to say. In the end, most everything that happens around you, including customer service, is about you and your choices.

Staying within your center circle

The revolution begins in your own heart. What others do will effect you, but it need not be anything greater than an occasional distraction.

Peter Block

Who you are is how you will serve. No matter how many training sessions you attend or how many times you are admonished to modify your behavior, at the center of your professional self are your own personal values, character, and principles. You can't be divided into a professional self and a personal self, one good and one bad. The untrue or false self will be weak and crumble under pressure. You are who you are. If you drive to work cursing everyone on the road, is it possible to genuinely care about those same people when they walk through the door as customers? You must live inside of your inner circle, know who you are, what you value, what principles you live by, and whether you are a person more concerned with image or character. The answers to these questions will be the foundation on which you will build your ability to serve.

Being in control versus taking control

One of the things many people fear most in life is losing control. People can be almost obsessed with being in control of their lives. We hear this when the elderly talk about going into nursing homes. When asked what they fear most, the answer is often "losing control of my life." This is true as well when people are in airplanes, or staying as a guest in someone's home. They often get anxious because they have lost the ability to be in control. This seems somewhat incongruent, however, with how people actually live their lives. For as much as we want to be in control, we seldom rise up and actually take control. This is how the blame game begins to escalate in our lives. When we choose to actually take control of our own lives, we choose whatever option is best for each situation as it arises. But when we want to be in control of everyone and everything, we often try to keep situations from arising at all. But that flies in the face of reality. To paraphrase a popular bumper sticker: Stuff happens. And lots of the stuff that happens is far beyond our control. What we can do is take control of our reactions and responses to those things that happen around us.

The cognitive pause

Life is often an action/reaction process. Someone is treated a certain way and then, almost instinctively, responds in kind to that treatment. If a person is treated rudely, she might snap back and be rude herself. Or if he is spoken to in a gruff manner, he might respond in a gruff manner as well. But this is not the way it has to be. Jeanne Johnson, a Minneapolis therapist, says that people have the ability to make behavioral choices using an innate tool called the cognitive pause. The other animals of this world have a stimulus/stimulus response mechanism built into their genetic make-up. You might have witnessed this in the behavior of a dog that you have loved and cared for over the years. One day, because you love him, you give him a meaty, juicy steak bone. Minutes later you reach down and try to take the bone away. Most dogs, no matter how great your affection has been, will growl, snap, and/or bite. This animal, no matter how pampered, does not have the cognitive pause or ability to stop and think, "I'd like to bite her right now, but this is the person who feeds and cares for me. Plus, I'd like a Milk Bone treat tonight before bed. So maybe I should make another choice." No, this dog sees your hand coming his way (stimulus) and does what comes naturally (response). Humans, on the other hand, can be faced with a stimulus, then pause and ask, "What is the best way to respond to this?" and then make a choice.

Self-talk

A memorable statement I once heard was, "Whether you think you can, or whether you think you can't, either way, you're probably right." Although many people blame their inability to provide good service on the two outer circles of the spheres of influence—the system, policies, phones, under staffing, poor management—the real breakdown occurs inside one's own head. Self-talk can make or break peak performance. In fact, many athletes work with psychologists and motivational coaches to keep their psyches, or self-talk, at the competitive edge. There is no question that their bodies can make the jump, scale the mountain, or round the track; it's that voice inside their head that worries them.

What does your voice say to you? When a certain type of customer comes through the door, does your voice say, "Oh no. Here comes big, bad Bob. What a pain! I sure hope he doesn't come over here." Or, "I can't believe it's only 2 o'clock. I can't stand it. And here comes another customer. Can't she go to another counter. Pleeeease! Oh no, here she comes." Or, "Don't tell me he's going to lead this meeting. That bonehead. He never gets anything done." And on and on. An incredible statistic about the *voice in our head* is that 80 percent of its messages are negative. Add to that the fact that people want to be right, and we have potential for disaster looming in most of our interpersonal encounters.

So what's the point? Left to its own devices, our self-talk will whine and complain about every person and every little thing. It's the easiest thing in the world to do. Our self-talk must be deliberately positive to overcome it's negative nature. The power of our positive voice must overpower the voice that says: This is dumb, or, Why should I treat customers well when my boss or the customers don't treat me well? Once again, you must choose to override your natural negative impulses. Not because it's easy or because anyone deserves it. But simply because it's the right thing to do and the only road to exceptional service.

Conclusion

Because service happens on the spot and is created in the moment, only organizations that turn power over to their employees truly will reap its benefits. This happens through genuine empowerment, stewardship, and partnership. In addition, each service provider needs to know (1) what they cannot control, (2) what they can influence, and (3) what they have the ability to control. It is each person's responsibility to serve, and the quality of that service will depend on the person's willingness to perform. In the end, one's own voice will govern the quality of each customer's experience. Choosing how to respond to other people's behavior, whether co-workers, managers, or customers, is a key element in exceptional service. We can choose to be above the negative fray or wallow in its midst.

14

Personal Power

Some say knowledge is power, but that is not true. Character is power.
Sathya Sai Baba

Power is not something one person bestows on another. We don't get empowered. We are offered the privilege of using our own power within environments that are free from hierarchy and void of rigid structure. In this environment, people can experience the thrill of utilizing their talents and expertise and become true participants in the organization's journey towards success.

Anthony Robbins, world-renowned motivational speaker and author, asked this question, "Why are some people in life successful and others are not?" Or in other words, why is it that some people seem to have the Midas touch? No matter what they do, they succeed. At first he assumed that people were successful because they had the power of **position.** Robbins reasoned that those people holding powerful positions were, in and of themselves, people of power. Yet, as he looked closer at successful people, he realized that a number of people had achieved great success with no position power at all. Lee Iacocca had been fired from Ford and was unemployed when he was picked up by Chrysler. Col. Harland Sanders was retired when he began to look for ways to bring his chicken recipe to the public. Fred Smith had received a poor grade and his idea was rejected in the class where he presented his business plan of overnight package delivery. Yet in spite of that poor grade, he still

Power to perform

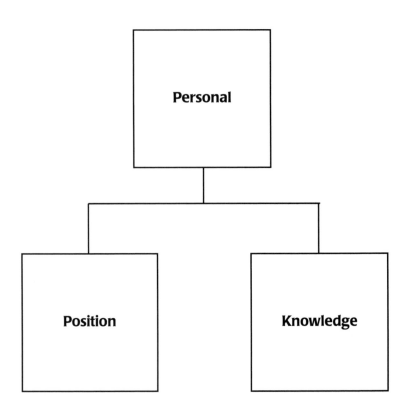

went on to found Federal Express. When Robbins took the time to think about it, he realized that he had known a lot of people who were considered to be in power positions who had not really experienced real success in their lives. And there were many who were not in powerful positions who had. He concluded that even though position certainly can be power, it is not the power that ultimately makes a person successful.

If position was not the power that creates success, then could the necessary ingredient be **knowledge?** Again, he reviewed information about the people who had achieved success in life and, though they were often bright, they were not always the most brilliant people in the world. And like many of us, Robbins knew a lot of people who were really smart who had not amounted to a hill of beans. It was clear that, although being creative and smart was a factor in success, it was not the definitive factor.

What Robbins found to be the definitive factor in success was **personal power;** in other words, the ability to act. It's the Nike commercial come to life: Just do it. People who know what's best for them or the organization, what will make them successful, and do it, are the people who experience genuine success in life.

Just knowing something or thinking something has no real value. How many times have you decided to do the right thing? Maybe you've wanted to quit smoking, or start exercising, or go back to school or whatever? Have you done it? Most people answer, "Well, to a certain degree," or, "No, but I tried." No matter how smart or great their idea, few people do what it takes to actually bring that idea to life.

You may have even been with people who see a product advertised and say, "Hey, that's my idea! I thought that up years ago!" When asked what they did with the idea, they reply in a whining, why-do-other-people-always-have-all-the-luck voice, "Nothing, but it really was my idea." Too bad. You lose. Nothing matters until it is put into motion. A decision is, in fact, only your last best idea until you put it into action. All of the smartest talk, biggest ideas, and three bucks won't even get you into the movies today. And they sure won't get you where you want to go in life. If you never act or do those things you know will get you where you want to go, you're wasting precious time.

"Just doing" service

What does all this just-do-it talk have to do with service? Over the years, many trainers and consultants have spent thousands of hours (not to mention the thousands of dollars the organizations have spent) working with employees and managers to improve service skills and habits. Yet often after the end of the training session when people have gone back to work, they are asked, "Since the training, what has changed in your work performance?" The most common answer, "Nothing." What a pitiful and depressing response! When asked why nothing has changed, most people start pointing the accusing finger in every direction. "Well, management didn't..." and, "We just got so busy and..." and, "They never give us enough..." and, "Well, they didn't do it in that department, so..." The blame game starts when these anthems are played and, in every instance, people abdicate ownership and responsibility for their own behavior.

It is interesting to get an employee alone and ask face-to-face: Regardless of what others did or didn't do, what did you do to integrate those new ideas into your work performance? A sheepish look usually comes over them and they realize that what really transpired was that they chose to do nothing. Each one of us, smack dab in the center sphere of influence, must choose to do or not do those things in life that make us winners or losers. It is about rising out of the ashes and above the fray and choosing to perform brilliantly, in spite of everyone else's behavior or choices. In the end, it's all about choosing to use our personal power to do things right and to do the right things.

Activating personal power

People must use their personal power to choose to provide impeccable service for their customers. According to Robbins, there are three steps that help us achieve our own sense of power. These steps teach that in order for us to experience our personal power, we must:

Be energized. It is probably safe to say that people who come to work with hangovers or who are depressed don't dazzle their customers with service. For them, the challenge lies in staying conscious, not in delighting customers.

Stay educated. One of the most powerful tools humans possess is the ability to pursue life-long learning. The movie, *Educating Rita*, showed how a young, lower-class, poorly educated woman transformed herself into a self-actualized, free-thinking, powerful woman. Entering the university against her husband's wishes, and with her own self-doubts about her capabilities, she found that every book and lecture opened a new window to her mind. Once the transition was complete, she was a different person. She had discovered power she had not known: her own mind, her own talents, and her own potential.

Overcome fear. People fear many things. Some fear snakes, rats, flying, intimacy; still others fear rejection, failure, or even success. The fear that often affects the changes required to provide impeccable service, however, is the fear of being different. People fear being different than, and separated from, those around them. There are certain things that we choose to etch out as part of our own identity. But one thing we don't want to be is odd or different from those around us.

Many people have attended customer service training sessions or read books on service. They know what it takes to provide good service. But they don't do it. Why? Because it's not cool to be on the bandwagon. It's more acceptable to walk out of a training session and mumble, "That was kind of dumb, wasn't it? You're not going to ask the customer how you're serving them, are you? I thought that was really dumb." That's what the status quo calls for. Few people walk out of a training session and say, "I learned something today. I'm going to change my behavior and do a better job in my relationship with customers. In fact, I'd like you to help me in my effort to provide better service." How uncool can you get?

This same kind of thing happened when I was in high school. On the day of the big test everyone would be milling around the classroom asking, "Did you study?" The standard answer was, "No, did you?" It wasn't cool to be perceived as someone who had studied, so no one would admit it even if they had. I found out at my 20-year high school class reunion that everyone had studied. Unfortunately, I had not. I should have gotten the hint when they all appeared on the honor roll every quarter and I achieved straight Cs. But they had to lie because it wasn't cool to stand up and say, "I want to do well and be successful so I studied."

Today it's often not cool to say, "I want to do a better job and apply some of the things I know are right to do." The others wouldn't like it. But in order to serve, this is exactly what has to happen. You have to overcome the fear of being different than your co-workers and strike out on a new path that leads to better relationships. It's about actually being the person that you had always hoped you would be.

Conclusion

"If it's going to be, it's up to me." That is the new battle cry of successful people. Luck and chance play minor roles in success. The real factors to success are knowing what truly matters and then doing whatever it takes to achieve those goals. People who do not succeed have only themselves to blame. Like my friend, Mary Quain, says, "You can have anything in life that you want. You just can't have everything." Know what matters to you, your organization, and your customers, and then use your power to bring those things to life.

15

Self-esteem and Spirit

Confident people have a philosophy about why they were created. They have a sense of purpose, a belief that they are important, that their lives matter.

David McNally

There are probably few elements more powerful in one's life then one's sense of self. Self-esteem lies at the very core of our personal power and paints the outlook for our day-to-day experiences. One can not attain true fulfillment in life without it, since achieving positive inner direction almost always precedes outer success. Self-esteem is our belief about who we are and our value in life. It is the heart and soul of who we are. As Andy Andrus writes in his article, "In Search of the Holy Grail" for *Executive Excellence*, "Companies must learn that their people are the heart and soul of their business. As re-engineering continues, people are losing their self-esteem. Everyone is looking over their shoulders to see if the changes will affect them and if so how. Uncertainty begets grave doubt over one's ability to effectively control one's future. Recovery of self-esteem is essential for organizations to be healthy at all levels. Low self-esteem often translates into low production, which in turn creates even lower self esteem and thus begins the downward spiral."

Self-esteem is at the center of much of today's downward spiral in business and industry. Because the contributors at the front line are suffering with self-esteem issues, everything suffers—production, creativity, cooperation, and energy, to name a few. To paraphrase Thomas Szasz from *The Second Sin*, self-esteem is to humans as gasoline is to cars. If it is full, you can go the long haul. If it is low, things get 'iffy. If it is empty, everything stands still. The CEO of Service Master adds about self-esteem, "Before you can make someone do something, you have to help them be something."

We are at the center of our self-esteem

From where does self-esteem come? William B. Swann, Jr., psychology professor from the University of Texas, writes in his book, *Self-Traps: The Elusive Quest for Higher Self-Esteem*, "self-esteem does not develop in a vacuum, but is maintained by a complex web of relationships. Parents play a big role in the early years. By age 18 months, you have already set kids on a trajectory." But even though our self-esteem is established early on, it can certainly be affected by our jobs, bosses, and others.

At its core, self-esteem is really about our relationship with ourselves. More important than what a boss, friend, or lover says is what we say about ourselves to ourselves. People with poor self-esteem often blame their boss or other significant people in their lives for their poor sense of self. We have probably all heard someone say: He treated me so poorly that I lost my self-esteem. But the truth is that a person's sense of self is usually damaged before they enter into that kind of a relationship or they would have walked away before any damage was done. In fact, we find that people with low self-esteem often inadvertently seek relationships that continue to re-enforce their poor self-image. According to Swann, "people cling to a poor self-image because of their strong drive to maintain a stable identity, even if it's a negative identity." He sees this desire for constancy as a contributor to people repeatedly seeking a abusive relationships. People with healthy self-esteem would walk out of any relationship where they were treated poorly. Not to say being treated poorly by someone doesn't affect us in some way. Swann reports that one in every four people suffer from chronically low self-image, and that low self-esteem can lead to depression and suicide. When any person is treated cruelly by another, there is the potential to affect self-esteem and shake one's confidence. But it is difficult to damage a healthy sense of self at its core. Even though the person with healthy self-esteem is affected by poor treatment, she or he views the reaction more as a sign that there is something wrong with the relationship and moves on before any real damage is done. Just like a person with a healthy sense of physical health will move his finger away from the flame before flesh is destroyed, people with a healthy sense of self will pull away from painful relationships.

One of the debilitating effects of leprosy is the inability to feel pain. Without feeling pain, those afflicted can severely injure themselves before they realize what is happening. The same is true for a person with low self-esteem. The pain of ridicule or humiliation is barely felt until after the damage is done. But as just as the flame will destroy the flesh, cruel behaviors destroy the spirit.

There are numerous examples of cruelty within organizations that damage or destroy people's spirit or sense of self. The glass ceiling damages the self-esteem of thousands of workers every day. People of color, women, those whose sexual orientation is different from that of the people in power, the disabled, and other disenfranchised workers feel blows everyday to their self-esteem.

"No Eileen, we're not promoting you. We think you have trouble handling ambiguity. It has nothing to do with your gender or race."

"But Mr. Boss, can you tell me exactly what you mean? What have I done specifically that makes you think I can't handle ambiguity?"

"Well, we don't have anything specific. It's just a gut feeling. We simply feel that Ron handles ambiguity better."

Based on what??? Many women and other unempowered groups hear these vague and damaging messages every day. And how do these messages translate inside of a person with an already shaky sense of self? "I thought I was a capable employee and now the people who know my skills see me as incapable. Although they can't tell me exactly what I have done (which is *always* a clue that there is something fishy), I must not be good enough." And a negative sense of self is re-enforced once again.

Shame, shame, shame on leaders and managers who send these messages to people within their span of influence! If a manager has nothing specific by which to judge a person (e.g., a behavior, an event, a specific issue), there should be no judgment at all. If gut feelings and judgments are made without being substantiated with specifics, an undeserving person's sense of self-esteem is once again attacked. And all because the person in authority does an ineffective job by making judgments not based on facts and reality.

Self-esteem and society

One of the saddest commentaries on society is that, even though little girls enter kindergarten with a pretty good sense of self, often, by third or fourth grade, that healthy sense begins to diminish. And sadly, that diminishing continues into the middle years of life. These little girls, in many cases, believe that they are less capable, bright, powerful, important, have fewer choices, and are less valuable than boys. And these little girls believe this at their very core. So what's the problem with that? People with poor self-esteem make desperate choices. They will do almost anything to fill the void. One example is the heartbreaking fact that we have an extraordinary number of teenage pregnancies. Many people believe the answer to this situation is punishment. But before bringing out the whipping posts and banishing these children to islands, people might ask: What's going on with these girls and their sense of self? Maybe what's going on with these girls is that they believe they have no intrinsic value. When a person thinks she has little or no value, she must create whatever sense of value she can. Unfortunately, being someone's sexual pleasure gives a hollow-spirited child a sense of misguided value. And misguided value often feels better than no value at all.

So what is teenage pregnancy doing in a book on customer service? It's here because little girls grow up to be the women in our offices, shops, and factories. And there they find their heads slammed against the glass ceiling and have their negative self-images re-enforced. The same organizations want these women to dazzle customers with their brilliant service and deliver quality products. Impossible! Oppression, whether of the body or spirit, destroys. And people whose spirits are being destroyed lose their spirit to serve or do quality work. No amount of slogans or customer service promotions or training can ever take the place of that emptiness and destruction.

These negative messages aren't just reserved for women. People who are different in any way or who have little power or privilege are often systemically diminished. This is always wrong and it often damages self-esteem which will, in the end, negatively affect the organization. Low self-esteem, no self-respect, resentment towards others—customers, colleagues, employees—and the world will almost always make it impossible for a person to deal with others in a generous and caring way. That lack of generosity and caring rears its ugly head in the form of bad service. That bad service becomes the organization's swan song as it disappears into the black hole of organizations with which few people want to do business.

Our choices and our self-esteem

Of all the judgments that we pass in life, none is more important than the one we pass on ourselves.

Nathanial Brandon

We talked earlier about how many people blame someone or something else for their hard luck and ultimately for their low self-esteem. For children, self-esteem often is, in fact, in the hands of others. Children find their sense of self by internalizing other people's images of them. But as adults, we no longer have to accept that. We now have other choices. At work we lament, "My boss acts like I never do anything right. I have to ask permission before I can do anything." We have to remember that, as difficult as these situations are, they are not always about us. To help protect ourselves when we are in such situations, ask, "Is this about me or about him? Is what she's saying or how she's acting about me or about her?" We must be absolutely honest with ourselves. Then ask within which sphere of influence the message belongs. Is it something over which we have no control? For instance, is the remark simply off-handed or thoughtless? If so, let it go. If it's not about us, but it's something we can influence, ask what you are going to do. And if it's something that we can control ask, "What is my plan?"

How we respond to someone else's behavior, not what they say or do, is what ultimately affects our self-esteem. If we truly are at fault, we must own it and move toward it; our self-esteem will only strengthen. There is a real power in taking responsibility for that which is rightly ours. If we are not at fault and we are the target of someone else's rantings due to their own low self-esteem, we must put up our emotional guard, tell ourselves the truth and let it go. And if this is a pattern (it happens more than once), it might be smart to start getting exit plans in order. This always sounds easier than it is. But ease comes with practice. We must bring clarity to our sense of self by asking the right questions, answering them honestly, and taking whatever action is ultimately in our best interest.

In addition to asking the right questions, we need to honestly assess ourselves. We need to know the truth about our strengths and our challenges. Once we have found the truth, we need to follow the basic tenets of the Twelve Step programs: change what we can, accept what we can't, and use our wisdom to know which is which.

Self-esteem: a balance between doing and being

Self-esteem depends on a balance between feeling competent and feeling lovable.
William B. Swann, Jr.

There are two basic components of self-esteem. First is the confidence we possess in facing life's challenges. The other is feeling worthy of happiness and fulfillment.

When we lack confidence or feel unworthy, we develop all kinds of defense mechanisms to create illusions to cover up our low self-esteem. Often, if we can't do something to hide our low sense of self, we simply withdraw. Low self-esteem will never be something that helps us, or the people we encounter. Part of recovery for negative self-esteem is to seek the real truth about ourselves—not what someone has told us, or some untruth we have learned to believe over time.

In practical terms, our self-esteem runs on the continuum between doing and being.

| 1 | 2 | 3 | 4 | 5 | 6 | 7 | 8 | 9 | 10 |

DOING   **BEING**

One of the ways that we get a sense of self is from what we do. Another is from our sense of being, or who we are. We run along the doing-being continuum throughout our lives. People who get their sense of self from **doing** tend to be closely identified with their jobs or with what they do and put a great deal of importance on performance. Those who get their sense of self from **being** are secure in who they are and feel they are worthy and valued regardless of what they do. The key to this continuum is balance. If someone stays solely at either end of the spectrum, their life will probably run into difficulties. Those who are stuck in doing will never feel adequate and will need to remain in constant motion to attain some sense of value. They are usually great performers who pay a high emotional price for their success. Those stuck at the being end of the continuum probably believe that life owes them a living, and they take little responsibility for much of anything. On the 1-to-10 continuum from doing to being, a healthy sense of self will probably be around 6.5 to 8. People need to believe that they are wonderful and special just because they were born (being) and yet know their contributions and responsibilities are vital to themselves and others (doing).

Recovering self-esteem

There are a number of ways to begin to recover self-esteem. As mentioned earlier, one step is to leave the situation you find damaging. Because this is often so difficult, it may be best to seek professional help from a counselor or therapist to help focus on what is the best solution to the problem. If you choose to handle the situation on your own, here are some steps to help change your understanding of who you really are and why you deserve to feel good about yourself.

Give yourself a break. As William Swann says, people with low self-esteem tend to be hypercritical. Set your standards realistically and with kindness. In other words, lighten up.

Gravitate toward people who think well of you. Maybe someday their impression of you will make an impression on you.

Beware of quick fixes. A whirlwind romance or inspirational slogan might move you towards a better sense of self, but since they are grounded on shaky foundations, they can also be a setup for disappointment.

Learn to love your own reality. You might be too short to play pro basketball or model. Or you might not have the talent to sing in a band. Face it. Accept it. And then let it go. Let go of whatever you are pining about that will never happen. It is tethering you back from the journey you can make happen.

Be honest about the mistakes you have made. As you look back at mistakes, ask if it is appropriate to make amends to those involved. If not, let it go and forgive yourself.

Finally, *pursue those things that you can change with passion and patience.* In order to insure recovery of your self-esteem, be sure you make a plan that you are confident you can achieve. Then, as Nike's ads admonish, JUST DO IT. (Remember, whether you think you can or whether you think you can't, either way you're probably right.) In the process, be kind to yourself and know that from time to time you will fall down and maybe even fail. Make a commitment that every time that happens, you will get up and start again. Just remember every day *to keep on keeping on.*

"I need to believe I'm important to feel important."

Some people think that because they are in positions low on the corporate totem pole or in jobs not as glamorous as others they have good reason for their lack of self-esteem.

But that is not necessarily true. David McNally tells a story about a shoeshine man by the name of Zee. By most people's standards, shining shoes is not one of the most prestigious jobs in the world. And yet Zee did his work in such a way that he was a sought after artisan of his craft. How could someone make an art out of shining shoes? He always let customers know that they were wearing a truly "fine" pair of shoes. He also made certain that the customer felt that she or he was the most fascinating person he had ever met. His enthusiasm was so infectious that he often worked with lines six-deep waiting for his services. When questioned about his work, he always responded, "I'm happy here; I love what I'm doing, and I make good money." The point is that it doesn't matter what you do but how you go about doing it. Zee was not subservient to anyone. He was happy to be *of service* and *in service* and it showed in everything he did. He served with dignity. And because it was genuine, it paid off in great tips, a very good living, and a wonderful sense of self.

This story is just one example of how a person found value in his contribution to life. Because feeling good about ourselves is such an important part of our ability to truly be in service to others, we need to be deeply conscious of our sense of self. You might find inspiration from this quote from Claudio Naranjo, author of *On the Psychology of Meditation:*

Naranjo's Rules to Live By

Live now. Be concerned with the present rather than with the past or future.

Live here. Deal with what is present rather than with what is absent.

Stop imagining. Experience the real.

Stop unnecessary thinking. Rather, taste and see.

Express rather than manipulate, explain, justify or judge.

Give in to unpleasantness and pain just as to pleasure. Do not restrict awareness.

Accept no should nor ought other than your own. Adore no graven image.

Take full responsibility for your actions, feelings and thoughts.

Surrender to being as you are.

Creating organizations that honor self-esteem

If there is little self-esteem in the people within an organization, there will be few organizational values enacted. The ability to bring values to life is equal to the degree of each contributor's self-esteem. For instance, if trust is one of an organization's values, it is exhibited through people feeling secure enough to express themselves openly and honestly. If people don't feel safe or valued, there is little possibility for open dialogue and, for them, the core value of trust does not exist.

In organizations where the structure and culture are hierarchical, low self-esteem is re-enforced. But within organizations where the positional powerful choose to allow the less powerful to use their power, high self-esteem is reinforced. Part of the problem is that in hierarchies, all of the attention focuses on one end of the spectrum. Everyone is interested in either the bottom line or the reaction of the people at the top to that bottom line. Is the bottom line of a company important? Absolutely! Without close attention to financial results, the entire foundation can collapse and there will be work for no one. And if that happens, everyone loses. But some of the bottom-line gawkers have lost sight of the significant factors that ultimately drive those almighty dollar results. Customer satisfaction has been minimized, workers are disillusioned and unhappy, and decisions are being made to avoid pain today regardless of their long-term implications.

The pain and discomfort that many of today's leaders face is the pressure of unhappy stockholders. If you or anyone you know have ever invested in the stock market, you may be familiar with the anxiety that accompanies a stock's declining value. People buy stocks with the hope that its value will someday (sooner rather than later) increase. Although most of the people we know probably don't have buckets of money in the market, there are plenty of people who do. And those people usually have the ear of someone who can rattle the chain of the person at the top of the organization in which they have invested: What's going on? Why is this stock losing value? I'll lose my shirt! So, what does the person at the top have to do? Raise the value of the stock. And there is usually one way to raise the value of a stock and that is for the organization to make money or show a profit. And there are two ways to make money or show a profit—increase income or decrease expenses. And when income goes down, there is only one thing left to do—decrease expenses. And what's the quickest and easiest way to do this? Downsize. Re-engineer. Lay people off. Let people go. Self-esteem struggles as these short-term decisions impact people's lives. And the self-esteem of the workers left on the job is shaken as they pick up the slack in areas that are outside of their expertise.

Antoinette K. O'Connell of Training Professionals, Inc., offers these suggestions to help managers create an environment that supports healthy self-esteem:

- Create a culture that lets people know you value them and their contribution.
- Be honest and sincere. Deal with issues openly and honestly and as soon as the situation occurs. Be able to forgive previous mistakes and move on. Don't continue to ambush employees with errors from the past.
- Encourage communication and listening. Be sure the communication is two-way. Be open with your thoughts and listen to the thoughts of others.
- See the humor in the situation. Try to separate the important issues from minor irritations and spills.
- As often as possible, back people's decisions. Second guessing de-motivates and is often about method. Let go of that behavior.

Leadership and self-esteem

One of the most critical elements in the success of an organization is the self-esteem of its leaders. Poor self-esteem in leaders can take on many negative dimensions, such as arrogance and rigidity. Those leaders seem incapable of having their ideas challenged without being personally threatened. On the other hand, people with healthy self-esteem enjoy having their ideas challenged and often learn from the debate.

Two-term President Bill Clinton seems to be a good example of someone with a good sense of self. Many articles have been written about how he valued debates, even when the debaters were strongly opposed to his position. He listened closely and, if the argument maked logical sense, changed his mind. This, unfortunately, had a somewhat negative effect on his image as president. Incredibly, some people would prefer leaders to stick to their guns even if their position no longer makes sense. In other words, they don't want them to let the facts get in the way of their leader's opinion.

Leaders with low self-esteem would prefer to have people around them who simply agree with whatever they say. These leaders hold meetings, not to get good feedback to make well-informed decisions, but to have everyone guess what they have already decided. In these situations there is little dialogue and, if anyone moves too far away from the leader's opinion, a quick end to the debate.

Evaluating your sense of self

Self-esteem is a critical part of every individual's and every organization's life. As you finish reading this chapter, ask yourself two questions. The first is: How is my self-esteem? Remember self-esteem is different from ego. Ego is often a replacement for self-esteem and requires a great deal of attention. Ego is about me: Look what I know. Listen to my stories. Here's what I think. Look at me. Me. Me. Me. Many times self-centered people appear to have a healthy sense of themselves, but this is a facade. Self-esteem requires little from the outside world and is quietly settled in at the core of a confident, fulfilled person.

The second question is: What am I doing that affects someone else's self-esteem? Do I build self-esteem, destroy it, or do nothing? Eric Berne wrote in his book, *Games People Play* that we all respond to "strokes of recognition." Even a nod when passing someone on the street is a stroke of recognition. We all have read the sad stories of how orphaned babies in third-world countries are bathed, fed, and changed on a regular basis, but seldom held or spoken to. They receive few strokes of recognition, and because of this many of them die. Babies have no way of rising up in their crib, walking to a mirror, and saying: There I am. I exist. They depend on others for that information—adults to give them recognition and assure them of their existence. Children usually get one of two types of strokes of recognition from adults, usually their parents. One is positive: What a nice baby. What a pretty baby. The other is negative: If you don't stop whining, I'll slap you. You sound just like your stupid mother/father when you carry on like that. Believe it or not, as horrible as the negative strokes are, they are still better than none at all. To get someone's attention is at least part of the reason that some children behave poorly and act out.

I experienced this first hand as a child. When I was two years old, my mother invited some of her friends over for a holiday coffee and lunch. Being a zealous housekeeper, she spent her days prior to the event baking, cleaning, and attending to every detail. Being an only child at the time, I felt positively abandoned.

An hour before the guests arrived, I had reached my limit of being ignored. I pulled over the Christmas tree. The house was in instant shambles. To my horror, and I remember this vividly, my mother picked me up, hauled me over to a neighbor and said, "Here, you take her. I can't deal with it any longer." In my two-year-old mind, I had just been given away for good. I hadn't really planned on getting this type of attention. Although in reality, the woman I was given to was the woman who was going to baby-sit me anyway, I didn't have the luxury of that information at the time. I remember sitting behind a chair in her living room crying until she brought me a cookie. Once the cookie showed up, I calmed down, and the idea of living there seemed a little better. We laughed about that day for years, but it wasn't until I realized what was at the core of my behavior that I really understood the dynamics. Everyone thought that I was just being naughty. In reality, being inadvertently ignored for that length of time challenged my sense of importance, and to some extent, my own existence. The tree was really my call for recognition—a little loud and messy, perhaps, but it did get my mother's attention, and I got the *stroke* I needed.

Even though adults can look into the mirror to assure themselves of their own existence, we still depend on one another for our strokes of recognition. If those strokes are filled with positive acknowledgments, our self-esteem is grounded. If they are negative, our sense of self is challenged. But if we have no strokes of recognition at all, our sense of self can become hollow and empty. Never miss an opportunity to fill someone's sense of self with positive reinforcement. The marvelous side effect is that when we are filling another's vessel with positive recognition, we are at the same time filling our own.

Spirit

One of the most taboo topics in the business world is that of spirit. It borders too closely on the realm of religion or, to some, the roots of the occult. Yet we know that the entire person, body, mind, and spirit, shows up at work every day. All people who walk the hallowed halls of business or industry do so in their entirety. We also know that the most powerful work issues, especially in reference to service, are not about tasks but relationships and issues of the spirit. We may not talk about spirit openly or even comfortably, especially at work, but we can't deny its significance in our lives.

The dictionary defines spiritual as (1) the animating or life-giving principle with a human being, (2) the real sense of significance of something such as our contributions, how we use our talents and our significance in our work. Simply put, spirit is our non-body self (or the non-bodied self of an organization). Spirit refers to our (and our organizations') aliveness or real self. Today as organizations are being re-engineered and reshaped, what is being sought is that which is real within the organization—that which gives the organization purpose, life, and meaning. Not only are organizations being re-shaped, re-structured, and re-engineered, but they are being re-spirited, which literally means to *take in new breath*.

Spirit and service

Spirit is central to the meaning of service. We can not seriously discuss service without discussing spirit. As Deepak Chopra says in his book, *The Seven Spiritual Laws of Success:* "Everyone has a purpose in life...a unique gift or special talent to give to others. And when we blend this unique talent with service to others, we experience the ecstasy and exultation of our own spirit, which is the ultimate goal of all goals."

When people serve in the spiritual sense, there is nothing else to teach them. They are already doing whatever needs to be done. Their sense of service is at the center of their motivation and drives every movement of the eye, every word spoken, and every action that is taken. One of the most powerful aspects of spirit-based service is that it never wanes. It is not dependent on good days, moods, rewards, or any external stimulus. It is always consistent and strong. Why? Because spirit is immutable—spirit itself does not change. You may know someone whose spirit has stayed the same even though they have faced unimaginable challenges.

I found this in the spirit of my friend, Paul Spangenberg. Though I had known Paul since junior high school, we hadn't really been friends. I only knew what everyone else knew about him—that was he was a nice guy and really smart. Paul went into the seminary after college and then on to become a Lutheran minister. When he was in his thirties and a successful pastor at a church in New York, he began to have trouble keeping his balance. He was soon diagnosed with multiple sclerosis. I met up with Paul at our 20-year high school class reunion. Few of us had been aware of his condition and were shocked and dismayed to see him in a wheelchair. Paul and I renewed, or I should say established, our friendship that night. From that night on, I learned countless lessons from him and experienced hours of delight just knowing him. I was deeply saddened by his death in 1994 and still miss him today. But what I found most amazing about Paul was that even though this brilliant man had lost his ability to care for himself, to speak with clarity, or to have any hope of recovery, his kind, wonderful, funny spirit never changed or diminished. Through it all, he was always the same. His spirit, now free and in the home of his faith, was immutable.

Once again, we return to choice. Paul chose not to let his illness or his challenges get in the way of who he was. In order to serve from the heart, people must choose this same thing. They need to do that which is right, no matter what the challenges may be. Organizations must choose to do the right things as well. They need to create systems that support service and reward people equitably for their contributions. Few organizations are aware of the spiritual impact they have on their customers and the community as a whole. According to the Reverend Allen C. Liles of the Unity Church, "Many organizations have lost their inner spiritual focus on the true reason that the company exists. This includes the real benefit their products or services give to their public. Are those products or services enhancing the lives of those touched by them?" This is a spiritual question that all organizations must answer.

The organization's spirit

Just as Paul's spirit never waned through his difficulties, an organization's spirit must not be allowed to wane during difficult times. Difficult times and challenges can destroy the spirit of an organization in the same way they can destroy the spirit of a human being. Organizations must embrace the same spirit that made them great in the first place, not retreat from it when times get rough. The collective spirit of an organization can be its strength and greatest hope for recovery during trying times. Unfortunately, leaders often choose to revert to old behaviors when faced with difficulties and challenges. Open-book management is thrown out the window and control and compliance return. Meetings are held in back rooms and whispering takes the place of open communication. The spirit that drives a great organization must sustain it through its painful junctures as well. If not, the organization goes back to zero, the lessons from the past are forgotten, and everything must be re-learned again and again and again.

Killing the spirit of service

Be kind. Everyone is fighting a tough battle.
Michael Lebeouff

Because most customer complaints regarding service have to do with the way they are treated, we must address the effect that employees' spirit has on the customers' experience. Customers depend on the service providers' willingness to serve, their service spirit. When the spirit of good service is alive and well, customer satisfaction soars. When the spirit of service is destroyed, failure is all around. The spirit of good service is destroyed by a number of things ranging from stress to conflicting values or priorities; boredom to inequities in power, pay, and privilege. In an organization where any of these issues are prevalent, the spirit of service can be destroyed and, in some instances, is even beyond recovery.

Possibly the greatest spiritual problem facing organizations today is the treatment of employees. Granted, there are a number of people in organizations who whine and carry on about every little thing. But most people want to do well and contribute to the success of their organization. After all, an organization is nothing more than a group of people joined together by a common purpose. As a part of that group, most people want it to succeed. Unfortunately, when faced with making the difficult decisions of running a business, many leaders make decisions at the expense of those same people. This, in turn, breaks their spirit, the effect of which is often transferred to the customer in the form of bad service. Restoring the organization's commitment to first serve the people who serve the external customer seems to be one of the quickest ways to resuscitate spirituality.

Revitalizing spirit starts at the top

Restoring spirit by serving the internal customer must start at the top and flow down through all of the channels and levels of the organization. Where extreme unhappiness is found among the staff, the source of that unhappiness is often with leadership. The people at the top have cultivated poor working relationships and are more interested in the bottom line than in people. Don't misunderstand this point. It makes good sense that leaders and managers be aware of and responsible for the bottom line. Somebody has to be! Can you imagine your organization being millions of dollars in debt and hearing one of your leaders lament: Gee, I wonder when that happened? Leaders must be cognizant of the organization's financial picture and take responsibility for the many decisions that impact it. But those decisions cannot be thoughtlessly made at the expense of the organization's people. The tough decisions must be made in balance with a sense of responsibility to the people who helped create the organization's success in the first place.

A modern-day leader of an organization who proved you can be nice to your people and successful was the late Sam Walton of

Walmart and Sam's Club. He started his business in a small-town general store and always believed that the "bigger he got, the smaller he'd have to think." He focused a great deal of that small-town thinking on how he treated his staff and customers. Because of the model he created, Walmart employees seem to have a unique dedication to their jobs, and it shows in the treatment of their customers. In turn, those satisfied customers have made Walmart one of the most financially solid businesses in the country today. Isn't it interesting how doing what's right translates into success? There are a number of organizations like Walmart where people say: I love working here and I love who I work for. We hear it from the employees at Saturn, Nordstrom, Federal Express, The Ritz Carlton Hotel, and Southwest Airlines, to name a few. Are there dissatisfied people within the ranks of these businesses? Certainly. But for the most part, the people who work for these organizations perform well and they do this, in part, because of the way they are treated from the top and on down.

Integrity

Organizations that treat people well and create the spirit of service from the inside out are usually made up of people with deep integrity. Integrity is wholeness, goodness, courage, self-discipline and, living by inner truth.

In fact, the integrity of the entire organization is only as good as the integrity of the people within the organization. An organization filled with people of little or no integrity is an organization that is usually void of spirituality. Just being in the presence of people with no integrity is a sickening experience; organizations with no integrity are indeed deeply ill. Integrity can't be trained or mandated or faked. Like service itself, it must be genuine and come from the very core.

There are some key ingredients that people of integrity seem to have. First, they are **genuine.** People aren't afraid that they have hidden agendas or sense something about them that they aren't sure about. What you see is what you get. In addition to being real, they are **fair.** They exude a sincere goodness or kindness. You feel trusting and safe in their presence. Third, they have the **courage to act** when they know something is right. They don't do it for the sensationalism but because it needs to be done. This courage includes telling the truth even when it's hard. Fourth, they **live by an internal voice** of self-control. When many of us are sitting, they're running or walking. They do the hard things because they know those things are in their long-term best interest. This can be exercise, returning to school, or going through the rudiments of learning a new skill. They just do it. And finally, they **live by their own truth.** They are not swayed by fads or gimmicks or the latest popular beliefs. They live as they are inside of themselves. Ultimately, integrity exists when the outer self and the inner self are one and the same.

I can't talk about integrity without mentioning my sister, Vina. We all know people who have integrity, and I have a number of friends and family members who are indeed people with great integrity. But I have known none more consistent or value-based than Vina. And this isn't just a sister's blind adoration speaking. She has always been this way. I have never known her to lie about anything. For a number of years she has been an executive with RTW, Inc. Over the years, she has had hundreds of people working under her leadership at any given time. And yet, I would venture a guess that not one of those people has ever questioned Vina's integrity. And, I would say that her integrity has contributed to making RTW one of the most successful companies in Minnesota.

Reverence and belief

At the deepest level of spirit lies reverence. According to Peter Block, reverence is an "intensified state of commitment which consists of dedication, enthusiasm, admiration, respect, conviction, and earnestness." Spirit, integrity, and reverence are foundational in providing extraordinary service. They are foundational because of how deeply they affect the worker. To be all of these things, spirit must be alive within the service provider at the deepest level. In order for people to work from the deepest part of their spiritual self, the organization must support them at that level. When a person is asked about the organization they work for, they rarely respond with specific information such as yearly sales or production quotas. Instead they talk about its humanness or that part of the organization that affects their spirit: What does it feel like to work here? What is the organization's integrity? Who are the people who work here and what do they stand for? How deeply committed are you to this place?

People are usually committed to those things in life in which they deeply believe. We hear a lot about service and quality, but do people truly believe in them? For service to be a reality, people within the organization must have a core foundation of spirituality called belief—a powerful mixture of faith, confidence, and trust. It is so powerful that some physicians say that it accounts for 75 to 90 percent of healing. What we believe will happen, happens. What we believe we are, we are. Whether we think we can or can't, we're right. Belief is the instrument of all possibilities. What does your organization believe about service? Does it believe that you need to get on the bandwagon because everyone else is doing it? Or does it live with the faith, confidence, and trust that service is a real and genuine part of the spirit of the organization? Without a deep-seeded belief in service, everything that is done will be on the surface and temporary. For it to be, it must be believed.

The spirit of forgiveness

Another topic that rarely comes up in the world of business is that of forgiveness. Many think the topic of forgiveness is too religious, so they don't bring it to the workplace. Heaven forbid that anything touching on religion should enter the sanctuary of commerce! But, again, the whole person comes to work and that person is often in need of a number of things in addition to tools and a place to do a job. People need to feel connected to those for whom they work and with whom they work. Unforgiven words and deeds put distance between people and separate them from those around them. Christians believe that forgiveness is theirs for the asking from a loving God who desires to remove the distance between them. And the distance between many of us needs to be removed through forgiveness at work as well as at home.

Thousands of careers have been ruined because of one stupid mistake, and countless opportunities lost because of a misunderstanding. There are people who function for years inside of organizations where their mistakes or foolishness continue to haunt them. In fact, many organizations have personnel files where people's errors are written up so they can never be forgotten. And those files never change. The errors are never deleted and the person is never allowed to make up for the wrong done. In other words, they are never forgiven.

Human forgiveness is different from divine forgiveness. A minister once said that when God forgives, the infraction is lifted off the page like the magic of an Etch-a-Sketch. Once the page is lifted, the imprint is gone forever. But when humans forgive, we tend to store it on a mental back-up disk just in case we need to use it in the future. How wonderful it would be if we would completely let go of whatever has happened and start anew! Is there someone who needs your forgiveness? Choose right now to forgive them. Choose to forgive that bad decision, cruel comment, or breach of trust. Choose to forgive the bad anything and begin to restore that person to a condition from which she or he can genuinely work and grow. Make the decision to forgive now—then do it.

Building team spirit

We hear a lot of talk today about teams, team spirit, and working together. The team concept is actually working in a number of organizations, but for many others it is not. Teams don't work when organizations talk teams but leave everything else the same—the organization still operates as a hierarchy and everything is done in the same old way.

How do we begin to think of coworkers as part of our team and create a team spirit? First, take the time to know what each member of the group contributes, what is their role and its significance to the organization's overall success. Next, never say to someone, "That's not my job." If you are asked to help a customer or a coworker, just do it. Third, don't be afraid to tell a teammate or coworker that they are doing a good job. Help celebrate service heroes. Fourth, treat teammates with respect and always work to maintain their self-esteem. And finally, be a part of each other's success.

To learn how to work better together within our organizations, we need to take lessons from some of our fine feathered friends. Jim

Belasco writes about the comparison between an organization and a flock of geese. Geese structure their flight so it works best for the good of all. Every capable member needs to be willing to assume a leadership position when, and if, needed. In flight, the goose at the head of the free formation takes on the greatest burden and does the most work. When that goose gets tired, a fresh one from the back moves up and assumes the lead position. Also vital to their journey is the commitment to care for one another. Instinctively knowing they are stronger as a whole than alone, they cooperatively work to reach their common goal. When one goose is wounded or goes down, two geese follow it and protect and feed it until it recovers or dies. Then together they join the rest of the group and continue their flight. By cooperating and working together, a flock of geese can fly 171 percent further than any one of them could fly alone.

Conclusion

Everyone's sense of self contributes to their sense of others. In order for service providers to care about customers and serve their needs, they need to first care about themselves.

Cooperating and working together is the basis for the spirit of an organization. By creating a spirit that never changes, whether in good times or bad, through leading and participating with integrity, by believing that service is your organization's crown jewel, and by letting go of other's mistakes, you can build an organization rich in cooperation and team spirit. And this organization will fly much, much further than an organization composed of individuals on solo journeys, vying for their separateness from the flock.

16

Stress

*Management must be interested in and
committed to creating a healthier workplace.*

Grace Gorringe

In order to provide stellar service, people must feel vital and capable of performing at the top of their game. Employees' energy needs to be viewed as a renewable resource that must be sustained and nurtured over time. Although there are a number of elements that affect that resource, from physical illness to poor lifestyle choices, nothing depletes a person's energy and ability to perform more negatively than stress. Although not all stress is bad, and some even necessary for people to function at effective levels, negative stress may cause repercussions that damage not only the individual but the organization as well.

We are seeing this today more than at any other time in history. Due to restructuring, downsizing, and re-engineering, fewer people are being asked to do more with less, and many are tired, discouraged, and broken. They are being pulled between the need to keep their jobs and the enormous price they must pay to do so. Until organizations sincerely address the processes, systems, and workloads plaguing many workers today, all of the wellness programs and health fairs in the world will not improve the workers' stressful reality.

Burnout

One of the most damaging casualties of stress is burnout. We, as well as our customers, see burnout in people dragging their bodies through the door in the morning with bleary-eyed *who cares* messages written all over their faces. Not all, but most burnout comes from working under conditions that are psychologically intolerable. It is occasionally caused by physical labor, but that is far more rare than psychological burnout. Burnout is often expressed by people saying things like: It's not my problem. I can't take it anymore! It's like the scene from the movie *Network* when the lead character opens the window and yells out, "I'm mad as hell and I won't take it anymore." In a variety of ways, workers are yelling out the windows of organizations all over America.

In defense of the organizations that do put the welfare of their work force as a top priority, there are a number of employees who are at the root of their own burnout. No matter what's happening, they just *can't handle it.* Assuming that these people are emotionally and mentally sound, the significant factor for their inability to cope seems to lie in the degree of their maturity. Life itself is stressful, and all people experience stress at one time or another. Stress accompanies good life situations as well as bad. People can experience stress with something as joyful as a wedding or the birth of a child as well as with losing a job or ending a relationship. The significant factor is not what happens but how one deals with it. And how one deals with it depends, to a great degree, on the level of maturity and willingness to face the facts.

CRITICAL AREAS OF WELL-BEING

> *Becoming enlightened is not just following the figures of light. It's about making darkness conscious.*
>
> Carl Jung

Healthy people tend to deal with stressful situations more effectively than people who are struggling in critical areas of their lives. We have discussed the importance of self-esteem and found that people with a healthy sense of self are able to deal with life's challenges more effectively than those with a low sense of self. In addition to having good self-esteem, people also need to be healthy in five significant areas of their life. If they are not, they may find normal, daily stresses more than they can handle. In order to be able to adequately cope with the effects of daily stress, we need to be healthy in these areas: emotional, mental, physical, financial, and spiritual.

Emotional and mental well-being

Everyone has ups and downs. But if downs are more frequent than ups, last longer, or are more intense, a person needs to pay attention to his or her emotional well-being. People stuck in the throes of depression generally find it hard to contribute at the level necessary for success, and often find themselves sinking deeper into an unproductive downward spiral. The effects of this spiral are not only devastating to the individual but to the organization. Many organizations have counseling services available for employees and offer insurance packages that cover emotional as well as mental health. Mental and emotional health are closely related and can be treated by a number of health professionals. The important point is to seek the help you need. A number of years ago, people were stigmatized by seeking mental-health care. Fortunately, today that has changed. Twelve-step groups are common and respected, and depression has been called the common cold of mental health. Untreated, mental and emotional illnesses negatively impact our lives. They affect our ability to enjoy life, in turn affecting the people whose lives we touch. When people suffering from mental or emotional issues ignore them too long, they lose friends, loved ones, and jobs. Compounded by depression, stress on the job can seem almost unbearable, exacerbating the underlying cause of depression, and the downward spiral begins.

Mental and emotional well-being are also affected by drug and alcohol abuse. There's little question that an employee can't effectively do his or her job when hung over from some type of substance abuse. In some organizations, mandatory drug tests are being given to stop the damage caused by abuse. Being sick from too much alcohol or too many drugs can also reduce good sense and judgment.

Most customers can sense when a person is not into their job, and most people suffering from substance abuse are incapable of caring about the quality of their work. Since it's hard for anyone to express a genuine desire to serve when their head is splitting and they're in a fog, a service-driven organization must realize the importance of the emotional and mental well-being of all of their contributors.

Physical well-being

The physical well-being of an organization's people is also a critical aspect of good service. The Bloomingdale brothers discovered this in the early 1940s when the sales clerks working in their retail store were asked to remain on their feet in high heels from ten to twelve hours a day. By closing time, they were so physically fatigued that many struggled simply to stand, much less serve their customers. Francis Perkins, Secretary of Labor for President Franklin Roosevelt, helped write laws that changed those destructive practices. People can't work well when they are in physical pain. They are distracted and incapable of making rational decisions. That's what physical pain does—it takes your mind off the work that must be done. You may be able to go through the act of helping customers or solving problems, but it's neither genuine or effective; in the end, it has little value to anyone.

Financial well-being

Being financially okay doesn't necessarily mean we have a million dollars in the bank. It does mean not worrying about the utility company turning off the heat or the car being repossessed from the parking lot. Financial issues plague many workers and disrupt their effectiveness on the job. The effect of financial stress can be a barrier to good performance and, ultimately, good service. And poor service loses customers, which means businesses lose money, which, in turn, causes people to lose jobs, which means there's no money, which drains the lifeblood out of people's spirits.

Spiritual well-being

> *Spirit is our higher reality.*
>
> Jack Hawley

In order for us to perform at our very best, we must experience some sense of spiritual health. This means different things to different people, but simply put, it's about the journey of one's higher self toward one's higher power. If there is a war raging inside us, or a deep-seated sense of being disconnected from what we believe to be true, it affects our ability to be at peace with ourselves. Many philosophers and theologians have written about the need for humankind to be connected to something we believe is greater than ourselves. The void caused by the of lack spiritual connectedness seems to have had an adverse effect not only on our ability to perform, but on our very humanity as well.

> I am not I
> I am this one
> Walking beside me, whom I do not see
> Whom at times I manage to visit,
> And at other times I forget.
> The one who remains silent when I talk,
> The one who will remain standing when I die.
>
> Juan Ramon Jimenez
> (Translated by Robert Bly) 1990

Our spiritual well-being is determined, to some degree, by how we value our work and our contribution to the greater good. When we believe that the work we do has no value, a part of our spirit dies. Writers such as Thomas Moore write about how deeply that conflict rages inside many of us. These writers believe that a spiritual war is at the center of much of our discontent and dissatisfaction with life. Moore writes in his book, *Care of the Soul*, that "fulfilling work, rewarding relationships, personal power, and relief from symptoms are all gifts of the soul." The idea that fulfilling work can actually be a "gift of the soul" puts a pretty heavy value on work and work relationships. One might even say that the lack of fulfilling work could be a void in the soul and the cause for a sense of spiritual bankruptcy. It can be further argued that this spiritual bankruptcy is at the core of the discontent in many of our organizations as well. When people at all levels truly value each other, when integrity and character, not strategies, are at the center of the organization, and when being successful includes more than the bottom-line, the spirit of the organization comes to life and the spiritual well-being of the individual finds its fulfillment.

Emotionally-challenging work

When an individual contributor who is basically okay mentally, emotionally, physically, financially, and spiritually burns out, it's possible that this individual works for an organization that takes more than it gives. This imbalance can come from relationships with people, either co-workers or managers, or it can simply be found in the nature of the work itself. In either case, people need be in touch with their levels of stress and know when it's time to get out.

There are some jobs where the nature of the work is more emotionally taxing than others. Healthcare providers in long-term or emergency situations, police officers, air-traffic controllers, people working in complaint departments, and others in emotionally intensive jobs, can suffer from the effects of burnout regardless of their sense of self-esteem, good health, or well-being. It's important that the people in these high-stress jobs take extra steps to take care of themselves. The organizations they work for must be cognizant of the damage that can occur when long-term stress goes unchecked. They need to create schedules that make sense, and provide mental health days for employees to take time off simply because they need it. Stress affects not only people's ability to enjoy life, but their ability to serve. Whether from burnout on the job or dealing with the rest of our lives, we can hit the wall and ruin everything. But that doesn't need to happen. Fitness and wellness expert Lonna Mosow makes these suggestions to her clients who are suffering the ill effects of stress:

> To get back in control and feel you have the power to regulate your emotional and physical response to stress, you need

to get into your body via your mind. The mind and body are inseparable. One speaks to the other and one depends on the other. The mind has the ability feed the "right" information to the body enabling muscles that are constantly contracted and over-taxed to relax and let go. And, believe it or not, this powerful relaxation process is accomplished by breathing. Take a deep breath of air, really deep. Imagine completely filling your lungs like a balloon filled with air. Hold it for a moment. Then exhale (preferably through your mouth) all of the air from your lungs. Once again feel the air re-entering your lungs. Listen to yourself breathe and control from *where you draw* the air. Breathing in such a manner will bring your focus into your very being. With every inhale, you can "cleanse" your internal self. With every exhale, you can rid yourself of tension in the chest, shoulders, neck, and back.

Along with *thoughtful breathing*, do exercises that can be done at your desk or break room. They have a cumulative effect and help prevent stress from building up. These exercises include shrugging your shoulders up and down; clasping your hands behind your back and lifting them upwards as you bend your body forward; twisting your spine while sitting in a chair and gripping the chair back; and clenching your toes and then letting them relax. Because of the negative effects of stress, it is important that everyone deal with stress on the spot and in the moment whenever possible.

Deadly indifference

Not everybody burns out. Some simply fizzle. They fizzle from boredom, being chronically ignored, or discounted. Others lose interest due to lack of challenges or growth potential. For whatever reason, people become filled with the deadly indifference that we discussed earlier. The problem is that this indifference eventually becomes part of the customer's experience with the organization. Indifference is a hard beast to tame. First, it is difficult to identify. Most people suffering from it show up for work each day on time and go through the motions of doing their jobs. They rarely act out, nor do they behave in a manner for which they would be reprimanded. They just don't care, and their mere presence reeks of it.

There are two factors that affect people's ability to climb out of the rut of indifference: (1)the individual's ability to choose to rise above it, and (2) the leader's willingness to serve. An individual can choose to remain mired in nothingness or choose to perform well in spite of difficult circumstances. Boredom is a symptom of a mind unchallenged, and no one can be ignored who relentlessly pursues new ideas and lives with a sense of passion. Leaders, on the other hand, can dig in their heels, remain top-down driven, and drain the life out of their employees. Or they can choose to inspire, get out of the way, and allow people the privilege of performing brilliantly, using their own skills and creative power.

Conclusion

Stress can be a barrier that eliminates all possibilities of good service. People suffering from burnout fail to rise to the challenges facing organizations today. A sense of emotional, mental, physical, financial, and spiritual well-being lays a foundation rooted in self-esteem that airlifts service providers over the valleys of indifference and despair. To overcome stress, use the relievers suggested by Lonna Mosow: breathe, move, and deal with stress on the spot and in the moment.

17

Communication and Measurement

Sometimes the only way to get 20/20 vision
is to look through the eyes of the customer.

Harvey MacKay

Once the organization has been restructured, policies re-written, and people empowered, it is imperative to measure the impact these changes have on the customer. Measurement can be accomplished only through communication. When we measure, we are really asking our customers, "How are we doing, are you satisfied, is there anything else we could do that would make it easier or more desirable for you to do business with us?" We are, in fact, communicating. But for some, the term communication sounds far too personal. Measurement sounds more antiseptic and puts us at a psychological distance from our customers. But do we really want to be antiseptic and distant in our communication with our customers? If communication is at the center of every successful relationship and has been found to be the most important factor in job enhancement, do we want our communication with customers and co-workers to lose any of its meaning? According to Performance Research Associates, 56 percent of all managers and 48 percent of front-line leaders believe that poor communication is the number one customer service problem. This includes communication both to and from the customer.

Communication: the service power tool

Your voice can inspire confidence and assurance or generate doubt and anxiety. Most people don't know if they're opening or shutting the door to success when they speak. Or losing customers.

Jeff Jacobi

If service is to be, it must be communicated. As we discussed earlier, communication is simply an exchange of meaning where the end result is mutual understanding. Diane Booher further states in an article for *Executive Excellence* that for communication to be effective it must be "clear, correct, consistent, complete, current, and compassionate." Service can be communicated at any juncture in the customers' experience with the organization, beginning with the ad, through the drive into the parking lot, to the first hello. From any one of these encounters, a positive or negative service image is communicated. Of these, the most powerful service image is communicated through the service providers themselves. As we discussed about moments of truth, an organization's most powerful impressions come from the *people* who represent the organization.

People have many methods of communicating. From our discussion on congruency, we know that we communicate through words, tone, and body language.

In addition to those methods of communication, we communicate with facial expressions (we have 200,000 possible facial movements), eye contact (culturally biased), gestures, posture and movement, overall appearance, colors, adornments, our environment, and our use of space (proxemics). With any one of the categories, we can communicate: I want to serve you, or, don't bother me.

Interpersonal barriers to communication

Although most people would say that they want to communicate well, barriers often get in the way. Some barriers to good communication include:

Time. Time is essential in communicating with others. Most couples who experience stress within their relationships often find that the lack of time spent together is at the core. And when we rush customers through the communication process, they may not be able to effectively share their issues, requests, or concerns. This could ultimately destroy the relationship itself.

Level of interest. Sometimes people tell us things that we don't find particularly interesting or supply us with too much detail or unnecessary information. When that happens, we often mentally check out and stop listening. This can be risky. Simply because something is not interesting or important to us doesn't mean that it's not important to them. Be gracious and open to customers as they speak to you.

Distractions. Particularly in business situations, there are noises and interruptions all around. These interruptions can distract us from communicating well. When communicating with customers, find a spot as private as possible within which you can interact. If that is not possible, work hard to maintain your full attention as they speak.

Age. Another common barrier to good communication is a gap in age. This was evident when George Bush and Bill Clinton ran against each other for the presidency. One of the differences between the two candidates was that George Bush had served in World War II, and Bill Clinton had not served in the Viet Nam war. The people from Bush's generation could not understand Clinton's perceived lack of patriotism. But the voters from Clinton's generation had a different understanding of the war in Viet Nam than their elders had of World War II. Age became a barrier to communication regarding that issue.

Gender. If there was ever a potentially dangerous topic, it would be the difference between male and female communication. Some simplify the entire issue by saying men never do and women never stop. In reality, both of those assessments are wrong. Men and women both communicate, but their communication styles are often different. Because broad generalizations are never accurate, the best we can conclude is that, in many instances, these differences do seem to be true.

First, women tend to respond more intensely to how things are said and men more to content. Men often disregard how the message is delivered. Men like to move immediately to the solution; women prefer to process the issue. Women may be more likely to respond: I just want to talk this through. Don't tell me what to do. Men tend to use communication to report; women to discuss. Neither one of these methods of communication is right or wrong. They are just different. At times, it is better to arrive at a solution; at other times it is better to discuss options. It is the difference between the predominant communication styles of men and women that can become a barrier. However, when treated with respect and openness, these differences can enhance the decision-making process and assure participants that the approach to the solution was thorough and thoughtful.

Cultural differences. Our cultural melting pot is continuing to grow creating new traditions and customs. Often we are not familiar with other cultures and the symbols that express their uniqueness. We are not as open to their communication and may close our minds to their needs. Be open to the requests of people from different cultures and be willing to serve them as they wish to be served.

Language. Sometimes we simply don't understand what another person is saying because of language differences. Don't pretend you understand the other person to avoid embarrassment. In the end, if what you perceived what the speaker was saying was wrong, it could prove more embarrassing than dealing with the issue up front. To deal with the lack of understanding due to a language barrier, simply ask, "I want to be sure that I'm understanding you. Did you say, _____?" Or you can say, "In order to make certain that I understand you correctly, would you please speak more slowly?" Most people will not find this offensive and will appreciate your genuine desire to help them.

Abilities of the speaker. Some people express themselves more clearly than others. You have probably had the experience of listening to a very small child and felt frustrated when trying to figure out what she was saying. Most adults have learned the words necessary to communicate, but some may not be able to properly use those words to develop ideas clearly and concisely. It is our job to understand what the customer is telling us. The best way to do this with someone who has limited communication skills is to ask close-ended questions.

These are questions that are most often answered with yes or no. For instance, "Did the gasket come off when you pulled on it?"

Physical limitations. Some of our customers will be people who have experienced some type of illness or have an impairment that makes communication difficult. They can experience difficulty speaking, hearing, or seeing. In any one of these instances, you may be asked to participate differently in the communication process. Be open to whatever these customers need and, as always, when in doubt, ask them what they would like you to do to help them.

Subject knowledge. Have you ever asked someone a question and found the answer to be filled with information and jargon far beyond your ability to understand? When you are communicating with someone, always have in mind their ability to understand what you are saying. It might satisfy your ego to impress them with your knowledge and words, but it will be an ineffective and meaningless communication.

Own agenda. I remember, as a young adult, sitting in the kitchen with my mother telling her what I was going to do with the rest of my life. As I spoke, she sat across from me nodding and responding with an occasional "okay," "aha," and, "I see." When I finished, I noticed her eyes fade to the ceiling, and she said, "I wonder if we have any brown sugar." During my entire dissertation she had been mentally traveling through the cupboards looking for brown sugar. In other words, she was not listening to me but working through her own agenda. (After that, until the end of her life, every time I told her anything that was important to me, I always asked, "Are you brown-sugaring me?") Because we can think from 800 to 1000 words a minute, we need to clear our mind and listen from the heart to avoid the *own agenda* barrier.

"I've heard this before." Our brain tends to categorize and store similar topics in the same *file.* When we hear something that sounds familiar, we turn off our listening gear, deciding we've already heard it. This happens in business situations most often when customers are complaining. "Everybody's got a gripe about the new color scheme. I don't need to listen to you!" But when you shut out a person's voice,

you limit your depth of information and you diminish the time and effort that person took to give you valuable feedback. Listen to every customer as if it were the first time you heard that information.

Prejudice. When people are different from us, we sometimes discount their value. This is called prejudice. When we pre-judge, we have an opinion before we know the truth. There are all kinds of prejudices, and they always interfere with communication, even when they are not intentional. If you believe that someone has less value than you, it is a barrier to communication. For instance, workers in a hospital's hospice area often have patients who are living out their lives with AIDS. If the care provider is prejudiced regarding people who are gay, do you think it will interfere with his ability to care for the gay patient? It's important that this patient and his partner be treated with the same compassion as a traditional family.

These are only a few of the barriers that get in the way of good communication and ultimately in the way of good service. Be aware of the barriers you may have to good communication, as they can make or break your positive service image.

Communication lies at the core of all relationships

Without communication, all other elements in a relationship lose meaning. If you have a relationship with a person you trust, but you have never communicated that trust, it has no meaning. Everything that matters within a relationship, whether it's trust, mutual understanding, honesty, respect, must always be communicated to have any value.

A therapist told about a couple who came to her crying about the pain they continually inflicted on each other. They would scream, hit, demean, and express all kinds of abuse in the name of love. Her response, "If that's how you love one another, get over it. End it! Stop it! Because love's not what's being communicated."

There are other relationships where people aren't abusive but are unable to show (communicate) their love. Any relationship where a person can't express love is most likely empty and without depth or meaning. For love to have meaning, it must be communicated through words and deeds. Simply feeling love is a selfish, indulgent emotion and defies the true meaning of love. Love is an action, something that is expressed; something that is communicated from one person to another.

The same is true for organizations and their relationships with customers. When asked if they value customers, most organizations respond with glee, "Oh, yes, yes, we deeply value and appreciate our customers." But when pressed as to how they express this appreciation, there is rarely an adequate reply, "Well we don't really show it. We just feel it in our heart." A lot of good that does in the eyes of the customer.

If communication is at the center of all relationships, including your customers' relationship with you, answer this question: How do you know, right now, at this exact moment, that your customers are truly happy with the way they are being served? If you are like most service providers, you will answer with one of these: "Surveys," "They tell us," "They're nice to us," "They return and continue to do business with us," or "They refer other customers to us."

Granted, all of these answers have some degree of validity. It is true that some survey respondents express themselves clearly and honestly. It is also true that many satisfied customers return again and again to do repeat business. We find that satisfied, happy customers generally treat us more positively than unhappy ones. We know that, on occasion, customers will tell us exactly how they feel about doing business with us. And we know that, when a customer comes to us through a referral, the referring customer was probably satisfied. But there are drawbacks to relying on these methods to measure the degree of customer satisfaction.

Surveys

"Many companies today are working really hard but they just might be working on the wrong things." Surveys might be one of those things. Surveys are one way to measure customer satisfaction. However, I don't know if you've noticed or not, but we seem to be living in a survey-mad world. The doctor, the car-repair shop, the restaurant, the hotel, everybody wants us to fill out a survey reporting our degree of satisfaction in doing business with them.

Unfortunately, when used alone, surveys can create the same distance that the lack of interpersonal contact creates in all relationships. However, used in tandem with sincere conversation and one-to-one interaction, surveys can still be quite valuable.

Making surveys valuable tools

To help make surveys a valuable tool in assessing customer satisfaction, you might consider integrating the following into your process:

- Let the respondents know why the survey is being done in the first place.
- Be certain that you are measuring the right things. The right things are those things that matter to the customer and where action can be taken once the information is complete.
- Finally, be certain that you're asking the right people.

In addition to those suggestions, Michael Donovan writes in *The Service Edge*, that good measurement systems should: meet real business needs and expectations, be expressed in numbers, easily tracked and converted into action, be fast in converting from figures to facts, and be easily understood by those being measured.

What you measure must be important to the customer and it must be something on which some type of action can be taken. For instance, it would make no sense to measure the number of customers who did business with you who had red hair. Of course, it would make sense if you were in the hair-care business or provided a product that could affect someone's hair. But if you repaired bicycles, that would have no meaning to the customer, nor could you really take any kind of action to improve it.

Customers as measurement partners

For measurement to work best, customers must view themselves as partners in the process. Measurement surveys can appear as an imposition if, without explanation or warning, they simply arrive in the mail or are crammed into their hands at the end of a transaction. If you include your customers in the plan by letting them know that a survey is an important part of your relationship with them or, better yet, by asking for their permission to include them in the survey process, your chances of getting a more committed response are increased. And be sure that you share the survey results with them.

Employees as measurement partners

In addition, utilize the survey as a learning instrument, as well as an opportunity to hear the customer's voice, by including employees in the process of creating the survey. Ask what they need to know in order to serve customers more effectively and consistently.

To create surveys that are genuinely effective, be sure to take your organization's culture into consideration as you begin the process. An important culture question is: Are the people being measured (employees) prepared to deal with the customer survey results? It's also important that you don't ask the wrong questions of the wrong people; the results can be demoralizing for the staff. Even when the results of an effective, valid survey are analyzed, and there is an extensive gap between the expectations of the customer and the organization's current reality, it puts employees in a difficult position. This type of feedback can result in defensiveness and even anger toward the customers. It's important to know what the truth is when implementing change based on survey results. Be sure to ask: Is this valid information? Can we trust the sources? How do we move forward in making changes with this gap in mind?

Survey results

The results from a good customer survey should provide the foundational information needed for continued improvement in both products and services. Surveys fail if customers take the time to respond, voice a need for change, and nothing changes. Soon they will begin to mistrust the process and will probably refuse to continue to participate. To strengthen the perceived value of surveys in the eyes of customers, advise them of the plans for action in response to the survey results. Then be certain that you do the things you said you would. Remember, the customer believes that your word is your promise. You must perform as if your job depends on living up to that word.

Types of surveys

Customer surveys can be written, conducted by telephone or in person, in focus groups or one-on-one interviews. Depending on the need, each type of survey seems to have its pros and cons. The good news about written surveys is that you can get responses to the specific questions you want answered. The bad news is that the scope of the survey is limited and, many times, some of the things that are important to the customer are missing from your questions.

Another concern with written surveys is that some people don't like to write. They will disregard your request entirely. Plus, as mentioned earlier, so many organizations today are asking for written feedback that many people are simply getting tired of responding to them. Thus, more and more people are ignoring requests for feedback. On the other hand, if you rely only on phone surveys, you'll lose people who don't feel comfortable expressing their opinions live and in person. Here there is a risk that they won't be open and honest, limiting the value of their feedback.

And finally, even though focus groups and one-to-one interviews are excellent ways to get real-time feedback, they require an added effort by the customer. Most customers today are busy, and taking time out of their day to meet with you can be viewed as an imposition. To soften the intrusion on their time, have the meeting over lunch or breakfast, and make certain you provide the meal or pick up the tab. For a focus-group interview to be most effective, it should be facilitated by an outside expert, and include questions you want answered as well as issues customers find relevant. One-to-one interviews should be handled by the top-ranking person on the team, in the department, or in the organization itself.

What seems to work best regarding surveys is to ask customers if they are willing to participate, then ask which method would they prefer: written, telephone, or in person. If the telephone or personal survey is their choice, ask when would be the best time to talk or meet with them. Although this extra effort takes time, the quality of the survey will be better and you will have a chance to create some goodwill by showing your sensitivity to the customer in the process.

Surveys and relationships

Though surveys, in and of themselves, are not bad methods of taking the pulse of the customer, they can be used inappropriately in the context of a genuinely good relationship. For instance, can you imagine waking up one morning, going down to the kitchen, and finding a survey from your significant other sitting next to the coffee pot? It reads: How do you like me so far? Check one. Do you expect that we'll be together 10, 20, 30 more years? Circle one. You would probably ask: What's the matter with you? Are you crazy? Why didn't you just *ask* me these things? And a number of customers are saying the same thing as we hand out more and more surveys: Why didn't you just ask me?

I wondered that myself on a recent visit to Milwaukee. Just before leaving the hotel to make a presentation to a group of executives, I discovered that I was short of a couple of essential handouts. I went to the front desk and very nicely asked the desk clerk behind the counter if she would make ten copies of the document for me. Her response included a clucking sound and rolling eyes as if to say: Can't you see how busy I am and how you're annoying me? Since I didn't have time to reach across the counter and choke her, I responded, "I know you're busy but I would really appreciate this." Like the good martyr she was, she consented to make the copies.

Upon returning from the presentation, I noticed a survey sitting on top of the television set in my room. It asked that I fill it out so I could let the hotel know what I had experienced during my visit with them. Since I am more of a speaker than a writer (which I trust is not glaringly evident in this book), I had no interest in taking time to fill out their survey. Second, everyone who had served me during my visit to Milwaukee had asked me to write about my level of satisfaction. The airline, car rental, and restaurants had all wanted me to spend my time helping them improve their business. The hotel assured me at the top of its written form that if I let them know about any negative experiences I had had with them, they'd change it before my next visit. The only problem was, after my first visit to that hotel, there wasn't going to be a next visit!

If a hotel representative had knocked on my door and asked me how I was enjoying my stay instead of relying on a survey, I could have immediately unloaded my negative baggage and, depending the representative's response, left the hotel with a positive impression and a willingness to return again.

The point is that surveys work well only when they are used along with a sincere: How are we doing in serving you? Without this interpersonal, face-to-face connection with the customer, a survey is only as meaningful as an obligatory card sent by a loved one on a birthday or anniversary. If that loved one expresses no intimacy or affection on an on-going basis and then writes a sentiment in a card, that sentiment may be perceived as shallow and empty. Relationships must be tended to and maintained daily in order to thrive. And at the very center of the thriving relationship is communication that is genuine and timely. Although the depth and intimate nature of this interaction can be uncomfortable for some people and a sacrifice of their comfort zone, it is the essence of real service and at the core of true customer satisfaction.

While staying at a world-class hotel on a visit to Santa Fe, I received a letter from the hotel manager at the door of my room. She expressed her pleasure regarding my stay and asked that I write any comments I would like to make on the letter and return it to her with my mailing address included. (I found this a bit of an imposition since the hotel had received my mailing address at the time I made the reservation and at check-in.)

Although this was intended to be a friendly gesture on the part of the hotel manager, what would have been more effective would have been a voice mail message with an invitation to stop by her office to introduce myself and share any feedback I might have. Another option would have been for her to stop by our table during any of the dining hours to introduce herself and open the door for honest, face-to-face feedback. Too often leaders rely on charts, surveys, market analyses, and focus groups at the exclusion of the face-to-face: How are we doing?

Although it is easier for organizations with one-to-one client contact to talk intimately with customers, it doesn't necessarily need to be limited to this type of organization. In a Minnesota Public Radio interview, Mike Veeck, then owner of Minnesota's St. Paul Saints, recalled how his father, Bill Veeck, set a marvelous example for dealing with customers. For years, the senior Veeck ran Comiskey Park in Chicago, home of the Chicago White Sox. Surprising to fans, Veeck, manager of this huge baseball enterprise, could easily be found in the park's front office. When asked about his visibility, he responded, "Market surveys are fine and good. But nothing beats the humanity of sitting down face-to-face with someone and asking, 'How are we doing?'"

The credibility factor

There is a vital consideration, however, when asking customers about the quality of the service they have experienced with you. The question must be sincere and believed if it is to hold any real value. For instance, imagine that you had just eaten dinner at a restaurant where the food was tasteless, the service poor, and the entire experience less than desirable. How would you respond when the host or hostess asked, in a perfunctory, disinterested tone, "How was everything tonight?" Most people would respond, "Fine," and then complain all the way home. (Remember that only 4 percent of dissatisfied customers will tell you when they are unhappy.)

But isn't this strange? When someone in a restaurant takes the time to ask how things are, why don't most people tell the truth? There are a number of answers to this question. One is that people don't want to make a scene. They are embarrassed to express negative emotions or reactions and, with others watching, they just don't need the hassle. Or they think that nothing will be done about it anyway. So why bother? Others don't respond because they had just eaten and don't want to get upset. After all, they've got a patty melt sitting in the middle of their stomach and they don't really need the indigestion. Others don't want to get anyone in trouble. They're just too nice to say anything. We Minnesotans talk a lot about *Minnesota nice*. But nice isn't always what we are. We are sometimes Minnesota passive-aggressive. We may act nice at the time, but, believe me, we'll get you in the end! (Is Minnesota the only state in the Union where the customers rather than the service provider say thank you when they pay?)

But there is another possibility as to why unhappy diners don't answer honestly—they may not trust the question. To many, it falls into the same genre with, "How are you today?" or, "Have a nice day." We simply don't believe that the person asking the question really wants to hear the answer.

Do you think that the diner's response would be different if the hostess or host sincerely asked, "Do you mind if I ask you a question? We're trying to make this a restaurant that you would come back to time and time again. Would you please be honest with me and tell me how the food and service were tonight?" Would you agree that most people would probably tell the truth if the question was asked in this manner? In most instances, when a question is posed in a manner that people can trust, they choose to tell the truth. And how the host or hostess responds to the customer's feedback will influence whether the customer will return again or simply go away.

AT&T/GIS story

An example of the power of asking customers, "How are we doing?" occurred when I worked with Prism Performance, Inc., when they put together a world-wide group of trainers to work on a project for AT&T. AT&T had just acquired NCR (GIS) and, as a part of the organization's transformation, employees were restructured into customer-focused, cross-functional teams. Managers became team leaders and employees became part of teams with well-defined relationships with their customers.

One of the jobs of the trainers was to prepare these teams to sit down, face-to-face with their customers, and ask the question: *How are we doing?* Even though it was important how the question was asked, the real challenge came in helping team members listen openly to their customers' responses without defensiveness or, "ya, but" responses. This experience was powerful, not only for GIS team members, but for their customers as well. Like many companies, GIS had communicated with their customers through surveys and other detached methods of communication. And, like most companies, they did receive some valuable feedback. However, almost without exception, customers found the face-to-face opportunity to express themselves candidly and without confrontation a new and revitalizing experience in their relationship with GIS.

Listening

Listening is a magnetic and strange thing, a creative force.
The people who listen to us are the ones we move toward,
and we want to sit in their radius. When we are listened to,
it creates us, makes us unfold and expand.

Karl Menninger

If we are asking our customers questions, then the art of listening to their responses must become a significant skill for everyone within the company. Ellen Langer, in her book, *Mindfulness*, shows that people often don't listen effectively to questions before they respond. To prove her point, she poses the following questions to her audiences:

What do you call a tree that has acorns? Oak
What do you call a funny story? Joke
What do you call a sound made by a frog? Croak
What do you call the white of the egg? (Yoke?) No, the white.

Because people assume the rhyme meter will continue, they don't listen effectively to the last question. This is a common problem in communication. People don't listen effectively to others because they assume they already know what the speaker is going to say. Unfortunately, the more familiar you are with the speaker, the more this seems to be the case.

Sometimes the longer you are in business, the further away from the customer you become. I remember having lunch at an upscale, suburban Minneapolis hotel on St. Patrick's day. The dining room was crowded, but since the hotel must have been aware that it was St. Patrick's Day, it should have been adequately staffed. However, this was not the case. My lunch partner and I waited an excessively long time for every aspect of the meal, from water being placed on the table to our final cup of coffee. After lunch, I went to the maitre'd and said firmly but politely, "I need to let you know that this is the worst service I have had in a long time." To which he stood at attention, smiled and said, "Oh, really?"

That was it. "Oh really?" To say I was let down is an understatement. This is a five-star hotel, we had paid a significant price for lunch, and I expected a much better response than "Oh really?" What I really needed was to be listened to and understood. I had taken the time, made the effort, and used my energy to give this business some important feedback, but I was never given the satisfaction that my comments were listened to or that they mattered.

Fifty-five percent of communication is listening. In fact, you could say that the keys to customer satisfaction are listening, acting and then, listening again. Listening plays an enormous part in our ability to interact with others. Yet, we really listen to only 25 percent of everything we hear. Because hearing is an automatic function of the body's aural system and listening is a choice, 75 percent of everything we hear goes in one ear and out the other. Granted, not everything we hear during any given day needs to be listened to. We have cubicles today instead of offices so interactions between co-workers are overheard. We inadvertently listen to other people's telephone conversations, radios are playing in the background, and other auditory stimuli surround us daily. But we need to be better at listening to those things that are important to us or to others. How do we do this? The following four steps will help assure customers, or anyone for that matter, that you are genuinely listening to them:

1. Be present. This is hard to describe but most people know instinctively what it means. It suggests an earnest desire to capture what the speaker is saying. To do this, your mind, body, and spirit are involved in the process of understanding. Being present also includes:

Eye Contact. As we suggested earlier, this is somewhat culturally biased. Eastern and mid-eastern people tend to avoid long periods of direct eye contact. Europeans are comfortable with direct eye contact and can maintain it for extended periods of time. Americans look directly into one another's eyes but maintain direct eye contact for only around six seconds. We tend to look and then look away. What does this mean? Only that you should not be concerned if someone else's eye contact is different than yours. In general, as you improve your eye contact, it will most likely mean that you are comfortable looking into someone's eyes and staying there for a comfortable or appropriate period of time—comfortable for you as well as for the other.

Verbal and non-verbal attends (back-channeling cues). Verbal and non-verbal attends are those oral or physiological comments we make that show the other person that we are listening. Verbal attends can include "Ah-ha," "I see," "Mmmm," "Okay." They are verbal indications that you are in sync with what the person is saying. This doesn't necessarily mean that you agree with them but that you have heard and/or understood what has been said. Be careful, as this can be overdone. Some people are so busy "Ah-ha-ing' and "I see-ing" that it becomes a distraction. The most powerful listening is done in silence with a committed presence.

Questioning. One of the most flattering responses to someone who is sharing information is to ask questions. Of course, this doesn't include the question, "Huh, what did you say?" That's a down-right insult! But probing questions that suggest: *Tell me more*, are welcomed by most speakers. As a good listener, you show interest through the process of asking questions. Questions can be used to clarify information such as: Which dress do you want me to bring home? Or they can open doors to further information: And then what did you do?

Active listening. Active listening allows the listener to check in to verify that the information that was perceived to be the message was indeed the message. Active listening includes repeating back to the speaker exactly what was heard. A common reflective response might be something like, "Now let me be certain I understand what you were saying. You want me to go to the office..." This helps eliminate confusion and misunderstanding that causes conflict in many relationships.

Stephen Covey teaches about another type of active listening—

empathic listening. Empathic listening checks for content ("This is what you said.") and for meaning ("These appear to be the feelings beneath that content.") Once again, this is important because many people have a problem saying what they really want to say. Our ability to dig deeper into the emotion beneath the customer's comments may allow us to find solutions to problems we didn't even know existed.

2. Value their opinion or feedback. The second step in being a good listener is to assure customers that you value their opinion, and that their experience with your organization truly matters. One of the reasons we don't tell the host or hostess at the restaurant when they ask, "How was everything tonight?" is that we don't really believe that they want to know. When customers are asked why they don't say something about poor service, they often reply, "Nobody seems to care anyway, so why bother?" In other words they don't believe their opinions are valued by the organization.

3. Tell the customer what you are going to do. Customers want to know what you are going to do about the issue they have raised. Just because a customer tells someone about poor service doesn't mean the problem has been solved, and most customers want the problem solved if they are going to return again. This doesn't necessarily mean that you can fix the problem yourself. All you might be able to do is pass the information on to the manager. But let the complaining customer know that that's the action you're going to take.

4. Thank the customer for their honesty. It's difficult for many customers to express their displeasure with an organization. When someone takes the time and risk to do so, they need to be thanked. Remember that when a customer complains, they are really giving you a second chance. If you don't blow it, your relationship can be saved and, in some instances, made even stronger than before.

Remember when I complained to the maitre'd at the fancy hotel outside of Minneapolis? When I told him that their service was the worst I had received, he sort of shrugged and responded, "Oh really?" Had he instead followed the four steps listed above, our interaction would have unfolded something like this:

Me: "I'm sorry I have to tell you this, but our service today was the worst service I've have received anywhere in along time."

Maitre'd: (Using good listening skills including eye contact, attends, etc.) "I'm so sorry to hear this. Would you please tell me what happened?" (He assures me he values my feedback.)

Me: "Well, we came into the restaurant today expecting a nice lunch and..." (He remains present as I speak.)

Maitre'd: "Once again, I am so sorry about your experience with us. (Remember: Don't defend your mistakes. The customer will forgive anything but that.) I'm not sure what happened today regarding your service, but I will find out. Could I have your name, and is there a number I could reach you at once I've had a chance to look into this further?"

Me: (Probably a little startled) "Well, my name is Petra Marquart and you can reach me at my office at..."

Maitre'd: "I want to thank you, Ms. Marquart, for bringing this to our attention. To let you know how sorry we are, here is a discount coupon to be used any time you like in the future." (It would have been better yet if there had been a discount on our current charges, but we had already paid the bill in this instance.)

To make this experience even better, that afternoon I would receive a phone call from the maitre'd or manager. It would go something like this: "Hello, Ms. Marquart, this is John, the maitre'd at the-hotel-that-shall-go-unnamed. I had a chance to look into the problems you experienced at lunch today and found that we had errantly assigned two people to one section of the dining room and only one to another. It was our mistake and we are truly sorry. Thank you again for drawing this to our attention. I'm not sure we would have caught it without your help. I hope to see you here for a meal again soon. Good-bye."

Would I go back to that hotel again had it been handled this way? In a minute! To truly serve, you need to be obsessed with the needs of the customer, and the only way you will ever know what those needs include is to listen to what the customer tells you.

Discovering latent needs through listening

"Listen" and "silent" have the same letters. But listening is not silence.
Customer Service Managers Letter, 3/25/95

Another reason listening is such an important part of business success is that instead of pushing products on the customer, it uses customers (who are listened to) to pull products through the market. Gone are the days of developing hit and miss products that are presented to the public through expensive marketing campaigns in the hope that people will buy them. Listening is about anticipating what people may want or need.

Peter Senge teaches that organizations must know what the customers' latent needs are, and then work to meet those needs. Those latent needs include things that customers value but may rarely, if ever, experience. In his article for MIT's Sloan School of Management titled, "The Leader's New Work: Building Learning Organizations," Senge writes that "leading-edge firms seek to understand and meet the 'latent need' of the customer. These are things that customers might truly value but have never experienced or would never think to ask for."

An example of this type of thinking was evident when Mazda created its popular Miata. To insure that their new sports car would be based on more than an educated guess, Mazda spent one year doing research before the car's design was formulated. Mazda had a variety of prototypes of essential items including the steering wheels, bucket seats, stereos, engine sounds, and so forth, from a number of popular sport cars such as the BMW, Corvette, Jaguar, Mercedes, on display at various dealerships throughout the United States. They then asked committed sports-car drivers to come in and test those items for preference and reaction. After one year, those preferences and reactions were the basis for the design of the Miata. The car was so popular that, for the first couple of years following its introduction, it could rarely be found on dealers' showroom floors.

How did this happen? After listening to the people most likely to buy this car, and then actually doing what they suggested, Mazda introduced a product into the market that people didn't know that

266

they wanted prior to its arrival. Once the product was introduced, millions of people not only wanted it, but came out in droves to buy it.

The same is true of automatic teller machines (ATMs). Prior to the introduction of ATMs, customers didn't know this was something that they would want or use. Few, if any, came into the bank and asked for a more automated, convenient way of banking. The introduction of the Miata and ATM are examples of what Senge defines as meeting latent needs or creating something that the customer might truly value but has never thought to ask for.

They tell us

The second response to the question, "How can you tell if your customers are satisfied?" is often, "They tell us."

Once again I will remind you that statistically, only four out of 100 dissatisfied customers actually will tell you that they are unhappy with your product or service. The other 96 will tell you about their unhappiness by going elsewhere and never returning again. We believe that even fewer than four out of 100 will tell you when they are happy or satisfied with your product or service. People are more apt to let others know how they feel when they are unhappy. This is because the behavior or infraction has violated the customer's pain threshold. If a customer is in enough pain, they're going to let you know.

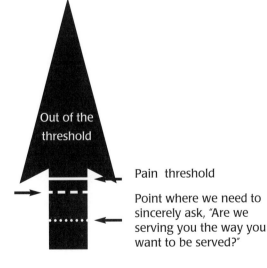

Out of the threshold

Point at which people complain or comment on service

Pain threshold

Point where we need to sincerely ask, "Are we serving you the way you want to be served?"

We have both emotional and physical pain thresholds. The doctor says, "Let me know when this hurts," and, depending on your pain threshold, you will at some point say, "Now!" The same is true with our emotional pain threshold. For instance, if we experience enough pain in a relationship or job, at some point we say, "That's it," and we leave. Because most customers say something only when reaching or hovering dangerously close to their pain threshold, we need to encourage their feedback long before their experience becomes painful. If we wait until they say something to us, they may already be planning their escape and the chances for mending the relationship are reduced.

They are nice to us

Humans are funny. What you see is not always what is real. A group of physicians was asked if they thought patients were angry with them after waiting in the examining room fifteen minutes or more. They all responded, "No."

They were then asked, "How do you know this?"

Their response: "Because when we finally get in to see them, they are usually friendly and nice."

"But Doc, do you know why they're nice to you? Because they know what you're going to be doing to them in the next ten minutes and, to be honest, they'd prefer you weren't mad at them in the process!"

Many patients in all kinds of care facilities hide the fact that they're dissatisfied with anything because, at some level, they fear retaliation. Does this mean that people fear their care providers will deliberately hurt them if they complain? Not necessarily. But it does mean that people are concerned that their care providers will not think as favorably of them, and may not treat them with the same care and consideration if they are confronted with the patient's or family member's anger.

The same is true with a number of other service relationships. How many of us really want our car mechanic, dentist, hair stylist, rabbi or minister, teacher, cab driver, food server, or any other person we depend on for service angry with us? Not many. There are people who don't care what others think and freely express themselves at any time, but most of us are uncomfortable expressing anger and, instead of being honest about our dissatisfaction, we cover up and fake it.

I remember being in a discount electronic store with a friend. She was interested in buying a CD player and needed some advice as to the various components available. Two or three sales people walked past her as if she were invisible and another, who said he'd be right back, was never seen or heard from again. After waiting for what seemed like forever, she began to stew. Her anger was clearly evident to me. So evident, in fact, that I moved slowly away from her pretending that I was looking at something at the end of the aisle. I didn't want to be in the area when she blew up.

But this is not what happened. Dr. Jekyl transformed to a sweeter-than-pie Ms. Hyde as soon as the salesperson approached. Her anger was gone and she was the picture of composure. Why? Because she had suddenly lost her irritation about being ignored? No. Because she didn't want to take the risk of receiving poor advice because she expressed her anger or complained. So the moment the salesperson walked up, she smiled and said in a cheerful voice, "I need some advice on a CD player. Do you think you could help me?" Gone was the angry, crazy woman, and in her place was a customer uncomfortable with her own anger and desperate not to lose the best advice this service provider had to offer.

What this shows is that just because customers are "nice" to us does not mean they are necessarily satisfied with our products or services. They may be subconsciously using that niceness to unintentionally manipulate an outcome and to insure that the relationship works in their favor. This, once again, confirms that if you can't depend on the attitude or behavior of the customer to show you how they feel about your service, you must make it a practice, as often as possible, to simply ask.

They return

Another indicator of customer satisfaction is whether they return to do business. We do know that customers vote on how we are doing everyday with their dollars. But can we assume that customers who return again and again are truly satisfied customers? To a certain degree, yes, but not completely.

Customers are sometimes like the couple married fifty years. One evening, when he came home, she asked, "Do you love me?" To which he tenderly replied, "I'm here aren't I?" From that reply, she could conclude that he does, indeed, love her. Or, he could be there simply because he's too lazy to pack. And that's true with customers as well. Sometimes they're just too lazy to pack. You have their billing information in your system, they know an easy route to your store, and your location is convenient. It's comfortable, easy and sometimes habit. But if they're not genuinely happy with the way you treat them, the new competitor coming down the road will make it easy and comfortable for your customers to switch.

What will happen when a new competitor makes the process of walking away from you simple and seamless? The transfer of information will be easy and silent as the night as it moves through electronic walls. There's a chance that you won't even know the customer is gone. All of their records will be masterfully transferred to the competitor, and those customers will never return again. When that happens, everyone in the organization will be shocked. "They've been our customers for years. Why on earth did they leave?"

"Because they weren't satisfied with your products or services."

"But why didn't they tell us?"

"Because, for whatever reasons, customers don't tell us. They simply go away. Oh, and by the way, another reason you didn't know is because you didn't ask."

Referrals

Other than asking, there is no better way to know that a customer is genuinely satisfied than by the people they refer to you. Customers who are satisfied like to talk about places where they do business. In

270

fact, many brag about the experience. "You should talk to the woman who does my taxes. She's just great!" "I tell you, I got a car mechanic who can fix anything and he's really reasonable..." But average or even decent service does not produce these kinds of comments. In order for people to brag about you, you need to truly dazzle them. They'll become the most cost-effective marketing department on earth.

How good is good enough?

The question is often asked: Once we measure and get feedback, how good do we have to be for our service image to be affected? What is good enough? Is being 99.9 percent effective in our service performance good enough? According to *Insight* magazine, the following are examples of other instances of 99.9 percent effectiveness. Do you think it is good enough in these instances?

If 99.9 percent is good enough, then....

> 12 babies will be given to the wrong parents each day;
>
> 2,488,200 books will be shipped in the next 12 months with the wrong cover;
>
> 20,000 incorrect drug prescriptions will be written within the next 12 months;
>
> 107 incorrect medical procedures will be performed by the end of today;
>
> Two plane landings daily at O'Hare in Chicago will be unsafe.

Just as no one would consider 99.9 percent good enough in these instances, organizations should never settle for less than perfect when it comes to service. Even if only one percent of your customers receive poor service, the people you turned off today could have been your greatest potential for revenue tomorrow. Looks, wardrobe, and mannerisms never tell the whole story. You might be surprised who you've really lost.

A number of years ago, a friend with an average income was looking for a financial planner. After making appointments with three different people, they all stood her up. Why? Because she was not a big hitter and meant little to their financial portfolios. What they didn't know was that she was in line to inherit millions of dollars within a few years. Do you think she called those financial planners when she became a wealthy woman?

Benchmarking

An important type of measurement is benchmarking. The definition of benchmarking, according to Christopher Bogan and Michael England, authors of *Benchmarking for Best Practices*, is "a process that seeks superior performance through systematic search for and use of the best practices in innovative ideas, highly effective operational procedures and winning strategies." In other words, to be the best, you need to model the best, and consistently strive to improve until you outshine your heroes. You must ask about every aspect of your business: How do the best do it? Once you answer that question, you need to ask: How can we do it better?

According to Stanley A. Brown in an article written for the *Customer Service Manager's Letter*, there are specific steps to follow when seeking improvement through the best practices approach. Organizations must:

• Pick companies that know the answers. In order to improve, you need to pick partners whose processes are more efficient than yours. In other words, if you want to know how to track root causes of problems, you should choose a company that has a sophisticated system in place for root cause analysis.

• Prepare for the interview. Know what you need and don't waste the time of people in the benchmarked organization. Open-ended questions work best in getting information as they will broaden the scope of the response. To further enhance the quality of your benchmarking interview, send any information and questions that you want addressed prior to the interview. In addition, send the company any information that will be helpful regarding your organization.

• Insure a productive interview. Describe your company and what you are doing. Explain the area that will be benchmarked. You lead the discussion to insure that you get the information you need effectively and efficiently.

• Establish a goal. A measurable goal should be set and clearly tracked to be certain that the initiative is succeeding. Brown used as an example tracking complaints more systematically and then reducing them by 50 percent.

• Follow up promptly. Send a thank-you letter within five working days. Within two weeks, send a summary of your findings. This will insure that you have indeed collected accurate information and it will reaffirm that you listened and captured relevant information.

One of the most successful grocery stores in the country is Stew Leonard's Dairy in Norfolk, Conn. Although plagued with legal issues in recent years, Stew Leonard often has been credited for creating successful practices that many organizations use as benchmarks. How do they continue to improve on practices that have earned them international recognition? One way is by seeking new ways to continually improve their current practices. How do they do this? By working at it. They own a bus that often takes managers and staff on field trips. Sometimes those field trips take them as far as 400 miles away. Their task: To visit grocery stores where each staff member is mandated to come away with one idea that they think that store does better than their store. For their benchmarking excursions to work effectively, everyone's ego needs to stay on the bus. Open minds and the willingness to learn are essential to discover diamonds in the rough that many organization's possess to some degree.

In its original use, benchmarking was used to mean a *distinctive mark* or *reference point* and that's still what we seek from other organizations. We look for those marks or points that stand out, those we all seek to attain. In seeking benchmarks to measure against, or in seeking to become a benchmark organization, we must identify something distinctive about the way something relevant is done.

One could argue that if an organization is really bad at something, it could also be viewed as distinctive. Of course, that doesn't mean it should be used as a benchmark of performance. An additional element in benchmarking is that it is has to improve the process or procedure in a area and in a manner that is relevant to you.

Are there organizations that other companies benchmark against today? Indeed. Organizations that others work to benchmark against are L.L. Bean, Nordstrom, Federal Express, Ritz Carlton Hotels, Southwest Airlines, and TGI Fridays, to name a few.

The future and communication

We are slowly moving into a business climate where more emphasis will be on individual clients than on groups of customers. In their book, *The One To One Future*, authors Don Peppers and Martha Rogers argue, "When the transformation from selling your product to as many customers as possible to selling as many products as possible to one customer is complete, communication will be at the center of the new relationship paradigm." Although communication has always been at the center of all good relationships, this new and more intimate business relationship model shows that good customer communication skills will become even more essential than before.

In view of what Peppers and Rogers are telling us, can you imagine the relationship you might have with a florist who consistently reminds you of your mother's or spouse's birthday each year? With this kind of transformation in your relationship, the flower shop becomes indispensable, a place that makes it easy and desirable for you to do business. Does the flower shop need a complicated, expensive system to provide this service for you? Not really. It needs a PC, a healthy dose of common sense, and a sincere desire to serve you.

Conclusion

Measuring the degree of customer satisfaction and the quality of the relationships we have with our customers depends on the quality of our communication with them. We know we can't depend on the fact that they continue to do business with us, that they're nice to us, that they will tell us, or that they will respond to surveys. Although there are a number of tools to measure customer satisfaction, there is one essential element that makes all other measurement tools meaningful. That essential element is asking customers, on occasion, what they want or need, how we are doing, and what we could do to improve our service to them.

18

Telephone

Total customer satisfaction is from the first
telephone contact through the life of the product.

John A. Goodman

We can't have a serious conversation about communication and not include the topic of the telephone. Even today, in a world filled with e-mail, fax machines, and computers, the telephone is still one of our most important links to the world around us. One reason for this is that, even in the twenty-first century, not everyone likes e-mail, fax machines, and computers. There are people who still long for live interaction with another human being. Until that longing is replaced entirely by automated processes, the telephone will remain one of the most critical aspects of business communication.

Every business must have a system in place for answering customer telephone calls at all times. But more important is the friendliness of the person answering the phone and their willingness to listen and help. The most precisely scripted greeting will never take the place of the genuine willingness to give callers exactly what they want in the most friendly and efficient manner possible. Polished greetings with terse or unfriendly undertones give a negative first impression and may be the last time a customer chooses to do business with you. The person answering the telephone represents the image of the entire organization and, often, is its first and most powerful moment of truth. With that in mind, it would make sense to put the organization's nicest, most efficient people at the telephone reception banks, and pay them as if the organization's entire reputation depended on them.

Answering the telephone

Organizations worry about how their phones should be answered: Exactly what should we say? Other than greeting the caller and identifying the organization, there are few basic telephone rules that are necessary. One thing is certain, however. A snippy, terse, perfectly worded, "Thank you for calling XYZ Company, this is Gloria, how may I be joyfully at your service?" is less valuable than a genuine, warm, "Howdy, ABC Incorporated. What can I do for you today?" Don't get me wrong, I'm not suggesting you answer your phones with "Howdy." But there are a number of organizations answering their phones with scripted messages that may be peppy and include all of the right things, but lose their value because there is zero sincerity. Genuine service can't be scripted or demanded. It comes from a deeper source from within us and is judged by each and every customer it touches. That said, if you want to be perceived as customer-friendly, there are several things you might consider including in your telephone answering process.

First, you need a *greeting* ("Good afternoon," "Thank you for calling," etc.). I don't think a service image would be communicated if you just picked up the telephone and said, "Ya?"

Second, use the clearest and shortest message to *identify the organization* (XYZ Corporation, Mary's Sewing Center). We want to be certain before going into the details surrounding our rash, that we are indeed talking to the clinic.

And finally, ask an *open-ended service question* ("How may I help you?" "How may I direct your call?"). This assures the caller that the phone call is welcome and that you are there to help them through the process.

If you want to offer anything more than these three suggestions, it is up to you. I will add a caveat, however. Too much information or too long an introduction is as irritating to the caller as too little. So don't over-do it.

276

Creating the telephone image

When we talk on the telephone, we lose 55 percent of our communication power: the physiology. In person, we can read thousands of messages in the speaker's face and body while hearing the tone of voice, and through those silent messages, interpret the meaning of the words as they are presented to us. Because the visual aspect of communication is missing over the phone, we create our visual image only through the words and tone of voice. In order for us to be clearly understood, we must project our image into the mind of the person with whom we are talking. Think about a time you've done business over the telephone with someone you have never met and then, at a later date, seen her/him in person. Did you think: That's her? She sounded thinner over the phone? How did this happen? It happened because she had painted a visual image of herself in your mind through her words and her tone of voice.

In order for you to project a positive image into the minds of the people with whom you are talking, think of the mnemonic PLEASE.

Pitch. Using the lower pitch of the voice makes it easier to hear over the phone. This is especially true for the elderly or hearing impaired.

Loudness. Speaking too loudly or not loudly enough are both bothersome to people over the telephone. Be certain that the volume you speak is comfortable to the caller. If you sense interference in the connection or any other interruption ask, "Are you able hear me?"

Emotion. Be careful that emotional reactions to other situations aren't inadvertently expressed over the phone. A bad moment with one person shouldn't be taken out on someone else.

Attitude. If you dislike the telephone or view it as interruption to your work, there's a good chance that people will hear that in your voice. Remember that communication is at the core of good service and the telephone is sometimes the best tool for that communication.

Speed. In person, we speak at around a 140 to 160 words per minute. Over the telephone we need to slow down and give the other person a chance to comprehend the message. This is most often true in the greeting. I have called companies when the person answering the telephone spoke so quickly that I had no idea what had been said.

Enunciation. This is verbally dotting your I's and crossing your T's. Make certain that you are understood through clarity of expression. Remember, communication is meaningless unless there is mutual understanding.

Telephone complaints

There are a number of behaviors that make people angry when doing business over the telephone. We must remember that even though the telephone is still the most powerful tool in business, it is one that many people dislike. Using the telephone well is a wonderful customer-driven skill and will enhance your organization's service image. Let's take a look a some of the telephone issues that customers complain about the most.

On hold

There are three things that bother people about being put on hold. First, that they have to be put on hold. In other words, the mere fact that they are going to be inconvenienced by having to wait is irritating. There's not much organizations can do about this, but understand that being put on hold affects the customer instantly.

Second, how they are put on hold. Have you ever called a company and the person answering the phone asks, "Can you hold?" and, before you are able to respond, you are put on hold? That irritates almost everyone. We think: If you're not going to wait for my answer, don't ask. The most customer-focused method of putting someone on hold is to ask, "Are you able to hold?" and then wait for their reply. Nine times out of ten, the person will say yes even if they are not happy about it. And in the case where someone says no, you need to respond immediately. It's common to get panicked when you are bogged down with a number of incoming calls. But when someone tells you they are not able to hold, it generally takes only seconds to deal with the caller. Either you will put them through to the person they are trying to reach, take a message, or put them into the call receiver's voice mail.

The final issue affecting the on-hold experience is how long the wait lasts. Research has found that most people are willing to wait on hold from 45 to 60 seconds without much dissatisfaction. After that length of time, however, someone needs to come back on the line and ask, "Are you still able to hold?" If not, take a message. If so, repeat the process and check in again after the next 45 to 60 seconds have passed.

There are mixed reviews as to whether music, company advertising, or nothing should be used in the background of the waiting process. Remembering the adage that you can't make all of the people happy all of the time, we have found that a number of people prefer music. It is not as self-serving as advertising and it lets the caller know that they haven't been cut off or disconnected somewhere in the waiting process.

Finally, when the person who finally answers the phone knows the answer to the caller's question, knows where to get the answer, or can refer the caller to someone they know has the answer, the aggravation of waiting on hold is softened.

Call centers or 800 numbers

Call centers are where you call to order products, complain about a product or service, or go to get questions answered. As wonderful and convenient as call centers sound, we know that call center technology is not good for all customers. The reason for this is that the technology being used sometimes seems more to the benefit of the person being called than the person calling—the customer.

In looking at customers' reactions, we find that it's not the new technology that customers seem to hate, it's the poor use of that technology. According to John Goodman of TARP, several conditions divide the good from the bad in call centers. Let's take a look at some of these.

1. Accessibility. In order for a call center to be genuinely accessible to a customer, it needs to be open or available around the clock, not just nine to five. Today customers are from all parts of the globe which can make time zones barriers to good service. In addition, people's work days are jammed full, shifts vary, and many have little time to take care of business during those hours. You need to encourage people to do business with you at their convenience, not yours.

2. People will find your call center accessible only if they are not asked to wait on hold for an extraordinary length of time. Let the caller know how long they can expect to be on hold. This can be done by with a message such as, "The wait time to speak with a representative is 17 minutes," or, "There are currently seven calls we must answer before taking your call." After you have advised them of the estimated length of time on hold, offer menu choices such as: "You can push one to leave a message, or you can speak with someone else in that department, or you can continue to hold."

3. Call centers should have no more than three options on the menu of choices. This is probably one of the greatest sources of frustration people have using the telephone today. We have found that their dissatisfaction is equal to the number of choices they have. For instance, if they have four menu choices it will create less dissatisfaction than if they have five choices.

4. For standard information such as office hours, keep the message short and concise.

Transferring

Many customers complain that they have to tell their story a number of times as they are transferred throughout the organization. This is eliminated, as we discussed earlier, when the person taking the call either knows the answer or knows who knows the answer. When this is not the case, we find ourselves being tossed around the system until we either get the answer or we hang up in frustration.

In order to keep people from being passed from person to person, and to eliminate redundancy in the telling of their story, consider the following suggestions:

First, *listen carefully* to the caller and either answer the question or get ample information so you will know who can answer their question.

Second, tell the caller *who you will be transferring them to* and that person's extension. Nothing is more frustrating for a caller than to be disconnected during a transfer and then, when calling back, not know to whom they were being transferred.

Next, *call the person to whom you are transferring* the caller and advise her/him about the call. This eliminates the need for the caller to tell their story again. You can advise the person receiving the call about the nature of the call, the details and the caller's mood. How nice it would be for a customer to hear, "Hi, Ms. Jones, this is Joe in accounting. I hear that you haven't received an invoice from us in the past few months. I'm sure we can straighten this out" instead of "This is Joe. What can I do for you?"

Safeguarding information

It is important that organizations have rules and policies that govern the information that can and can not be given out over the telephone. Having rules and policies eliminates the possibility of improper information being shared and helps protect employees from legal entanglements. However, customers dislike the terms *rule* and *policy* sufficiently enough that alternative responses need to be considered. The words policy and rule have a slammed-door effect and are viewed as curt and inflexible.

For instance, if a caller asked for an employee's home telephone number, most respondents would answer, "I'm sorry, it's against our policy to give out home phone numbers..." That same information could be shared in more customer-friendly terms such as, "For the privacy and benefit of our staff, I would prefer to take your phone number..." This makes it possible for callers to receive the denial to their request more positively. If you have a policy that asks that you do not even acknowledge that the employee works for your organization, again position the response to the request in a benefit statement, as opposed to a policy statement. "For the protection and privacy of our staff, we refer all telephone inquiries regarding personnel to human resources..." If a caller becomes rude following this friendly approach, remain firm. If the caller is persistent, at some point you may need to say, "This is our policy," but try to use it as a last resort.

When someone is not available

It would be nice if everyone was always available to take all of their calls all of the time. But that's not the real world. Most people are away from their desk or work station more often than they are there. When people are not available, customers get frustrated. Even though customers understand rationally, like most of us, they are often driven by their own anxieties for answers and solutions. Because of the energy that surrounds the need to speak with someone, or to get a question answered, customers don't want to hear, "She's out to lunch," "Gone home for the day," "On vacation," "Sick," "In a meeting," or whatever. Even though one of these may indeed be the case, the customer doesn't want to hear it. In fact, it's none of the customer's business. All customers need to know is when they can expect to hear from the person they're trying to reach! Here's how the conversation unfolds:

Caller: "Hello, is Mary there?"

Organization: "No, Mary's not in the office today. She will be returning tomorrow after one. May I take a message or would you like to speak to someone else in that department?"

or "No, Mary's not in the office today. She will be returning on March 25th. May I..."

or "No, Mary's not in the office at this time. I expect her in an hour. May I take..."

Screening calls

One of the most offensive questions a caller might hear is, "May I tell her who's calling?" It becomes offensive in this scenario:

"Good afternoon. ABC Incorporated. How may I help you?"

"Is Anne Smith there?"

"Yes she is. May I tell her who's calling?"

"This is John Jones."

"Hold on, Mr. Jones." [Time lapses.] "I'm sorry, Anne's in a meeting (on the phone, out to lunch, tied up for the moment, blah, blah blah). Could I have her return your call?"

Whether it's true or not, John Jones thinks that Anne didn't take the call because it was *his* call. He believes that had it been someone more important or someone Anne really wanted to talk with, she would have taken the call. John felt slighted because the person who answered the phone gave no indication of the possibility Anne might not be available. If instead the person answering would have said, "She's in the office. But she may be on the telephone or tied up in a meeting. Let me check...," it would have given the caller fair warning that Anne may not be able to take the call. The best way to avoid this all together is to have your central answering area have a consistently up-dated in and out board so that the person answering the phones can refer to at a glance. Another systemic solution to this is a telephone system that shows which extensions are in use so callers can be honestly apprised of people's availability.

Voice mail

Voice mail is one of those aspects of technology that people either love or hate. People who hate it usually don't dislike the technology per se, but rather how the technology is used. They resent people who never answer their phone but rather filter all of their calls through voice mail. They are also fed up with people who never return voice mail messages. Voice mail, like any other business tool, must be used properly to be effective.

Here are some tips for voice mail to be viewed as effective:

Update it daily. "Hi, this is Bill. I'm out of the office at this time (You don't need to say where. Who cares?) I will be back in my office at three and returning calls at that time. Thank you for calling."

Keep it friendly, but not goofy. Remarks or quips that seem funny or entertaining to you may be seen as silly or unprofessional to others. You may sound flippant or like someone who doesn't take their work seriously. I'm not sure you would have a great deal of faith in an attorney whose voice mail recording said, "Hi. It's a beautiful day at Joan's law offices. Don't let life's little worries get you down. You got a problem, we got a solution. So leave a message and..."

Just as you do when answering the phone live and in person, on voice mail you (1) greet, (2) identify, and instead of asking a service-focused question, (3) advise. For example: "(1) Thank you for calling.

(2) This is John Jones. (3) I will be out of my office until two o'clock and returning calls at that time. If you would like to leave a message, please do so. If you need to speak to someone immediately, please push zero..."

Always provide access to a live person. One of the most frustrating things about voice mail is never being able to talk with a live person. Many organizations simply route callers through loops of the voice-mail maze from one person's voice mail to another's and it drives people crazy. Voice mail that is done with the customer in mind does one of two things: The call comes into a living, breathing person who then asks if the caller would like voice mail. Or, the call goes directly into voice mail but has the option of being transferred out to someone who is guaranteed to be there.

E-mail

The future will find us communicating more frequently through e-mail and the future is now. There is little doubt about it. The ease of sending messages through the privacy of one's own keyboard is a wonderful communication tool. Once again, however, technology is ahead of people's comfort levels. A number of organizations today use e-mail to the exclusion of telephone voice messaging. But there are still a number of organizations, and people within those organizations, who are not e-mail users and it may take some time before they are.

There are several suggestions that will make e-mail work well for your organization:

Let customers know they have options. Don't assume that just because someone has an e-mail address they prefer to receive their messages through e-mail. Many organizations get on the technological bandwagon and dump new technology into employees' laps, whether they want it or not. Whenever you need to send information to someone, instead of saying, "I'll e-mail that to you," ask, "Would you like me to send that through e-mail, fax, regular mail, or leave it on your voice mail?"

Respond to e-mail in a timely manner, just as you would to voice mail or any other methods of communication.

If a message is urgent, you may want to *call the person receiving the e-mail* to make certain they read it. With portable computers, not all people are connected to e-mail at all times. Those who aren't will only receive the message once they are connected to the system.

Be careful how you present your written message. Spelling, grammar, and punctuation all still play a role in this method of communication. Also, don't send your message in an all-upper-case format. Upper case lettering represents *shouting* and it can leave a negative impression on the reader.

Conclusion

Good telephone techniques are essential for organizations serious about their service image.

Make certain that everyone in your organization knows the rules of good telephone etiquette and those things that matter most to customers. People rarely have a chance to make a second impression once they've blown the first; and that first impression is often made over the telephone. Organizations must remember that automation should enhance personal relationships, not take the place of them. Used properly, the new communication tools should simply offer new ways to connect with people in a more efficient and timely manner.

19

Dealing with Complaints

There is no traffic jam on the extra mile.

Anonymous

If you are communicating effectively with your customers, they will be telling you their complaints. And if it's perceived that you're not listening to their complaints, their dissatisfaction may be sufficient enough that they will leave and tell others on their way out the door. A story written in the *Minneapolis Star Tribune* told about a man who ate lunch every day at a Burger King. One day, the drive-through speaker was broken and orders were being taken by an employee walking from car to car. Because of this, the wait for lunch was around ten minutes. Ten minutes is not a terribly long period of time unless you are waiting in line at a fast-food restaurant. Then ten minutes takes on a whole new dimension.

Once he arrived at the pickup counter, he said to the woman behind the window, "How about charging me the price of the small fries for the large fries that I ordered?" The woman responded tersely, "I'm sorry, I can't do that." A little irritated, he cajoled, "Come on. I eat here every day. Couldn't you do this to show me that you're sorry I had to wait so long?" To this she responded, "No I can't!" With that, he put his food back on the drive-through counter and said, "Forget it then. I'm going to McDonald's." As he drove away, the woman stuck her head out of the window and yelled, "I hope you choke!"

Well, she yelled at the wrong guy. Furious, he went back to his office and copied every story and article he could find on customer service. He then sent those articles, along with a letter, to the Better Business Bureau, the head of the Burger King franchises, the parent company of Burger King and all of the local newspapers. Did it do any good? You decide. His letter was printed in one of the largest newspapers in a major metropolitan area. He was given free lunch for one year from another Burger King, and he and his wife were flown to Chicago and put up at a fancy hotel where he spoke at the franchise owners' annual meeting. The Burger King organization ended up spending thousands of dollars on something that would have initially cost a few cents.

This story shows the damage unhappy customers can cause if they take the time to get even with an organization that they believe has offended them or treated them poorly. Even if the organization doesn't know that the offense has taken place, an offended customer can wage a war that is almost impossible to win. Bad will is passed on from person to person and no marketing ploy or ad campaign can overcome the negative impression that angry customers create.

Mark Stevens, syndicated columnist for the *Minneapolis Star Tribune*, adds that what customers really want are "answers to their problems and solutions to their needs." Customers aren't out looking for a fight. But so many are fed up with the battles they face as they try to get their needs met, that they often walk through the door dressed in their defensive armor (usually disguised as *attitude*) and ready for war. As Stevens says, "Although customers dislike the words expensive, late, or discontinued, what they really hate is 'no.'" That's what initially got the guy at Burger King so upset. Don't tell me what you can't do. Tell me what you can do. The Burger King employee could have said, "I'm sorry I'm not able to change the price of the fries since this has already been logged into the system. But I can give you this coupon for a free order of fries the next time you come in. By the way, I'm really sorry this happened."

Losing customers costs $$$

Service companies have their own kind of scrap heap: customers who will not come back.
Frederich F. Reichheld and W. Earl Sasser, Jr.

Why is it vital to make certain that each customer you want to retain is indeed encouraged to remain? One reason is that service organizations depend on existing customers for 85 to 95 percent of their business. In other words, they're dependent on customers being happy. On average, companies lose about 25 percent of their customer base per year. This can prove to be an extraordinary financial loss. But, according to Frederich Reichheld and W. Earl Sasser, if a company retains as little as 5 percent of those potentially lost customers, they can increase their profits from 25 to 125 percent.

According to statistics presented by Minneapolis-based Performance Research Associates, Inc., 68 percent of car owners switch to another make because they are disappointed with the service, while only 14 percent of car buyers switch because of the product itself. TARP further reinforces the need to deal with customer's complaints by the following statistics. They found:

- Of those disappointed customers who say nothing, who just walk out the door, only 9 percent will return to do business in the future.
- Of those who say something but don't receive a satisfactory response, only 19 percent will return again to do business in the future.
- Ninety-one percent of customers with a major complaint (over $100) and 63 percent with a minor complaint ($1 to $5), who say nothing, will not buy from you again.
- An average of 89 percent of customers will return when their problem was handled with "wow." Only 62 percent will return when their problem was resolved, but there was no "wow."

Disappointment versus disillusionment

There's a big difference between disappointment and disillusionment. Disappointment means to fail to live up to an expectation. Disillusionment is about being deceived. Customers get over disappointments but they rarely overcome the broken relationship that deception and disillusionment create. Most people have stories about times they have been disappointed by an organization's decision, policy, or behavior. We are human beings and we are going to disappoint one another from time to time. Handled correctly, disappointments are forgiven and, usually, the relationship is saved. But stories of disillusionment usually end with lost customers.

I was disillusioned by a small-town business when my sister and I were refurbishing our family cabin in northern Minnesota. I learned that a wonderful little shop in Pequot Lakes filled with cabin accessories not only re-covered furniture but also picked the furniture up and dropped it off when finished.

Because our cabin is some distance from the shop, the upholsterer wasn't able to come out to measure the furniture. So I spent Thanksgiving weekend measuring every possible inch of the furniture we planned to re-cover. I drew diagrams and even brought along several cushions to insure accuracy. At the shop owner's suggestion, I met with "Nancy," the woman who would be doing the upholstering, to decide how much material was needed and to get a price for the job. Nancy estimated the amount of material and quoted what sounded to me like a reasonable price. I wrote down all of the estimates so I could "sell" my sister on the details of the project. She agreed that the price sounded fair, so we ordered the material. Once it arrived, I began to make arrangements for the couch and love seat to be picked up.

This is when the disappointment began. I was told, "Well, we can't come this weekend because the guys are going snowmobiling. How about next weekend?" [Next weekend arrives.] "No. It's so nice this weekend, the guys are snowmobiling, maybe next weekend." [Next weekend arrives] "No. We're going out of town snowmobiling. For sure next weekend." That "next weekend" arrived but the disappointment continued. After driving for three and one half hours alone over Minnesota's winter roads (not fun), spending the night in a cabin that takes forever to heat up, and waiting until 1:00 PM for the "guys" to arrive, the truck finally pulled into the driveway. But it wasn't a furniture truck. It was a pickup truck and instead of guys only Nancy and her two children got out. Not wanting to risk the children being injured, Nancy and I proceeded to move the large couch out of the house. We couldn't get it out the back door, so after banging it against the wall and scraping the new kitchen wallpaper, we had to carry it through the sliding doors, out over the deck, through a five-foot snow bank, around the house and finally up the hill to the truck. The strain was significant.

Weeks passed and the phone call finally came. The couches were finished. Hooray! They were delivered. Hooray! They looked fine. Hooray! (Except for a couple of little holes in the seams, but that's another story.)

Days passed before I received a phone call from the store owner. Disillusionment began. She said the bill came to $1,000 more than Nancy had quoted.

Me: "What? Help me. I'm hearing things. This can't be true."

The owner: "How could you possibly think that you could get a couch and love seat recovered for the price Nancy quoted?" (Good tactic, she's shaming me.)

Me: "I've never had anything upholstered before. It sounded fine to me. Plus you told me to talk to Nancy and I trusted she knew what she was doing."

The owner: "Well, that's not her job. All she does is the work. She had no business quoting you prices."

Me: "I can't believe that you won't honor the price quoted by your employee. We made our decision to go ahead with the work based on her quote and it was you who told me to meet with her."

The owner: "Look, you've got a beautiful couch and love seat. You got your money's worth. Plus, Nancy needs the money, she's got six kids blah, blah, blah" (Owner expresses zero remorse regarding the fact that we had been completely misled.)

Me: "I need to let you know that I'm very unhappy about this and I don't think it's fair. Plus, I had wanted pillows made and now that's out of the question."

The owner: "I'll tell you what I'll do. (Still no remorse.) We'll throw in the pillows as part of the deal."

Me: "Okay. Thank you." (At least I had some concession to help lessen the blow when I told tell my sister to cough up another $500.)

Because there had been an error with Nancy's estimate (disappointment bordering on disillusionment) as to how much material to order, we needed more fabric (around $200 worth) in order to make the pillows. But once the material came in, I dropped it off at the store and finally picked up the finished pillows several weeks later. The owner wasn't there so I told the clerks to let her know that I had come to get them.

Later that week, I received a phone call at work from the owner and experienced disillusionment to the *nth* degree:

The owner: "Hi, this is (name withheld to protect the guilty). I'm just calling to get your credit card number so we can get the pillows paid for."

Me: "What???? You said that you were going to throw those pillows in to make up for the extra $1,000 we paid for the upholstering."

The owner: "You've got to be kidding. We're not in business to give things away. This cost me $75. I've already paid Nancy and I expect you to pay me."

Me: "I can't believe that you'd throw me away for $75. You've called me a liar, you've betrayed your word, and you've destroyed my relationship with a place where I loved to shop."

I never paid that $75. Not because I couldn't afford it but because I was completely disillusioned. The relationship was over and I knew I would never do business with her again. In the end, everyone lost. I lost the pleasure of doing business at a place where I valued the quality of the products, and they lost a loyal customer who, in one year, had spent more than $4,000 and who had, in addition, referred a friend who spent over $3,000. We had also intended to have many of the rest of our cabin's furnishings done through this shop. But all of that ended for $75.

A second chance

Remember that when customers complain, they're really giving you a second chance. A decrease in the number of complaints is a sure sign that the relationship is in trouble. When a customer is willing to expend the time and energy to give you negative feedback, jump for joy. It's when your customers stop complaining and letting you know what's on their minds that you need to panic. When customers complain, they are still seeing themselves in the relationship with you. They may be in pain, but they still want to work it out. But when they retreat in silence, they have started to disengage and the process of doing business elsewhere has begun.

If you lack customer complaints, you are also lacking significant feedback. Feedback is something you can't live (long) without. Not knowing whether or not a customer is satisfied leaves the door open for all kinds of alternatives. But once you know about a customer's problem, the solution to that problem becomes one of the most significant elements of your relationship.

The good news about complaints is that 1) they point out areas in which the organization is weak or areas in need of improvement, and 2) they can actually strengthen your relationship with your customer if the problem is handled well. Every complaint gives you another chance to differentiate yourself from the competition.

You hear it, you own it

Customers don't care if you are full-time or part-time, union or management. They just want decent service.
Excellence in Customer Service Calendar, 10/4/95

Organizations that empower their staff to make the decisions necessary to solve customer complaints on the spot have a decided edge over those companies that insist employees go through red tape and hoops to get a complaint resolved. In fact, organizations adopting the "you hear it, you own it" philosophy, find the greatest customer satisfaction in the resolution of complaints. With this philosophy, the employee who first hears the complaint follows the process all the way through to a resolution.

The Ritz Carlton Hotels have adopted that philosophy. Any employee who hears a complaint owns that complaint and does whatever it takes to solve the problem and satisfy the customer. In part because of this, the Ritz Carlton Hotels have become one of the most successful hotel chains in the world.

As unbelievable as it might seem, customers who have had a complaint satisfactorily resolved are more likely to purchase products from you in the future than those who have experienced no problems at all with the organization. Customers who do not complain simply wait for an opportunity to go elsewhere. This means that when a customer says something to you, you need to startle them with your positive response. To be certain that your customers are willing to open up and talk to you, make it easy for them to complain. Let them know who they should talk to and when and how to reach that person. If they like to write, give them self-addressed, stamped envelopes and anything else that would make it easier to communicate through writing. If they prefer telling their story, make it easy and comfortable for them to do that. Finally, if possible, have someone available twenty-four hours a day (or at odd hours) who is capable of effectively handling complaints. Everyone hates: I'm just the night manager. You'll have to wait to talk to someone else during the day.

The ill effects of unhappy customers

Richard Whitely writes in his book, *The Customer-Driven Company*, that customers leave for a number of reasons. According to Whitely:

    1 percent die;
    3 percent move away;
    5 percent develop other friendships;
    9 percent competitive reasons;
    14 percent dissatisfied with product;
    68 percent indifference by owner, manager, and employees.

Although 18 percent of customers leave for reasons mostly outside of the organization's control, a whopping 82 percent of customers leave because they have an unsatisfactory relationship with the organization. Few organizations have control over someone's dying or moving away. And organizations may or may not be able to influence customers' desire to shop around. But every organization must take full responsibility for not resolving problems satisfactorily or allowing the walking dead to drain customer loyalty through the deadly sin of indifference.

Why customers complain

According to Crocker and Associates, Newport News, Virginia, there are five primary reasons that customers complain. First, they **don't get what they were promised.** To make certain that customers don't experience this with your organization, accept the premise that your word is your promise. When I was in the property management business, I received a telephone call from a resident from one of our communities. She asked me when she would be getting her new carpeting. This took me back since we seldom replaced carpet during a resident's tenancy. When I asked her what made her believe she was getting new carpet, she responded that the on-site manager had told her she would after she had been there for six months. I immediately called the manager and asked if he had told this resident that she would have new carpet installed. His response, "Yes, I did, but I didn't promise." We must live each day with the understanding that our word is our promise.

The second major reason for complaints is that the customer believes someone within the organization was **rude.** Rudeness can be experienced in a number of ways, from a flippant remark to a terse reprimand. However it may be experienced, it is never welcomed by customers and is always unnecessary.

Third, customers resent and complain when they perceive that **no one goes out of their way to serve them.** This is another description of deadly indifference. People who only do what is easy and obvious give the message that they don't care loudly and clearly.

The fourth reason that customers complain is that **no one listens** to them. (This should really read: they perceive that no one listens to them.) Have you ever spoken to someone who is reading or watching TV while you are talking? Many times when you ask the person to pay attention, they respond that they are, and can often recite verbatim what you have just said. Whether they heard you or not, the communication was unsatisfactory because you didn't perceive that you were heard.

Finally, customers get upset when the person serving them projects a **negative or can't do attitude.** We never seem to grow out of the resentment of being told no. Just like a child, when we hear "no" we realize we're being denied something; it brings out our sense of indignation more powerfully than just about any other expression. Don't tell customers what you can't do. Tell them what you can do, "No sir. We don't have a 100-foot hose. But we do have two fifty-foot hoses and I would be happy to get them for you."

Relationships at the core of complaints

According to TARP, 66 percent of the complaints about a product or service really have nothing to do with the product or service itself. What is really at the core of the complaint is the relational issues that accompany the product or service. For instance, a customer might complain that a certain product doesn't work the way it had been advertised, or that there were problems with a service performance. But what that customer is not talking about is the indifference they experience when complaining about the faulty product or service. We know that mistakes are going to be made and things are going to break down. These are part of the human experience. Customers don't expect everyone to have all of the answers all of the time, or for products to always work perfectly. But they do want solutions, not rationalizations or delays. We also know that people will accept a mistake. But what they will not accept, is defending that mistake or being indifferent to it.

According to Sue Morem, columnist for the *Minneapolis Star Tribune* and the *Chicago Tribune*, there are specific behaviors customers experience when doing business with companies that make them mad. Those are the companies that apologize but offer no solution, fight to defend their policies, and simply do not care. Morem further states that companies faring the worst are "those who offer to do something, but then never follow through."

If you want to make customers really angry, here are four behaviors that are guaranteed to do the job. You can:

- Fight back;
- Run away;
- Explain (disguised fighting back);
- Operate with mixed goals: meaning that you want to calm the customer down, win your point, and keep the customer, all at the same time. Common sense will tell you that this is nearly impossible.

Dealing with angry customers

In dealing with difficult or angry customers, we need to stay separate from the customer's anger or emotion. I often hear workers share their frustration when they are forced to deal with angry or emotionally-charged customers. In many instances, the flight or fight mechanism comes into play and the employee dealing with the angry customer either retreats or becomes defensive and fights back. Although these are both knee-jerk human responses to the stimulus of anger, neither work well in dealing with emotional behavior, in solving problems, or in saving relationships.

There are two types of anger most employees will face. One is appropriate and the other is not. When a customer threatens an employee physically or verbally abuses them, their values, or their sense of decency, the interaction must come to a halt. This can be accomplished by an empowered employee saying: If you use that language with me again, I will hang up. If that language is used again, the employee must hang up. In addition, this is a systemic issue. The staff must know when a supervisor should be asked to intervene. This should be made clear to the employee at the time of hiring. No employee should be subjected to the fear of attack or abuse. As soon as there is any indication that the interaction is inappropriate, someone in authority needs to step in and take control.

But there is another side to dealing with people's anger. When a customer is indeed angry, whether you believe she/he has the right to be or not, extraordinary service is about allowing her/him the privilege of expressing the human emotion of anger in your presence. Although your instincts will say fight or flee, those instincts need to be overridden by your willingness to help the person through this emotional process. Stellar service reputations are born in these emotionally-charged moments.

There are steps that service providers can take when they believe that a customer is angry or upset. Using these steps allows the service provider to help the angry or emotionally-charged customer instead of pretending they don't notice anything is wrong. Remember Steve Martin's reaction in the movie, *Trains, Planes and Automobiles*, when the car rental agent was oblivious to his distress. This is what happens when service providers ignore the obvious, and this is why taking charge and helping the customer through the emotion of anger is so important.

Step by step process in dealing with emotional behavior

The first step in dealing with a customer's anger is to **acknowledge the emotion.** Most often when we confront someone who is upset or angry, we are inclined to ask: What's wrong? But that's not the best first step in dealing with an emotionally charged situation. The best first step is to let the person know that you get it, that you see how deeply upset she or he is.

I have a friend who has been married to her husband for thirty years. As soon as he even suspects that she's angry about something, he apologizes. He doesn't even know what's wrong, but he still says he's sorry. This frustrates her. She usually responds, "Don't tell me you're sorry. You're going to be very soon. But not now!" What she wants first is her day in court. She wants him to know how angry she is and, by him short-cutting to, "I'm sorry," she feels robbed of the opportunity of letting him know the extent of her anger.

To acknowledge a customer's emotion, a service provider's response might be, "You appear to be upset," or, "It sounds like you're unhappy about this," or whatever is appropriate for the situation.

Remember, for the interaction to be genuine, whatever you say must be congruent in words, tone, and body language.

The next step in dealing with a customer's anger is to **ask an open-ended question.** Open-ended questions give the customer a chance to purge or get whatever is bothering them out of their system. The two best open-ended questions begin with *what* or *how*. For instance, "What happened? How did this happen?" Technically, *why* is another option to begin an open-ended question, but it can sound accusatory and may fuel the fire instead. For instance, the question, "Why are you crying?" may cause the receiver to become defensive.

While the customer is purging or getting the grievance out of his or her system, the best advice is to stay present. Simply be there. This is shown through eye contact, body language, and occasional verbal responses such as, "I see," or "really?" or whatever would be considered appropriate. Don't overdo the verbal responses. They can become irritating and distracting if you do.

The third step in dealing with emotional behavior is to **ask at least two close-ended questions.** Close-ended questions have definitive, one-word answers which are most often yes or no. While the customer is purging he is usually telling his story. Asking close-ended questions shows you listened and that you care. Close-ended questions might sound something like this:

"You say you have called here four times?"

"Yes."

"And nobody has ever returned your call?"

"No."

These close-ended questions not only show you listened and care, but they help clarify anything that you may have misunderstood.

Next, **validate the emotion.** A response that might validate the emotion would be, "You have every reason to be upset with us" or, "I can understand why you are angry. I'd be angry, too, if I had left messages for someone to call me back and no one had done so." Note that this is different than saying, "Oh, you probably left a message for George. He never calls anyone back." Validating the emotion is not about dragging co-workers through the mud. Some workers believe that if they get on your bandwagon against the organization, that you will somehow bond with them and get satisfaction out of knowing they, too, believe the organization is substandard.

I experienced this one evening when I went to pick up dinner at Kentucky Fried Chicken. In a hurry, I went through the drive-through where I ordered chicken and a biscuit. Having placed my order, someone blared back to me over the speaker that they had no butter. "What? No butter?" I couldn't imagine a biscuit without butter and I'm sure the disappointment in my voice could be heard even through the fuzziness of the speaker phone. As I waited in somewhat of a sulk for my chicken and butterless biscuit, the pass-through window flew open and out popped a man who proclaimed, "I want you to know our buyer's a moron." I was startled. "Who was this man and why was he revealing such disparaging information to me?" I'll tell you who he was. He was a KFC employee who wanted to get back on my good side by joining me in my snit. He, like me, was disgusted that there was no butter. But in his effort to show his solidarity, he instead made me worry about eating chicken at a place where the buyer was a moron.

The next step in dealing with an unhappy customer is to **offer three suggestions to solve the problem.** For instance, one could say, "Would you like me to transfer you to the head of that department so you can tell her what happened?" Or, "Would you like me to talk with the manager and tell her what you have told me and then I can get back with you?" Or, "Would you prefer to talk with someone else in the department who could solve your problem today?" People need choices in solving their problems to help recover their sense of power and control.

By offering three suggestions instead of saying, "This is what I will do," you are not limiting their choices and you are showing that you are willing to go out of your way to make them happy. If you offered three suggestions and none of them met the customer's approval, ask them what they would like you to do. If you are not able to do that which the customer asks, at least you have a point from which you both can begin to compromise your positions.

One seminar participant argued that it would be best to ask the customer what she/he would like immediately and not offer three suggestions. The risk with this, however, is that you might not be able to give them what they ask for, and then they may become even more angry. At least by offering them your three suggestions, you are letting them know that you are willing to do something.

Next, **come to an agreement** with the customer regarding the solution. This may mean that the customer has chosen one of your suggestions, you allowed the customer his or her wish, or you came up with a compromise that you can both live with. The fact that neither of you may like it, but are able to live with it, is a sure sign that you reached a genuine compromise.

Probably the most important step in the process of dealing with someone's anger is to **do whatever you promised to do.** If you slip up here, there is a good chance that you have lost the customer. "Oh boy! Did I blow it. I told this customer that I would have the manager of the accounting department call him back and I simply forgot!" Bye, bye, relationship. If you don't follow through here, your credibility on anything else in the future is at risk.

And finally, **go the extra mile,** or do something that the customer is not expecting. This could be a "We're sorry" card giving them 20 percent off of a future purchase; a personal, hand-written note; or a phone call to simply say, "Hi, Ms. Smith. My name is Mary and I spoke to you yesterday from XYZ Company. I'm just calling to let you know how sorry I am about everything and to check to see if the manager has called you." This can't sound perfunctory or part of some customer satisfaction program. It has to be a sincere, in-the-moment response to a relationship in trouble.

A lot of people respond that they don't have the time to do things like make phone calls or write letters of apology. But this we know for sure, if you are not doing everything in your power to keep customers happy, especially if the organization has made a mistake, you'll have plenty of time to spend on the telephone and writing letters because you will be out of job.

Remorse

Customers know they can't always get what they expect. But they want you to care, listen, and respond to them and go as far as possible to satisfy their needs. Taking responsibility for a mistake or a missed expectation is part of the servant's heart. It is also an important part of empowerment. As we acquire rights and power, we pay for them with responsibility. This is humbling—not shameful. We are not humble or responsible when we defend our mistakes, blame someone else, or discount the event's importance.

Customers really hate the absence of remorse when a mistake has been made or an encounter has been less than desirable. People are starving for someone to stand up and genuinely say from the heart, "I'm sorry." "I feel bad that this happened." Or ,"I don't know what happened but I'm just sorry that it did."

Fear versus remorse

Some organizations don't express remorse because they fear litigation. By saying, "I'm sorry," they fear an implied admission of culpability, and in today's sue-happy society, few are willing to risk it.

I believe that fear was the root cause of the lack of remorse in an experience of mine. I had been a long-time patron of a quaint inn and restaurant in a small Minnesota town on the Mississippi River. My friends, family, and I had celebrated many events at the restaurant and had stayed at the historic hotel on special occasions. The bill of fare was substantial for an evening meal and overnight stay, but I had always enjoyed the experience and willingly paid the cost without complaint. That is until one, unforgettable overnight visit. That evening, I had ordered the dinner special—a shrimp dish prepared table-side. During the process, the woman preparing my food commented that she was really over-worked because the other table-side preparer had called in sick. In an obvious hurry, she finished the dish and quickly left our table. That night, I became violently ill. We checked out before dawn so I could go home to die.

After several days of recovery, I called the owner of the inn, not to complain, but to let him know what had happened. The owner, who did not return my first phone call, immediately informed me that he had heard that I had gotten sick and had taken the shrimp to the health department to be tested. They had found "nothing wrong with the shrimp." I responded that I was not trying to lay blame but to recover my shaky feelings regarding the restaurant and hotel that I had long enjoyed. The owner tersely responded that he would, "Take care of it." I assumed that I would get a letter expressing his regret for the situation and maybe a gift certificate towards a meal or another stay. But I heard nothing. And after ten years of visiting this special place and gladly spending hundreds of dollars, I have not gone back.

Why didn't the owner of this upscale restaurant and inn do the right thing? Because he was afraid if he admitted any remorse, he might be held legally responsible. All I wanted was a little, "I'm sorry," but all I got was defensiveness. He was too afraid of culpability to express any real concern at all.

But this owner could have handled my situation in such a way that no culpability would have been attached. He could have sent a letter to me saying, "I'm not sure what happened to cause you to become ill that night. As I told you, the shrimp was tested and there was no problem found so I'm not sure what caused your illness. But I do know that I'm sorry that it happened and I would like to make it up to you by asking you to be my guest for dinner with this $25 gift certificate or this certificate to deduct 15 percent off of your next stay." Had I received that letter, I would have returned again and again, and continued to bring my family and friends.

Another side-stepping of remorse, due to the fear of culpability, came in 1996 when the State of Minnesota admitted that in the 1950s it had wrongfully institutionalized people who were mentally handicapped. Many of those people asked the State to simply say it was sorry. But lawyers advised against it to keep the wronged parties from deducing culpability. As a Minnesotan, I am embarrassed and saddened by their decision.

The United States government, on the other hand, did the right thing when President Clinton stood before America in May of 1997 and apologized to the men who had been involved in the Tuskegee Study. The United States government had denied penicillin to 400 African-American men for their syphilis. Fifty-years later, the president stood up and sincerely said in front of the world, "We are deeply, deeply sorry." Is this generation of Americans culpable? No. But are we sorry that it happened? Deeply, and from the heart.

Pride versus remorse

Another stumbling block to remorse is pride. If I admit I am wrong, I look bad. I look diminished. So consequently, I will keep from looking bad at all costs. But the expense to the organization is the customer's loyalty which is sometimes lost forever. Pride has no place in the servant's heart. Confidence, self-esteem, satisfaction of a job well done, all belong to the servant; but pride simply gets in the way. Even in these most modern of times, pride is still one of the most deadly, and costly, sins.

Remorse can be expressed in the same way today as it was when we learned it from our parents. Often, what parents wanted from us when we had done something wrong was the same things our customers want from us today—to admit our mistake, make it right, and be sincerely, from the heart, sorry.

Recovery

The principle of "paying the uttermost farthing" is to apologize when you make a mistake or fail to meet expectations. And then to behave better.

Stephen R. Covey

In their book, *The Profitable Art of Service Recovery*, Christopher W.L. Hart, James Heskett, and W. Earl Sasser, Jr. write that "errors are inevitable but dissatisfied customers are not." They offer the following example.

A Club Med vacation started out as a disaster for a group of vacationers. First, the plane took off six hours late, made two unexpected stops along the way, then circled the airport for thirty minutes before landing. At 2:00 AM, after ten hours of travel, long out of food and drink, the plane landed so hard that luggage came tumbling down from over head and oxygen masks dropped, ready for an emergency landing.

But waiting for them at the airport was a mariachi band, a red carpet, and lots of food and drinks. Even though it was the middle of the night, the Club Med manager spent time with each person, apologizing and making certain that their every need was met. This tired, crabby group of people, drank, danced, and ate until sunrise, and all agreed that that evening was one of the highlights of the entire vacation. There was no way to undo the horrific flight. But what this club manager did know was that she had to recover the lost good will of all of the people on the trip, and the only way she could do it was by blowing their socks off in the process.

Making amends

Part of recovery includes acts of atonement. But in order for your acts of atonement to have any meaning, you have to go the extra mile. L.L. Bean, known for going the extra mile and maintaining quality customer relationships, offers this example of an act of atonement. They had learned that one of their sport shirts was fraying at the collar after only a few washings. Once aware of the problem, L.L. Bean wrote letters to everyone who had ordered the shirt (being a mail-order catalog company that was relatively easy to do) explaining the problem and urging that the shirts be returned. To make it even easier to do business with them, they stated that if the customer should find it inconvenient to return the shirt, the L.L. Bean customer service department would make the arrangements for having it returned. In other words, their mistake was not going to add a burden to their customers' lives. So, in the process of making atonement (taking back the shirts), they went the extra mile by making it as simple as possible.

Stew Leonard's Dairy and Market is another high-profile organization that often goes the extra mile in service recovery. In one instance, Stew Leonard, Jr. read a suggestion box note from a disgruntled customer. The customer had written, "I only stopped by to pick up a chicken for dinner and you were all out. I guess that means TV dinners for us tonight." Just as he finished reading the note, a Perdue Chicken truck drove up to the store. Within minutes, someone was heading to the woman's house with a complimentary two-pound package of fresh chicken.

Random acts of empathy

If you really want to be someone's service hero, pay attention to things going on around you. Imagine the impact you will have when you recover from a problem you didn't create.

Take this example: The day after a fire had destroyed their home, the family was out raking through their possessions. Everyone was in a state of disbelief. Just then, a Domino's Pizza delivery man approached carrying two pizzas. The homeowner looked up and said, "I didn't order any pizza. Our house just burned down." The delivery man responded, "Yes, I can see that. I was driving by, saw what had happened and I just wanted to help. These pizzas have everything on them so if you don't like them, I'll take them back and get anything you want." As you might guess, the entire family was deeply touched and there is no doubt it created a powerful impression of Domino's Pizza.

An important ingredient in recovery is **empathy.** You don't need to have sympathy, but you do need empathy. The difference is that with empathy, we feel *with* the person. Feeling sympathy, we feel for the person. If someone falls into a hole, and you feel sympathy, you, too, get down into that hole. If, however, you feel empathy, you remain outside of the hole and do whatever you can to help the person out. Obviously you do more good by standing on solid ground than by jumping in and becoming part of the problem.

Acts of empathy don't have to be grand to be effective. An act of empathy might be shown as you arrive at the theater and realize that you have forgotten your tickets. The usher who understands your plight and allows you in, is showing empathy. If she showed sympathy, she might respond, "Don't you hate when that happens. That's awful. But there's nothing I can do."

Recovery tools

Employees must have certain tools to recover well. When these tools are lacking, recovery is nearly impossible. On a recent summer outing, I stopped to buy some popcorn at a quaint-looking popcorn stand. Feeling like splurging, I ordered the more expensive buttered popcorn. After the first bite, I realized that it not only didn't taste buttered, it barely tasted like popcorn. I stepped back and said, in almost unbelief to the young server, "This can't be butter!" With that, she picked up the container marked *Butter* and responded in garbled utterance, "Well, that's what it says." My knee-jerk response to her was, "But it tastes terrible!" Her atoning response to me: "Well, I like it!"

She was obviously lacking the three critical tools of recovery. First, she probably had **little authority** to make the decision to refund my money or make it right some other way. Second, she believed she had a greater responsibility to **maintain the sale** than to satisfy me. And finally, she had **no desire** to make me happy.

Breaking down organizational barriers to satisfaction

When organizations discover that they do have roadblocks or barriers to satisfaction, the important question to ask is: How do we break these barriers down?

The first step in breaking barriers down is to find out what the actual barriers are. The two most effective methods are 1) asking the customers and 2) asking the employees what they perceive the barriers to be. This can be done through one-to-one interviews, focus groups, or custom-designed, written surveys.

Once the barriers to satisfaction have been discovered, ask these same two groups how they would suggest eliminating the barriers. If these groups are part of the solution, they will be more committed to the process and dedicated to the resolution.

Finally, do whatever has been decided. Nothing creates more frustration than when people have taken the time and energy to offer suggestions for solutions to problems, and none of their ideas are implemented and nothing has changed.

The not-so-nice customer versus the abusive customer

In customer service, you are working with moods, tempers, expectations, and misunderstanding.
Price Pritchett

There are some organizations that act like their customers must earn the right to be treated well. But as Ron Zemke writes in the

November 1995 edition of *The Service Edge*, "even rude customers deserve our respect." According to Zemke there seems to be a "myth of the deserving customer." In that myth, service providers treat good customers well—those who speak respectfully, say please and thank you, and who are nice. Those who are demanding or perhaps short-tempered tend to be treated with whatever mood the service provider is in that day (and that's often not good). Even unattractive, crabby, difficult people deserve our best efforts.

Different from the surly or ill-tempered customer, and a real killer of the spirit of service, is the abusive customer. Michael Schrage, author of *Shared Minds*, argues that, "Some customers are value sub-tractors. What they cost in time, money, and morale outstrips the prices they pay." Organizations are discovering that, both internally and externally, some people are just not worth the aggravation they cause. After warnings and attempts to help them overcome their abusive behaviors, some people need to be separated from their relationship with the organization. Fortunately, this usually accounts for only a small fraction of an organization's customer relationships, but sometimes that small percentage does an enormous amount of harm.

Tom Peters writes in an article entitled, "Firing Customers" in his "Executives Only" column in the *Minneapolis Star Tribune*, that Herb Kelleher, CEO of Southwest Airlines, has taken a decisive stance on his commitment to employees in their relationship with abusive customers.

When customers are abusive to Southwest Airlines' employees, management steps in and deals with it. Kelleher sees it as a betrayal of their employees' trust if they do nothing. If a passenger has been abusive, they receive a letter suggesting they "fly elsewhere."

Although I applaud Southwest's dedication to its staff, this policy needs to be carefully enforced. Why? Because it is difficult to answer the question: What is abusive? Many times customers have a right to be angry, extremely angry, and employees are often the target of that anger. If a customer is angry for any reason, even if that anger is misdirected, the customer should not fear that she or he is running the risk of being automatically "fired." In any relationship, people have a right to be heard. Sometimes they are simply frustrated about something and all they need to do is vent. If we don't allow people the privilege of expressing anger in our presence, we will damage the quality of the entire relationship.

Don't misunderstand me. I am not condoning abusive behavior in any way. But I am worried about customers being punished for expressing a strong, negative emotion.

Every organization must spend time training its staff as to what is abusive and what is simply human anger and frustration. Although there is a fine line between them, abuse usually includes verbal attacks that are personal or insult someone's values. For example, cursing or using profane language is considered, by many people, to be against their value system. If a customer is threatening in any way, a supervisor or someone in authority needs to immediately step in and protect the employee.

But if a customer is simply extremely angry, we need to allow them the privilege of being angry in our presence. We must choose not to take it personally but instead use the eight-step process we discussed earlier to help them through it. Anger is a natural human emotion and we need not run from it or become defensive. Listen carefully to what the customer is really telling you. Then ask: Is this about me, or is it something I can influence, or is this completely out of my control? Go back to the spheres of influence and decide within which circle the issue belongs. Take responsibility for and fix those things that are within your control. Tell the customer what you will do to influence the situation if it must be remedied elsewhere. For instance: I'm going to write up what you told me and give it to the manager of that department. May I have your name and number so we can let you know what we have done? And if the customer is angry about something you can do nothing about, for instance the weather, listen patiently, then let it go.

One of the keys to working well with unhappy and difficult customers is to stay separate from the emotional behavior. In other words, stay detached. Just because someone is rude, doesn't mean you must be rude. As Ron Zemke says, "The difference between a customer-service pro and an amateur is the recognition that we aren't in the business to deal only with people who are nice or who meet our personal standards of worthiness."

Conclusion

Unhappy customers are at the core of most failed businesses today. The cost of one angry customer is enormous when you consider the number of other people who will be told and the amount of energy that accompanies negative experiences. Although no business can ever insure that customers won't be unhappy on occasion, they can insure against losing the customer by using techniques that resolve and recover negative customer situations. In fact, customers who have had a negative experience handled well, will tell five other people how wonderful the organization was to work with. What's amazing is that if you dazzle them with extraordinary service in the first place, they only tell three people. If there is a problem that is handled brilliantly, customers rise to the occasion and tell others how happy they are with your service. Why? Because when they are angry or upset, their adrenaline is pumping and their senses are keener. This makes their impression of you indelible and powerful.

20

Leadership

Leaders should lead as far as they can and then vanish.
Their ashes should not choke the fire they have lit.
H.G. Wells

In the process of putting together the material for this book, one of the most difficult decisions was where to place the chapter on leadership. Leadership is so important to service that the material needs to shout from the pages. Leadership is the flip side of the service-success coin. On one side is the service provider's willingness to choose to create dazzling service for every customer; on the other side is the leader of a team, division, department, or organization being committed to supporting the service provider's efforts, creating a service-driven vision, and operating from service-based values.

An interesting twist to this is that each side of the coin, people choosing to perform and people leading people, are actually intertwined on both sides of the coin. Leaders must also choose to perform and, since leadership is not the same as authority, individual service providers must often be leaders regardless of their position or level within the organization.

Although most organizations have managers and leaders at many levels, it appears that more and more organizations are being over-managed and under-led. How can you tell which is which? If you focus on policies, practices, procedures, or rules, you are probably over-managing. If, on the other hand, you are not practicing empower-ment, trust, mission, and vision, you are not only over-managing but you are under-leading as well.

Managerial structure and hierarchy

The problem is not that businesses are not managing well.
They are simply managing too much and leading too little.

Jack Hawley

Within many organizations, the terms manager, leader, and supervisor are used almost interchangeably. But do they really mean the same thing? The terms manager and supervisor have very little difference in meaning from a structural standpoint. Certain organizations put supervisors in charge of managers, and still others put managers in charge of supervi-sors. For many, it is a matter of semantics rather than a thoughtful and deliberate decision. The word supervisor literally means "to see what oth-ers cannot." By that definition, the word supervisor should be more closely associated with leader than it is with manager. But in today's gen-eral use and understanding of the word supervisor, it seems to have more to do with tasks and structure than it does with seeing what others cannot.

The difference between the meaning of manager and leader is some-what clearer. Manager is about today, and leader is about tomorrow. We manage tasks, we lead people. Management is about structure while lead-ership is almost spiritual.

Management = Control and coordination
Leadership = Caring and respect

Although all organizations need leaders at all levels, not all organizations need managers at all levels. But good managers can make a positive con-tribution to the organization, and often prove valuable in helping utilize resources, making processes flow effectively, and removing obstacles that impede service or production. Good managers are not controllers, they are facilitators (to "make easy"). Good managers help make everyone's job easier. But to be effective, good management must be attached to good leadership or people have no clear direction or understanding of goals.

How many organizations today are made up of people who work really hard but never seem to get to the organization's intended goals? This is often because workers often aren't clear as to what the organization's goals actually are. In fact, as stated earlier, according to Louis Harris, two-thirds of the work force in the United States reported that they have "no idea" what their leaders really expect of them or what genuinely matters to the leader. In other words, people don't have a clear vision of where the organization is headed, nor do they know by what standards or values their work should be performed.

Who is responsible for this lack of direction and information? The organization's leaders. Leaders must create the vision and values of the organization, make certain that everyone involved knows what they are, and make sure that everyone is committed to them. Managers, on the other hand, must attend to the details of the vision and values, how they will be achieved, at what cost, and when.

A rose by any other name

Although leader, manager, and supervisor are still the most common labels for positions of authority, many organizations today are using terms such as head coach, coach, or team leader. These new terms work well as long as there is also a change in behavior and not just in semantics. If people in authority are called coaches or team leaders, but they still act like managers, the new terminology is uninspiring. In fact, it often adds more aggravation to relationships that are already strained. To avoid negative reaction to new terms and labels, be certain that your organization is structurally prepared to support a new behavior of authority as well.

The role of leadership

Leadership is an art. It must be experienced or created.
Max DePree

One of the roles of leadership is to look for problems before they occur and opportunities before they disappear. This also applies in an organization's quest for quality service. Part of a leader's job is to make certain that the organization is customer-driven from the top

THE POWER OF SERVICE

down. This happens when leaders make a genuine commitment to the customer and the employee, and break down the organizational boundaries that get in the way of quality service delivery.

Leaders must align the organization's entire operating model—culture, business processes, and management systems—to support the service value. And they need to develop systems and processes that primarily support the process of serving the external customer. If those systems or processes are encumbered because of procedures, policies, rules, or culture, they cannot serve the customer. Ultimately, those systems destroy the relationships they were meant to support.

Another role of leadership is to be certain that the talents and skills of those within the leader's span of influence are nurtured and grown. This includes people's leadership skills. Sajeela Moskowitz Ramsey said that an "artful" leader will give everyone within the organization the opportunity to lead at one time or another. She believes that being a leader is each person's birthright. This is especially important in service. Since service is created in the moment, each person needs to be in charge of whatever the situation demands.

Another role of leadership that Moskowitz Ramsey found important was the ability to build and nurture intimacy. Although intimacy sounds incompatible with business, it is necessary because it is the bedrock of communication. Communication falters if there is perceived or real distance between the communicators. Intimacy is about connecting with another and closing the gap that keeps people separated. Harvey MacKay is so committed to intimacy that he wrote, "You need to be in the physical presence of people you need or want to influence. This includes customers as well." In other words, you can't hide in your office and let the little guys do the dirty work. You must be moving toward people (intimacy), not away.

Good leaders as coaches

Whether the term is used or not, skilled leaders often work as coaches to help people develop their own skills. In order to do this effectively, leaders must be certain that they're not focusing on controlling people's outcomes. Just as coaches in sports are concerned with the score in a game, leaders of organizations are concerned about results. Good coaches know that if they bring out the best in each player, the scoreboard manages itself. The August 1993 *Pryor Report* offers the following suggestions to help leaders coach people's skills instead of manage their outcomes:

> Listen openly and without judgment.
> Extend the benefit of the doubt.
> Follow through on agreements.
> Sincerely congratulate successes.
> Build bridges, not walls.
> Manage by wandering around. (Thanks, Tom Peters)
> Help people grow as people as well as professionals.

In addition to these suggestions, Kristin Anderson, from Performance Research Associates, Inc., writes in her book, *Knock Your Socks Off Service*, that in order for leaders and managers to contribute to dazzling service, they need to integrate the following into their leadership practices:

> Find and retain quality people.
> Know their customers intimately.
> Focus their department, team or organization on its purpose.
> Create systems that serve.
> Train and support their staff.
> Involve and empower their staff.
> Recognize and reward good performance.
> Celebrate success.
> Model the behavior desired.
> Lead a service culture.

The role of vision in leadership

> *People today need a covenant, not a contract.*
> Max dePree

Peter Senge talks about the vision required in leadership. Vision is something that most organizations talk about but few actually embrace. Leaders who have a vision and communicate it with clarity and passion can make the difference between mediocrity and greatness. Vision includes the question: What is our or my purpose? Although data is important in planning an organization's future, the answer to this question can shape its destiny.

Analysis is never a substitute for vision. Leaders who bring numbers and structure to the table, but no vision, can not sustain the energy required to compete in a painfully competitive marketplace. The job of leadership is so important and difficult that many leaders immerse themselves into the manager's role to avoid the responsibility of creating the big picture, the vision. Instead of being the artist who paints the picture of the beautiful structure of tomorrow, they prefer the work of the architect who will bring the vision to life.

With the picture of the finished product in place first, the work of the skilled architect is relatively easy. But without a picture or an image of the desired end result, the architect's (manager's) job is almost impossible. The job of the artist or image-maker is so critical that many leaders recoil from the pressure and, instead, micro-manage the details involved with building the structure. Though micro-managers are indeed busy, and may even come up with wonderful ideas, their real work is going undone. The people hired to do the detail work are frustrated and angry at the intrusion and the implication that they are not capable of successfully performing the work they were hired to do.

Leaders create strategy based on mission and vision

Leaders must not only create the vision, but must have a plan or strategy to insure that their strategic leadership is driven through the mission and the vision of the organization. According to Frances Hesselbein, contributing editor to the book, *The Organization of the Future*, there are ten behaviors that help leaders connect vision with strategy.

1. Understand the global and the local environment and be aware of trends and their implications.
2. Revisit the mission and ask: Is it still visible and do we steep all other issues into it?

3. Answer three of Peter Drucker's questions:
   What is our business?
   Who is our customer?
   What does the customer consider value?
4. Communicate the vision until it permeates to the outer edges of the organization.
5. Ban the hierarchy. When people are boxed, they're contained. Have flexible and fluid staffing designs. Become leaner, flatter, circular, and cohesive.
6. Challenge the status quo. Be certain there are no sacred cows in policies, procedures, or assumptions.
7. Disperse leadership. The more power you give away, the more you have. Get rid of the idea of power and instead share responsibility.
8. Lead by example. Just do it, and be consistent.
9. Be aware of the messages of language—leader versus manager.
10. Lead from the front. Don't push from the rear.
11. Walk the talk.
12. Keep promises.
13. Show that people are the greatest asset.

Leadership traits

Leadership ultimately becomes moral in that it raises the level of human conduct...of both the leader and led, and thus transforms both.

James McGregor Burns

Leaders are made, not born. Through life, job experiences, role models, and the pain of rising through the ranks, leaders are created. They are about how to be not how to do it. Effective leaders all have one indispensable quality—personal integrity. In fact, a leader's integrity and character are more important than any strategy or perfectly laid plan. To accomplish the work that has been set before them, leaders also need patience, wisdom, and common sense.

Warren Bennis writes in *Executive Excellence* that leaders who make a difference seem to have the following traits:

- A great deal of self-knowledge about who they are as human beings and about their own character.
- A strongly defined sense of purpose while creating an environment where people know why they are there.
- The ability to generate and sustain trust by being candid, communicating effectively and exhibiting a sense of constancy.
- A bias toward action.

Nurturing the leader within

We all possess the leadership traits and skills to lead others effectively. We need to find those skills and nurture them from within. How do we recognize and nurture the leader inside? First, we need to **know who we really are.** We need to ask questions about ourselves, our motives, our skills, our hopes, and our dreams and then answer those questions honestly.

Once we know who we are, it is important that we **stay true to that person** and to the person we want to be. We stay true to ourselves by working from our higher selves or from that part of us of which we are most proud. We have the option of working from our dark side or, as Thomas Moore calls it, our "shadow." But destructive behaviors come from our shadow, and those behaviors will never enhance our valuable leadership skills. To be fully involved as a leader, be true to who you genuinely are. Don't play games or act a part that you know is not really you. Sometimes when promoted to a position of authority, people believe that they need to change: Now that I'm the team leader I have to act more disinterested about other peoples' problems. Or: I have to act like I have all of the answers. In the end, these charades always fail because they take too much energy and no one can fake it all of the time. Instead, find the leader from within and present it as is from your higher self.

In addition to staying true to your higher self, **be clear on your personal goals and vision.** Ask: Does this leadership role fit with my personal goals and vision? If not, don't waste your time pursuing it.

It's a well-worn axiom that we only have one chance in this life and we shouldn't waste it doing work that has no value or meaning to us.

Also, as you nurture your role as leader, place a **high sense of value on your own self-esteem as well as the self-esteem of others.** To maintain your own self-esteem, consistently operate from your principles and values, and perform with personal integrity. Sometimes people believe that if they satisfy their desires, or get what they want, they will feel good about themselves. But if they get what they want, unethically, illegally, or at someone else's expense, they often lose their self-esteem in the process.

Dennis Longmire, CEO of Darling International, Inc., the company that was fined $4 million for polluting the Blue Earth River in Minnesota and lying about it, said that they were *embarrassed* about what had happened. They should have been embarrassed. When people get what they want at someone else's expense, by acting unethically or illegally, there is often a sense of shame and damage to their own sense of self-esteem.

In nurturing the leader within, be aware that leaders who people are willing to follow have a way of **showing people respect and regard** at all levels of the organization. We've all heard the horror stories of leaders who treat people poorly just because they can. Respect and regard are shown through the behaviors and words we choose to use when interacting with others. If we belittle, discount, or show little interest in a person's opinion or performance, we are showing that person disrespect. In addition, we often destroy their spirit and commitment to the job in the process.

Respect is so important that, when employees were asked to rank what they valued most in return for their work, the answer that was consistently at the top was "knowing that they were doing work that contributed to the success of the organization." People have to believe that they matter and that what they do has real value.

The final skill that needs to be nurtured to be a quality leader is to **know the skills and talents of the people within your span of influence** and help them develop those skills to their fullest. Too often leaders have people working with them who are gifted and capable of contributing great things to the organization. But for a number of reasons, including the fact that many leaders don't want to be upstaged, they give little help to the employee to nurture and develop those skills. In addition to fearing that they will be shown up, some leaders fear that if they develop the employee too effectively, the employee will leave. But employees who feel they are dying on the vine leave anyway. Truly effective leaders nurture each person's rising star, then do their own job of creating the vision of the future, so that these emerging talents have continuous opportunities to grow and remain challenged within the organization.

Inspirational leaders

> *The spiritual dimension—the inspiration, enthusiasm, vigor, etc—is always involved in situations of great achievement.*
>
> Peter Vaill

Leaders play an enormous part in setting the service model for their organization. How does dazzling service become part of an organization's culture? Leaders model the behavior all the time. Employees may listen to what leaders say, but they'll believe what they do. We rarely question our leader's talents or skills. Instead, people question their leader's motivation, trustworthiness, and ability to inspire. Quality service can't be bought, demanded, imposed, or extracted. It can only be modeled and passed on from one person to another.

Being inspirational and modeling good service behaviors paid off handsomely for one world-class service company—Nordstrom. Kathy McKenna, President and CEO of McKenna Management Company, was curious to know how managers at Nordstrom, a nationwide department store known for its incredible service, got their people to perform at such consistently high service levels. Eager to recruit any ideas for her own management staff, she spoke with several of Nordstrom's managers. "How do you get your people to be so good at customer service?" she asked. Their surprising response: "We treat them just the way we want them to treat you." Kathy pursued this further. "There must be something else. Don't you give them bonuses or something to support this wonderful behavior?" "No," they replied, "it would be easier if we could. But you simply can't buy this from people. They have to see us everyday, under all kinds of circumstances, maintaining our service commitment to them. That way they know this is who Nordstrom is and how we treat people. They really have no other option but to do the same for you." Nordstrom has earned a world-class reputation for their dazzling service due to the behavior models provided by their leaders and in a sense, it hasn't cost them a dime. The only expense involved is the daily commitment of each leader to be the person they want others to be.

Traits of inspirational leaders

There is a type of person who inspires us all. She or he exhibits behaviors that have been honed through practice and deliberation. And this isn't about just being nice. There are many nice people in positions of authority who are not necessarily inspirational. According to Lou Tice in *Executive Excellence*, inspirational leaders tend to **think positively**. They say yes a lot. In fact, they often want to say yes so badly that they actually look for reasons to say it. If those reasons can't be found, they will say no. But they desire to be more positive than negative in most situations.

One of the most important aspects in finding opportunities to say yes is to **listen carefully**. If a leader doesn't listen well and doesn't get the basic concepts or ideas being suggested, the safest answer is no. In many situations, if the idea is truly heard, the answer is often yes. How many times have you tried to convince someone, using many passionate moments of persuasion, only to have the person look up at you and say, "Well, I didn't know *that*." Never mind that you mentioned *that* every time you had the discussion.

Tice also teaches that inspirational leaders have the ability to **look at mistakes or failures as educational opportunities.** We all make mistakes; good leaders are aware of that. And, in most instances, we learn from those mistakes. Good leaders need to be aware of that as well. Such an educational opportunity occurred at IBM a number of years ago. An employee made a mistake that cost the blue-chip giant $500,000. Soon after the mistake, CEO Tom

Watson called the remorseful but terrified bungler into his office. "I suppose you know why I want to see you?" Watson asked. To which the employee said, "Well, sir, in light of everything that's happened, I assume you're going to fire me." "Fire you?" Watson shot back. "Are you kidding? I just spent half a million dollars educating you!"

It's important when dealing with human beings, who are prone to error and bad judgment, that we clearly separate the deed from the doer or the performance from the performer. People will not learn from their mistakes if they feel attacked or threatened. Sometimes people in authority seem to think of themselves as guards waiting for someone to do something wrong. Instead, those in authority need to ask, "How can I reinforce and support you when you're doing a good job, and how can I help you overcome the obstacles you face?"

Achieve Global, a training and development firm, has adopted this as one of its basic leadership principles: When good leaders are dealing with an issue, they must always focus on the situation, behavior, or event and not the person. Instead of the accusatory, "You're late!" which causes either defensiveness or retreat, a better approach might be, "Our starting time is 8:00 and you're arrival time was 8:20. What happened?" When people don't focus on the situation, the end result is usually blame. But when the focus is on the situation or behavior, the desired result is to find solutions and ways to insure that these things won't continue to occur.

Leaders who inspire people to action **aren't afraid to do the work.** They are willing to jump into the fray and deal with whatever has to be dealt with. A wonderful example of this is retired Major General Bernie Loeffke. He is one of the most highly decorated officers in U.S. military service. He speaks six languages, has been responsible for 15,000 service members, and, in 1992, directed an investigation of MIAs lost in the Soviet Union. But when he was introduced at a conference and asked what he was most proud of, he responded that his greatest accomplishment was his certificate as a midwife. Later, at that same conference, he overheard several hotel employees discussing that some of the kitchen help had not shown up for work. What did this highly decorated general do? He offered to help with the dishes—like any servant leader would do.

Another trait of inspirational leaders is that they **value both process and outcomes.** In other words, they know that they can't sacrifice one for the other. Leaders who get results at any cost will eventually fail. And leaders interested in the process but are not focused on outcomes will also fail. Both results and processes are essential for success over the long haul.

People will follow leaders who **know that they don't know it all** and don't pretend to. What they have instead is the ability to ask great questions and then listen intently to the answers. However, the third leg of this equation is the most important. In addition to asking the questions and listening to the answers, the inspirational leader acts on what was just heard.

Acting on information is an essential trait of inspirational leaders. Inspirational leaders actually use the ideas and suggestions offered by people at all levels of their organization. A startling statistic about employee feedback and the implementation of that feedback came to light several years ago. In Japan, front-line workers offer, on average, twenty-six suggestions each year on how to improve a product or service and, of those twenty-six suggestions, over 77 percent are implemented. In the United States, on the other hand, front-line workers offer, on average, 0.14 suggestions each year on how to improve a product or service and American business implements only 24 percent of those suggestions. Is it any wonder that American business and industry has lost its edge in many of the global markets? Inspirational leaders know that the people closest to the product and/or customer—the employees—know the answers to most of the questions. Because of that, inspirational leaders ask, listen, and act.

One of the most powerful behaviors exhibited by inspirational leaders is **compassion and concern for all living things.** They believe that what affects one affects all and what hurts one hurts all. Instead of focusing solely on winning, they believe that coming to consensus or mutual understanding is in everyone's best interest.

This thinking, unfortunately, hurt President Bill Clinton while in office. As was discussed earlier, the philosophy he modeled was, "Let me hear from all sides and then let's come to an agreement that meets somewhere in the middle." He was, and probably still is, a consensus builder. But his critics would prefer that he take a stand and live or die with it. Leaders who adhere to this philosophy would rather fail than take someone else's advice. They also make most decisions alone. On occasion, it appears that they are listening to others, but at the decision-making level, the only person they really want to hear is themselves.

Finally, inspirational leaders **know what they can and can't do.** They know their strengths and shortcomings, and their self-esteem is healthy enough for them to work with others who complement them. They have no problem saying, " I don't know," or, "Yours is a better way of doing it than I had suggested." They simply believe that the most important part of their work includes achieving the organization's goals and allowing people to perform and grow.

Inspirational leaders speak the truth

Ed Penney, Minneapolis-based consultant, has been working with CEOs from various size companies throughout the country. He has found a common thread. Many of these individuals (most have been men) are searching for a way to balance their own humanness (what they can't do) with their image as a leader (what they can do). Many are tired of the front they believe is required of them to keep the company on its competitive edge. They want to be able to reveal the chinks in their armor, but they are afraid of what exposing themselves might do, not only to their ability to lead, but to their future. Will they appear weak or will they be perceived to have lost it? Will the person behind them on the ladder sabotage them if any weaknesses are exposed?

These are enormous questions, all with many different implications. Yet Ed has found that everyone—front-line workers, managers and leaders—is looking for something honest and genuine to replace the facade many leaders create. The leader needs to be able to come into a meeting and say, "Is anyone else scared about this merger? I know I am." In most cases, this opens the door for others to begin to express their fears and offer solutions based on real concerns. When leaders pretend they feel one way but actually feel another, a sick game is perpetuated. This game is communicated from one person to another, and everyone knows that this organization is no place to deal with the truth. Consequently the myth continues and nothing is ever honestly resolved.

Servant leadership

The first responsibility of a leader is to define reality.
The last is to say thank you. In between, the leader is a servant.

Max dePree

If, as we discussed in chapter three, people who serve for a living are called servants, then we must conclude that those people in leadership, management, or authority positions are super servants. In other words, leaders, managers, and those in authority are in place to serve those who serve the external customer. The purpose of their work is to remove obstacles, create opportunities, communicate vision, and model the behaviors they value. Leaders must come to work every day willing to serve those who serve the creators of the bottom line, the customer. If leaders encumber people's ability to perform or create rather than remove obstacles, then they must work on their servanthood. Or if employees fret and stew before they share bad news with their leaders, or wonder what kind of mood they are in, those leaders must work on their servanthood.

Many people at the top resent the notion that they be considered servants. After all, they have worked hard for their positions and have often spent a great deal of time and money on their education. Being relegated to the lowly position of servant is a bitter pill to swallow. But that is, indeed, what effective leaders must be. Any leader who feels diminished by the thought of servanthood should consider the Latin translation for the word pope, *servs servorum*, or the servant of servants. The pope is the leader of millions of people throughout the world and considered a man of great power. Yet, in order for him to do the work set before him, he must accept the humble position of servant of servants.

Ron Zemke and Chip Bell, customer service specialists, had this to say about the role of leaders and their relationship to service:

"Leaders need to see their roles as helping service people do their jobs,...enhancing the culture, setting expectations of quality, providing a motivating climate, furnishing the necessary resources, helping solve problems, removing obstacles, and making sure high quality job performance pays off." In other words, leaders and managers are there to serve.

We also talked about the servant's heart and the need for true servants to be humble. In humbling yourself to serve, you need to:

- Leave your needs at the door.
- Leave your ego at the door.
- Leave your need to be right at the door.

The same is true for the leader, manager or person in authority. As a leader, to serve those who serve the external customer, you need to:

Leave your needs at the door and put the needs of the people within your span of influence at the center of your attention every day.

Leave your ego at the door. Every leader or person in authority needs healthy self-esteem. But let go of that puffed up part that believes that the world revolves around your thoughts, ideas, or opinions.

Leave your need to be right at the door and let others be right as often as possible. There are hundreds of ways to solve a problem or achieve success. Let someone else's way be the right way, and let go of the idea that your way is the only or best way.

Stephen Covey teaches about leadership from the heart. He writes in *Executive Excellence* that to achieve the humbleness that servant leaders require, the following must be a part of the leader's behavior and skills.

Leaders must build new relationships with the people they serve. They can't just use new words with old meanings. In other words, they can't be wolves dressed in sheep's clothing. To build new relationships, they work from a base of mutual respect, roles being equal but different (worker, manager, and leader), and relationships steeped in trust.

Servant leaders create a new performance basis that:
• specifies quantity and quality of desired results;
• teaches that principles should be the guide, not procedures nor policies;
• is honest and clear regarding all available resources (financial, human, etc.);
• clearly defines accountability, measurement and reporting;
• clarifies and defines both positive and negative consequences.

Once these things have been established and communicated, the leader needs to let go. Servant leaders believe that their primary responsibility is to serve the worker so goals can be successfully achieved. Once the foundation has been laid, the servant leader simply becomes a resource the worker can use to accomplish the task. However, in the process, the servant leader not only has the right, but the responsibility, to ask employees:

How's it going?
What are you learning?
What are your goals now?
How can I help you?

Reality shows us time and time again that the person working for a servant leader has more accountability and responsibility. And in turn, once the leader lets go of methods and focuses on results or outcomes, he or she is freed to continue to do the work of vision and values that will, in turn, secure the organization's future.

As rare as it is today for leaders to think of themselves as servants, there are those who are leading the way. Horst Shulze, President of the Ritz Carlton Hotels, is an example of a servant leader. Max dePree and Bob Greenleaf are pioneers in spirit-based leadership. So are Skip LeFauve of General Motor's Saturn division and Ken Melrose from Toro. Ken Melrose believes that he is accountable to all of Toro's stakeholders (all those who have a stake in Toro's success or failure). To support this belief, he posts his goals outside his office for all to see. He also prides himself in keeping both his office door and his mind open to anyone who wants to offer an opinion. He is committed to sharing information with everyone, even when it is bad, and to inviting involvement from all levels to gain the commitment of truly empowered employees.

Servant leaders give unity to the organization—a oneness that lifts them beyond all other competitors. They also tend to have longer tenure within the organization than traditional leaders. This is due in part to the fact that their contributions tend to be more subtle and that the effects of those contributions more long term.

Servant leadership is really an act of giving. Servant leaders give:
• whatever the situation needs;
• themselves;
• others the freedom to purse their dreams;
• personal values;
• sense to situations; and
• heart-felt support for human dignity and excellence.

Like good service, if any of this is to make a difference in other's lives, it must be given freely, with no strings attached.

Servant leaders serve from the heart

All leadership is spiritual.
Jack Hawley

Lou Tice writes, in *Executive Excellence*, about Robert Greenleaf, one of the first champions of the concept of servant leadership. He quotes Greenleaf as saying, "The servant leader is servant first. It begins with the natural feeling that one wants to serve, to serve first. This conscious choice brings one to aspire to lead. That person is sharply different from one who is leader first, perhaps because of the need to assuage an unusual power drive or to acquire material possessions."

Greenleaf advanced the belief that "artful leaders want to make a positive difference in the lives of other people." Many, if not most, leaders shy away from the truth that how they treat people or help them grow will affect their entire lives not just their work. When someone abuses people in any way, victims' entire being is affected. We do not have the capability to consistently separate ourselves from our situations. We do have facets of ourselves that are more capable in one setting than another. But everything that we hear, see, or experience, no matter where it happens, is deposited into the same memory bank. Those memories and how we process them add up to our life.

Stewardship and the spirit of service

The key questions of today's leaders and managers are no longer issues of task and structure but are questions of spirit.
Jack Hawley

Leaders need to have knowledge about the products or services their organization provides. But none of that knowledge matters if the leader doesn't inspire its people to perform. As Peter Block states, "Servant leaders are stewards to the people they lead and to the organization's mission."

In organizations where leaders are stewards and not simply task masters or bosses, there are still people in charge. But, as Block says, "stewards will hold power and inspire people to perform without using rewards, punishments, or directives." Thinking as a servant or steward will not come easily or naturally. But leaders at any point in their career can choose (here's that word again) to change. Partnership, empowerment, and service can be taught to anyone at any level depending on their desire to change and grow.

Humbling oneself to serve others for the greater good comes from the core of one's own spirit. To many business people, talk of spirit comes too close to religion for the topic to be comfortably broached in management meetings or business settings. It is too soft. But there is not one leader who has inspired people to greatness who did not gather that ability from their core being or spirit. When he won the Nobel Prize, the Dali Lama was asked: "What question do most executives ask you most often?" His response: "How can we introduce more ethics and spirituality into our business and everyday lives?" His answer to that question: "Do it from the heart, within your own culture."

In his book, *Reawakening the Spirit in Work: The Power of Dharmic Management*, Jack Hawley says, "When leaders follow their hearts, others rise to those heights." Spiritual responses to issues gather energy and ignite enthusiasm in others. One of the most powerful results of servant leadership is that it ignites enthusiasm or creates a spirit of energy. Enthusiasm can't be demanded, imposed, or legislated; it can be set on fire only by a leader with a servant's heart who reaches into the hearts of others and touches their very spirit.

Assessing your servant-leadership traits and skills

Do you ever wonder how you are perceived as a leader? Lou Tice poses these four questions to help you evaluate your servant-leadership capacity:

1. As a result of my leadership, are others growing as persons?

2. Are they, while being served, becoming healthier?

3. Are they becoming more autonomous, more free, wiser, more capable?

4. Are they more likely to become servant leaders? This becomes an unending chain built on the legacy of the last generation, which subsequently hands down a new legacy to those who follow.

Another way to evaluate the effectiveness of your servant-leadership abilities, would be to respond to these questions posed by Robert C. Kausen in an article written for *Executive Excellence:*

- Do the people who report to you feel respected and understood?
- Is a significant part of your focus on how to better serve employees?
- Is your mind sufficiently composed (uncluttered, calm, worry-free) so you can concentrate and be present with others?
- Do you avoid making people prove themselves?
- When people problems arise, do you approach them as a symptom of the system?
- Do you recognize people's state of mind and a connection with performance?

- Do you conduct frequent coaching sessions with your direct reports, and do you use the opportunity to learn as well as coach?
- Do you continually look for ways to turn over responsibility and authority?
- Do you seldom seem stressed?
- Are you and the people who report to you enjoying your jobs?

Finally, if you really want to know what the people within your span of influence honestly believe about your leadership capabilities and your ability to serve, have them complete the following questionnaire:

1. How well did I create an environment of freedom for you to perform at your highest level of capability?

VERY POORLY   EXCELLENT
1   2   3   4   5   6   7
Explain

2. How well did I coach you to develop your professional skills and talents?

VERY POORLY   EXCELLENT
1   2   3   4   5   6   7
Explain

3. How effective was I as a role model in my service to you and to others?

VERY POORLY   EXCELLENT
1   2   3   4   5   6   7
Explain

4. How well did I provide information for you to stay current with today's challenges?

VERY POORLY   EXCELLENT
1   2   3   4   5   6   7
Explain

5. How well did I listen to you when you had an idea or concern?

VERY POORLY   EXCELLENT

1   2   3   4   5   6   7

Explain

6. How much did I inspire you to perform beyond standard expectations?

VERY POORLY   EXCELLENT

1   2   3   4   5   6   7

Explain

7. Please share anything else that might help me improve my service to you.

_____

_____

_____

Leadership barriers to good service

Leaders must know both their strengths and their weaknesses or shadows. If not, their shadows are often cast into their organization making theirs a dangerous and careless stewardship.

Sajeela Moskowitz Ramsey

Leaders play a significant part in the process of delivering extraordinary service to customers. Their decisions and treatment of staff affect external customers and are often at the root of customer complaints. But leaders are not always as free to make decisions or take action as people might imagine. They often have stockholders or boards of directors to answer to. The people on these boards usually are not integral parts of the organization, nor do they know the employees or what is happening on a day-to-day basis. Yet they have a powerful impact on the decisions that govern everyone involved.

Stockholders primarily want one thing—a reasonable return on investment. No one can blame them for that. But when return on investment is the primary goal of an organization, as opposed to long-term, steady growth, it colors how, when, why, and what leaders decide to do. Most leaders are under pressure to make everyone happy, and that is difficult or even impossible to accomplish. But painful decisions aren't the destructive barriers that kill the spirit of service. The killers of spirit come in the form of stress, abusive interactions, and de-motivating behaviors.

Stress creators

I once worked for a man who proudly proclaimed, "I don't have stress, I give it." And was that ever the truth! People wore out like bald tires working for him and, because of it, the turnover within his company was extraordinarily high. People just can't take constant, chronic stress. Leaders can be one of three things.

Stress creators—making mountains out of molehills.

Stress carriers—making sure everyone is aware of the mountains.

Stress buffers—making sure molehills remain molehills.

Good leaders carry their share of the load and don't dump unnecessary stress and strain on others. Many times leaders who do put extraordinary stress on others exhibit this type of abuse to sustain their own egos. Leaders who create crises and dump baggage on *underlings* just because they can, make certain that their position of authority is clearly defined and not forgotten. But, in the end, leaders who impose unnecessary stress on others lose because good people don't need to endure it. They emotionally reject the organization (on-the-job retirement), lose loyalty to its goals and success, and eventually leave.

Abusive interactions

> *Autocratic governance withers the spirit.*
> Peter Block

Some employees display poor service behaviors because they fear the wrath of their supervisor. They are afraid that, if they make the wrong decision or do the wrong thing, that they will be punished through their manager's abusive behavior. In their book, *Driving Fear*

Out of the Workplace, authors Kathleen Ryan and Daniel Oestreich discuss the continuum of fear tactics that some leaders use:

> Silence
> Glaring eye contact or the look
> Brevity or abruptness
> Snubbing or ignoring people
> Insults and put-downs
> Blaming, discrediting and discounting
> An aggressive, controlling manner
> Threats about the job
> Yelling and shouting
> Angry outbursts, loss of control
> Physical threats

Some leaders within organizations who level these kinds of abuse are not aware of the effects of their behavior. But from silence to physical threats, these behaviors break down relationships, and never work in anyone's favor.

One of the most frequent abusive behaviors is silence, or giving the cold shoulder to someone who has fallen out of the leader's favor. Granted, sometimes it's better to remain silent than to say something regrettable. But that is not the kind of silence being discussed here. The silence we are talking about is the silent treatment that provokes one to question: What's going on? Did I do something wrong? Why won't anyone tell me what's happening? This type of silence forces people to question their own capabilities, their own value, and even their own being at times. This silence is destructive and has no value in interpersonal relationships, professional or personal.

Ryan and Oestriech's list does not represent all of the behaviors that cause relationships to break down. Whatever gets in the way in any relationship needs to be dealt with and resolved. Some methods to overcome relationship breakdowns include:

- Taking the time to listen;
- Giving people the benefit of the doubt;
- Following through on whatever you say you will do;
- Being present and available during the work-day;

- Giving good, constructive feedback in an effective and timely manner; and
- Working to constantly maintain the self-esteem of others in any interaction you might have with them, no matter how difficult the situation might be.

Negative behaviors and outbursts are unwelcome no matter who is exhibiting them. When they are expressed by leaders or people in authority, they have a greater impact on the receiver because of the power and authority the leadership position carries. When leaders use silence, yelling, glaring, or snubbing, people feel particularly threatened.

Consider Scrooge, the despicable boss in Dickens' *Christmas Carol*. He was hated by his staff and, by all appearances, he also hated them. Their working conditions were horrible, and not one person could find a good word to say about this man of misery. I can't imagine anyone wanting to be thought of as a modern-day Scrooge, but according to many front-line workers, there are plenty of leaders today who certainly would be contenders. Although few walk around yelling, "Bah Humbug," many do grumble, pick apart, second guess, discount, ignore, belittle, and destroy people so subtly that only those closely involved see it happening. Don't be fooled. These behaviors destroy the human spirit and ultimately the image of service for the entire organization.

Looking at Ryan's and Oestreich's "fear tactics" continuum, ask yourself: Do I do any of these things to the people in my world? If the answer is yes, then get help in resolving this destructive behavior. Even though you may win your points and get tasks completed with these behaviors, ask yourself at what or at whose expense?

De-motivating behaviors

In addition to behaviors that are abusive and that destroy the spirit of service, there are behaviors that simply deaden people's desire to perform. Leaders' behaviors and decisions can inspire people to action, or they can de-motivate them into lethargy. Once again, the employee still has the option to choose how to react to the leader's decisions and behaviors. But there are certain actions by leaders that can take the steam out of a person's energy and out of his or her willingness to perform and serve.

Actions that de-motivate employees from performing include:
• Pay low, get by with paying as little as you can;
• Don't train or only train on the essential job tasks;
• Don't share the pie or reward people financially;
• Give only negative feedback;
• Put more effort into marketing and ignore customer retention;
• Put up banners and signs that don't pass the snicker test;
• Be certain there's a clear line between front-line staff and management, especially in the customers eyes; and
• Use front-line people as bad news messengers to customers; stay hidden in your office and avoid customer contact.

How to get leaders on the service bandwagon

In almost every class or seminar I teach, the question arises, "Where are the head honchos? Why aren't they taking this service class? Don't they care?" My assumption is that they do indeed care but they see themselves apart from the day-to-day service reality. Unfortunately few CEOs come in contact with their external customers. How then do leaders and senior managers get on the service bandwagon?

First, leaders need to know what customers, both internal and external, want. There's one good way to find this out: spend time with them. Instead of being in the back office or on the 29th floor, be in their presence and listen to their thoughts, ideas, and needs. As successful business man Harvey MacKay contends, "Sometimes the only way we get 20/20 vision is through the eyes of the customer." Twenty-twenty vision comes through the eyes of the employees, as well.

Second, be cognizant of the data that tell you what you are losing due to poor service. If most leaders were aware of the financial losses to their business due to bad service, they would jump on the service bandwagon in nano-seconds.

Finally, take a look around at your competitors and see what they are doing better than you. It may shake up your ego to see that you are not the best, or at times, not even a contender. Although this peek at reality can be painful, it's not as painful as going out of business or losing one's job.

Conclusion

It is common knowledge that people will bend over backwards for leaders who treat them well. And this isn't about allowing people to perform at low-quality work standards. This is about choosing to use good leadership skills and to be thoughtful and deliberate in the treatment of others. It is about being a leader for whom people love to work and to whom they are deeply loyal. It is not about being a boss who gets things done through destruction, but about being a leader who can move people through inspiration and consistent personal behavior. No matter how hard the task, or how difficult the problem, people will trust leaders who maintain their service integrity.

Final Remarks

In the end, we know that service is a combination of brilliant individual performance, simple, effective systems, and inspirational leadership. At the center of each of these is choice. Individual contributors and those in authority will choose every day, in every decision and at every juncture, whether they will do what's right and best or what's easy and self-gratifying. Because extraordinary customer service is essential for mere survival, it is no longer optional. Average service will not allow an organization to become a serious contender. Service at all levels, internal and external, must be powerful and dramatic to make a lasting impression and transform the spirit of service. There are no excuses for bad service. If each contributor asks, "What can I do to serve this customer in such a way that it will create a sense of indebtedness and devotion," organizations will see a genuine, lasting transformation in their service reputation. Don't look around at others for this to happen. This is ultimately about you and what you choose to do. Choose to do the right thing.

References

Albrecht, Karl. *The Only Thing That Matters.* New York: Harper Business, 1992.

Anderson, Kristen and Ron Zemke. *Delivering Knock Your Socks Off Service.* New York: AMACOM, 1991.

Balm, Gerald J. *Benchmarking: A Practitioner's Guide for Becoming and Staying the Best of the Best.* Schaumburg, Illinois: QPMA Press, 1992.

Carlzen, Jan. *Moments of Truth.* Ballinger Publishing Company, 1987.

Chopra, Deepak. *Seven Spiritual Laws of Success.* San Rafael, CA: Amber-Allen Publishing and New World Library, 1994.

Covey, Stephen R.and Roger A. Merrill and Rebecca R. Merrill. *First Things First.* New York: Simon & Schuster, 1994.

Covey, Stephen. *Seven Habits of Highly Effective People.* New York: Simon & Schuster, 1989.

Deming, W. Edwards. *The New Economics for Industry, Government and Education.* Cambridge: MIT, 1993.

Devito, Joseph A. *The Interpersonal Communication Book.* New York: Harper Collins College Publishers, 1995.

Frankl, Viktor F. *Man's Search for Meaning.* New York: Washington Square, 1984.

Hanson, Dan. *A Place to Shine: Bringing Special Gifts to Light.* Minneapolis: TPG Press, 1992.

Hawley, Jack. *Reawakening The Spirit in Work: The Power of Dharmic Management.* San Francisco: Berrett-Koehler, 1993.

Bern, Eric. *Games People Play: The Psychology of Human Relationships.* New York: Grove, 1964.

Block, Peter. *Stewardship: Choosing Service Over Self-Interest.* San Francisco: Berrett-Koehler Publishers, 1993.

Bogan, Christopher E. and Michael J. English. *Benchmarking for Best Practices.* New York: McGraw-Hill, 1994.

Janov, Jill. *The Inventive Organization.* San Francisco: Jossey-Bass, 1994.

Koob Cannie, Joan. *Keeping Customers for Life.* New York: AMACOM, 1991.

Kuhn, Thomas. *The Structure of Scientific Revolutions.* Chicago: University of Chicago, 1970.

Langer, Ellen. *Mindfulness.* New York: Addison-Wesley Publishing, 1989.

Large, Peter. *The Micro Revolution Revisited.* London; Totown, New Jersey: F. Pinter; Rowman and Allanheld, 1984.

LeBeouff, Michael. *How to Win Customers and Keep Them for Life.* New York: Putnam, 1988.

Levering, Robert and Milton Moskowitz. *The 100 Best Companies to Work for in America.* New York: Penguin, 1994.

Main, Jeremy. *Quality Wars: The Triumphs and Defeats of American Business.* New York: Free Press, 1994.

McDermott, Lynda C. *Caught in the Middle.* Englewood Cliffs, NJ: Prentice Hall, 1992.

Mehrabian, Albert. *Silent Messages.* Florence, KY: Wadsworth, 1981.

Moore, Thomas. *Care of the Soul: A Guide for Cultivating Depth and Sacredness in Everyday Life.* New York: HarperCollins, 1992.

Morem, Susan. *How to Gain the Professional Edge.* Minneapolis: Best Books, 1997.

Narjano, Claudio. *On the Psychology of Meditation.* New York: Viking, 1971.

Nash, Linda. *The Shorter Road To Success.* St. Louis: Prism, 1996.

Peppers, Don and Martha Rogers. *The One to One Future.* New York: Doubleday, 1993.

Perri, Vicki. *Treating Your Customers Like Gold.* Minneapolis: Hennepin Technical College, 1991.

Peters, Thomas J. and Robert H. Waterman, Jr. *In Search of Excellence.* New York: Harper & Row, 1982.

Pietrofesa, John J., Alan Hoffman and Howard H. Splete. *Counseling: An Introduction.* Boston: Houghton Mifflin, 1984.

Pritchett, Price. *New Work Habits for a Radically Changing World.* Dallas: Pritchett, 1996.

Pritchett, Price. *Service Excellence.* Dallas: Pritchett, 1989.

Reichheld, Frederich. *The Loyalty Effect: The Hidden Force Behind Growth, Profits and Lasting Value.* Boston: Bain, 1996.

Ryan, Kathleen, and Daniel Oestreich. *Driving Fear Out of the Workplace: How to Overcome the Invisible Barriers to Quality, Productivity and Innovation.* Jossey-Bass Publishers, 1991.

Sashkin, Marshall and Kenneth J. Kiser. *Putting Total Quality Management to Work.* San Francisco: Berrett-Koehler, 1993.

Schaaf, Richard, and Ron Zemke. *The Service Edge.* [city]:New American Library, 1989.

Schrage, Michael. *Shared Minds: The New Technologies of Collaboration.* New York: Random House, 1990.

Senge, Peter. *The Fifth Discipline: The Art and Practice of the Learning Organization.* New York: Doubleday/Currency, 1990.

Sewell, Carl and Paul B. Brown. *Customers for Life: How to Turn that One-Time Buyer Into a Lifetime Customer.* New York: Doubleday, 1990.

Silverman Goldzimer, Linda. *I'm First: Your Customer's Message to You.* New York: Rawson, 1989.

Stack, Jack. *The Great Game of Business: The Only Sensible Way to Run a Business.* New York: Doubleday/Currency, 1992.

Sviokla, John J. and Benson P. Shapiro. *Keeping Customers.* Boston: Harvard Business Review, 1993.

Swann, William, Jr. *Self Trap: The Elusive Quest for Higher Self-Esteem.* New York: W.H. Freeman, 1996.

Szasz, Thomas. *The Second Sin.* Garden City, NY: Anchor, 1973.

Tschohl, John. *Achieving Excellence Through Customer Service.* Englewood Cliffs, New Jersey: Prentice Hall, 1991.

Weiser, William E. *Selected Readings on the Role of Training in Economic Development and High Performance Organizations.* Minneapolis: Minnesota Technical College System, 1992.

Whiteley, Richard. *The Customer-Driven Company.* Reading MA: Addison Wesley, 1991.

Zemke, Ron and Chip R. Bell. *Service Wisdom: Creating and Maintaining the Customer Service Edge.* Minneapolis: Lakewood Books, 1989.

Movies and Videos

City Slickers, Castle Rock Entertainment, 1992.

Discovering the Future: The Business of Paradigms, Charthouse Learning Corp., 1989.

Educating Rita, Columbia TriStar Productions, 1983.

Mr. Saturday Night, Castle Rock Entertainment and New Line Cinema, 1992.

Network, Metro-Goldwyn-Mayer, 1976.

Pretty Woman, Touchstone Pictures/Silver Screen Partners IV: distributed by Touchstone Home Video, 1990.

Trains, Planes and Automobiles, Paramount Pictures, 1987.

Periodicals

Chicago Tribune, Tribune Publishing, Chicago, IL.

Customer Service Manager's Letter. Bureau of Business Practice, Waterford, CT, 1996.

Executive Excellence. Executive Excellence Publishing, Provo, UT.

Harvard Business Review. Harvard Business School, Boston, MA.

Inc. Goldhirsh Group, Inc., Boston, MA.

Insight. The Washington Times Corp., Washington, D.C.

Minneapolis Star Tribune. Cowles Media Company, Minneapolis, MN.

Nation's Business. U.S. Chamber of Commerce, Washington, D.C.

New York Times, The. The New York Times Company, New York, NY.

Service Edge, The. Lakewood Publications, Minneapolis, MN.

Sloan Management Review. Massachusetts Institute of Technology, Cambridge, MA.

Time. Time Warner, Syracuse, NY.

Wall Street Journal, The. Dow Jones & Co., New York, NY.

Washington Post, The. The Washington Post, Washington, D.C.

Index

Petra Marquart is a native Minnesotan with a colorful and diverse professional background. She was a singer who toured extensively for more than seven years during which the highlight was working with Elvis Presley at the grand opening of the International Hotel in Las Vegas.

Today, she is a certified trainer for the widely acclaimed customer service program, *Treating Your Customers Like Gold.* This program was the basis for the customer service programs she wrote for the Mall of America, US Bancorp, Target Center Arena, Fairview-University Health System, and Isle of Capri Casinos, Inc. She is also a certified trainer in Achieve Global's *Frontline Leadership, Leadership 2000,* and *Working for Self-Directed Teams.*

She has served as a member of Honeywell's Adult Continuing Education Board and as an educational partner with the American Institute of Banking, Hennepin County Government Center, Northern States Power, and Unisys.

When she is able, she spends time at the family cabin in northern Minnesota where she tends to her wildflowers and watches the world go by.

The Power of Service is the foundation for a customer service training program by the same name. She and her staff enjoy traveling and would be happy to spend time with you and your organization to help you achieve your service goals. For further information, you may contact Petra Marquart and Associates at 952-470-1998 or through our website address below. We look forward to serving you.

www.petramarquart.com
info@petramarquart.com

Quotes from Satisfied Customers

"Petra is the comsummate trainer. Her material is always cutting edge and absolutely on target for your specific audience. Her delivery is beyond superb. Her sense of timing and humor is without equal. Once you have scheduled Petra for a session, all you need do is sit back, relax, and wait for the cheering to subside."

> Kathleen McKenna-Harmon
> President
> McKenna Management Associates, Inc.

"Petra is a dynamite presenter. She is able to creat electricity in the training room."

> David R. Wilson
> Area H/R Manager Asia Pacific
> 3M Company

"As a presenter/trainer, Petra's enthusiasm, high-energy, and sense of humor are contagious. She captivates audiences with her dynamic approach and fun personality. Petra is a 'WOW!'"

> Susan G. Mortensen
> Adult Education Coordinator/Administrator
> Honeywell, Inc.

"Petra is a dynamic, motivating, crowd-engaging speaker who brings to life the rationale and practical aspects of becoming a customer-focused organization. She keeps your attention, stimulates your brain, tugs at your heart...and she teaches."

> Pamela L. Tibbetts
> Senior Vice President
> Fairview Riverside Medical Center

"Petra's deep subject knowledge, real life examples, and direct style revolutionized our employees' perceptions about service in merely one session. Additionally, her quick wit and sense of humor entertained everyone and elevated their retention. I highly recommend Petra Marquart if you are serious about outstanding customer service."

> John F. Healey
> Vice President
> Healey Ramme Company

"Petra is Dynamite! Every time we have her speak, she packs the house the leaves them wanting more. She is by far one of our members' favorite speakers. I recommend her very highly."

Lora A. Peterson
Director of Education
Minnesota MultiHousing Association

"Petra was a wonderful delight to work with in developing the Casino America, Inc. Guest Service Training Program. I found her ability to be flexible and creative, while meeting the needs for customization, an essential qualification for the successful completion of our project."

Robert F. Boone
Vice President, Human Resources
Casino America, Inc.

"From planning to execution, Petra Marquart exceeded my expectations. She showed business savvy in the program design and clearly identified behavior objectives. Her presentation skills are superior and engaging. Petra Marquart really delivers."

Jane I. Erdmann
Sr. Vice President, Managing Director
Drake Beam Morin, Inc.

"Petra is one of my all-time favorite presenters. I always leave the presentation knowing I can make a difference in whatever the topic area was. She is well researched, knowledgeable, and best of all, enthusiastic. Petra really cares that you get what you came for."

Ann Coates
Adult Program Coordinator
Eden Prairie Schools District 272

"Petra does an excellent job motivating employees and leaders to 'treat customers like gold.' Her informal, yet professional, style; sense of humor, and her obvious enthusiasm and expertise, ensure a continued partnership on various training activities."

Melody McKay
Training Consultant
Northern States Power Company

"Petra is a dynamic speaker/trainer. Her enthusiasm and humor captivate an audience! She is a first-class presenter."

Tina Cronin
Training Manager
Aequitron Medical